Best Editorial Cartoons of the Year

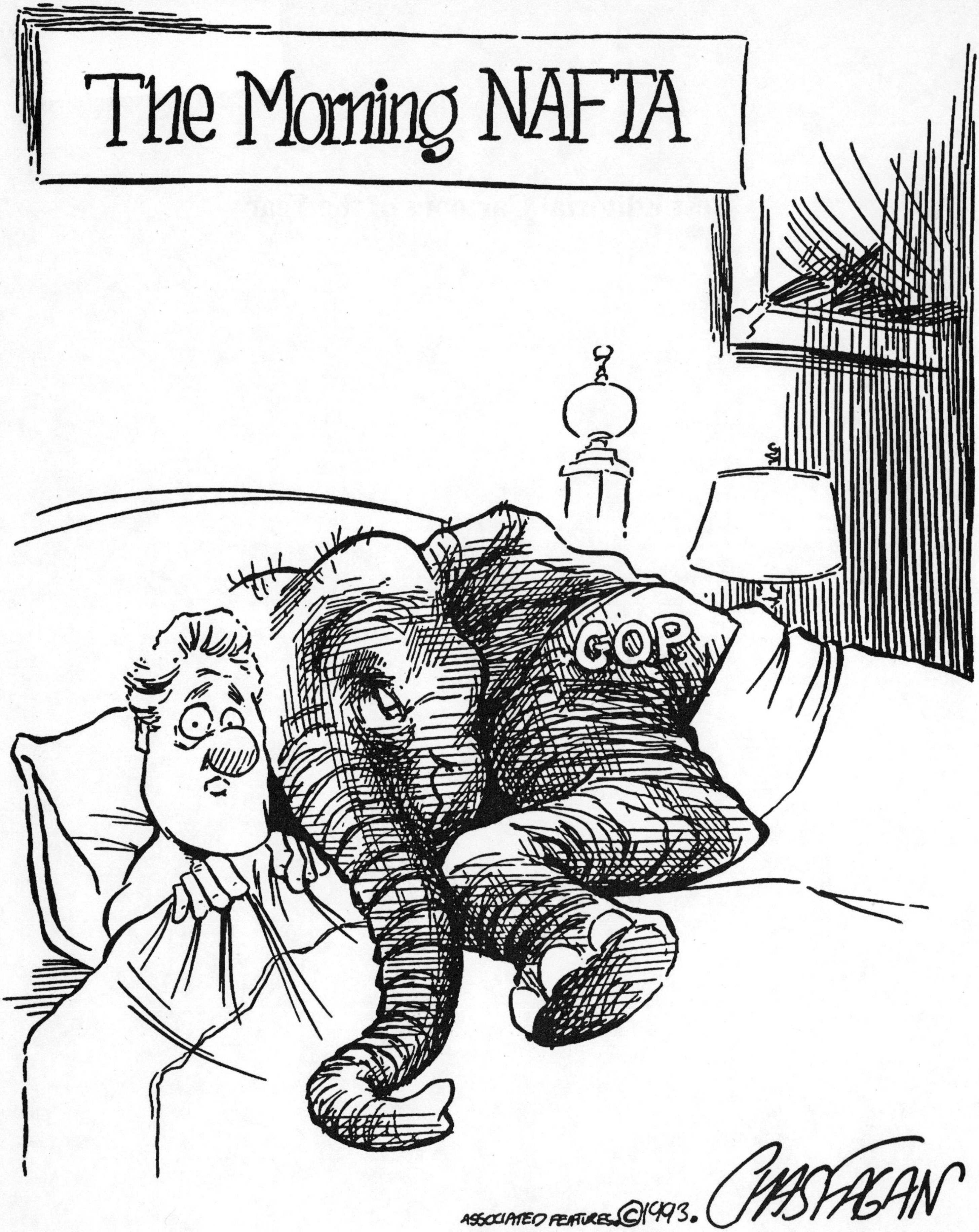
The Morning NAFTA
G.O.P.
ASSOCIATED FEATURES ©1993.
CHAS FAGAN

CHARLES FAGAN
Courtesy Associated Features Syndicate

BEST EDITORIAL CARTOONS OF THE YEAR

1994 EDITION

Edited by
CHARLES BROOKS

PELICAN PUBLISHING COMPANY
Gretna 1994

Copyright © 1994
By Charles Brooks
All rights reserved

The cartoons in this volume are reproduced with the expressed permission of the individual cartoonists and their respective publications and/or syndicates. Any unauthorized reproduction is strictly prohibited.

Library of Congress Serial Catalog Data

Best editorial cartoons. 1972-
   Gretna [La.] Pelican Pub. Co.
   v. 29 cm annual-
"A pictorial history of the year."

   1. United States—Politics and government—1969—Caricatures and Cartoons—Periodicals.
E839.5.B45   320.9'7309240207   73-643645
ISSN 0091-2220   MARC-S

Manufactured in the United States of America
Published by Pelican Publishing Company, Inc.
1101 Monroe Street, Gretna, Louisiana 70053

Contents

Award-Winning Cartoons 6
The Clinton Administration 13
Health Care 35
Russia 51
The Middle East 59
NAFTA 65
The Family and Society 75
The Economy 83
Foreign Affairs 91
Politics 107
Congress 111
The Courts 119
Crime 125
U.S. Military 143
Education 153
The Environment 161
Canada 169
. . . and Other Issues 175
Past Award Winners 187
Index of Cartoonists 190

Award-Winning Cartoons

1993 PULITZER PRIZE

STEVE BENSON
Editorial Cartoonist
Arizona Republic

Born in Sacramento, California; cum laude graduate of Brigham Young University and graduate of the Minneapolis Art Instruction School; served as editorial cartoonist for the Senate Republican Policy Committee and the Washington Post Writers Group; editorial cartoonist, Arizona Republic, 1980 to the present; winner of the National Headliners Club Award, 1984.

1992 NATIONAL SOCIETY OF PROFESSIONAL JOURNALISTS AWARD

(Selected in 1993)

ROBERT ARIAIL
Editorial Cartoonist
The State

Graduate of the University of South Carolina; editorial cartoonist for The State, Columbia, South Carolina, 1984 to the present; winner of the National Headliners Club Award, 1990.

1993 FISCHETTI AWARD

BILL SCHORR
Editorial Cartoonist
Kansas City Star

Born in New York City, 1948; graduate of California State University, Long Beach, 1973; editorial cartoonist for the Kansas City Star, 1973-78, the Los Angeles Herald Examiner, 1978-87, and the Kansas City Star, 1987 to the present; formerly cartoonist for the Los Angeles Times Syndicate; creator of the comic strip, "The Grizzwells," for the Newspaper Enterprise Association.

1992 NATIONAL NEWSPAPER AWARD/CANADA
(Selected in 1993)

CANADA VOTES A RESOUNDING "NO" ON PRIME MINISTER BRIAN MULRONEY'S FINAL CONSTITUTIONAL PROPOSAL.

BRUCE MACKINNON
Editorial Cartoonist
Halifax Herald

Born in Nova Scotia; studied fine arts at Mount Allison University and the Nova Scotia College of Art and Design; editorial cartoonist for the Halifax Chronicle-Herald and Mail-Star, 1985-86; editorial cartoonist for the Halifax Herald, 1986 to the present.

1993 NATIONAL HEADLINERS CLUB AWARD

WALT HANDELSMAN
Editorial Cartoonist
New Orleans Times-Picayune

Born in 1957; graduated from the University of Cincinnati; editorial cartoonist for the Patuxent Publishing Corp., 1982-85, the Scranton Times, 1985-89, and the New Orleans Times-Picayune, 1989 to the present; winner of the National Headliners Club Award, 1989, and the National Society of Professional Journalists Award, 1991.

Best Editorial Cartoons of the Year

PAUL CONRAD
Courtesy Los Angeles Times

The Clinton Administration

President Clinton did not get off to a flying start in his first year in office. First, he jumped into bitter controversies over gays serving in the military and over abortion rights. Then he made page-one news everywhere when he delayed landings at Los Angeles International Airport for fifty-six minutes while getting a $200 haircut aboard Air Force One. He stumbled in trying to fill several top jobs with nominees he later had to withdraw. His job stimulus package was defeated, and his deficit-reduction plan squeaked by on a 50-49 vote.

The president left a trail of broken promises, but he managed some solid accomplishments in the area of trade. His wife Hillary's health reform was announced, but stiff opposition formed immediately. Candidate Clinton had promised a middle-class tax cut, but President Clinton pushed through the largest tax increase ever.

Vice-President Al Gore championed something he called "reinventing government," but Clinton was distracted from domestic issues much of the year by foreign problems. His inexperience in foreign affairs was spotlighted by miscalculations in Somalia, Bosnia, and Haiti.

Over bitter labor opposition, the Clinton-backed North American Free Trade Agreement passed late in the year. Les Aspin resigned as U.S. secretary of defense, and the historic Israeli-Palestinian accords were signed at the White House by Yasser Arafat and Yitzhak Rabin.

ED GAMBLE
Courtesy Florida Times-Union

BOB GORRELL
Courtesy Richmond Times-Dispatch

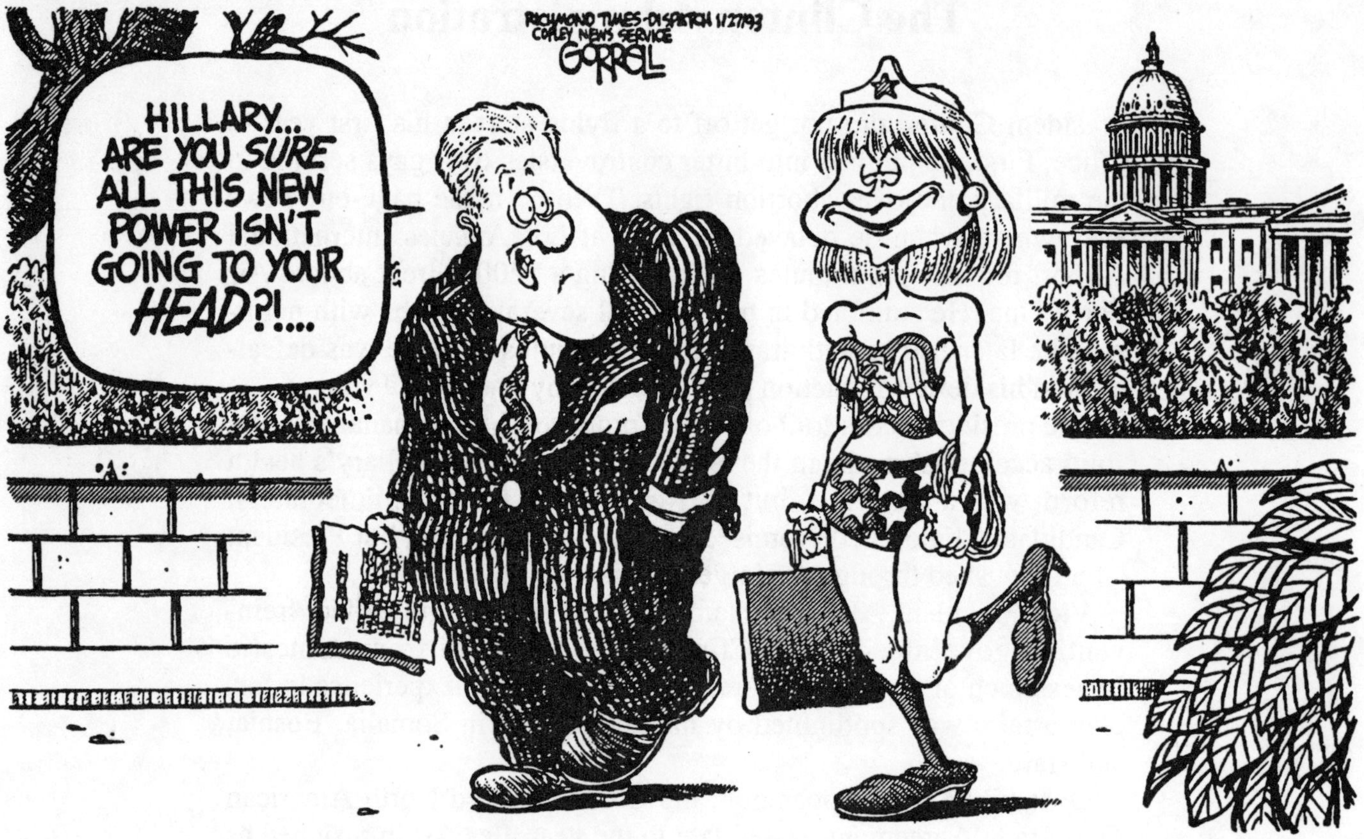
RICHMOND TIMES-DISPATCH 1/27/93
COPLEY NEWS SERVICE
GORRELL
HILLARY... ARE YOU SURE ALL THIS NEW POWER ISN'T GOING TO YOUR HEAD?!....

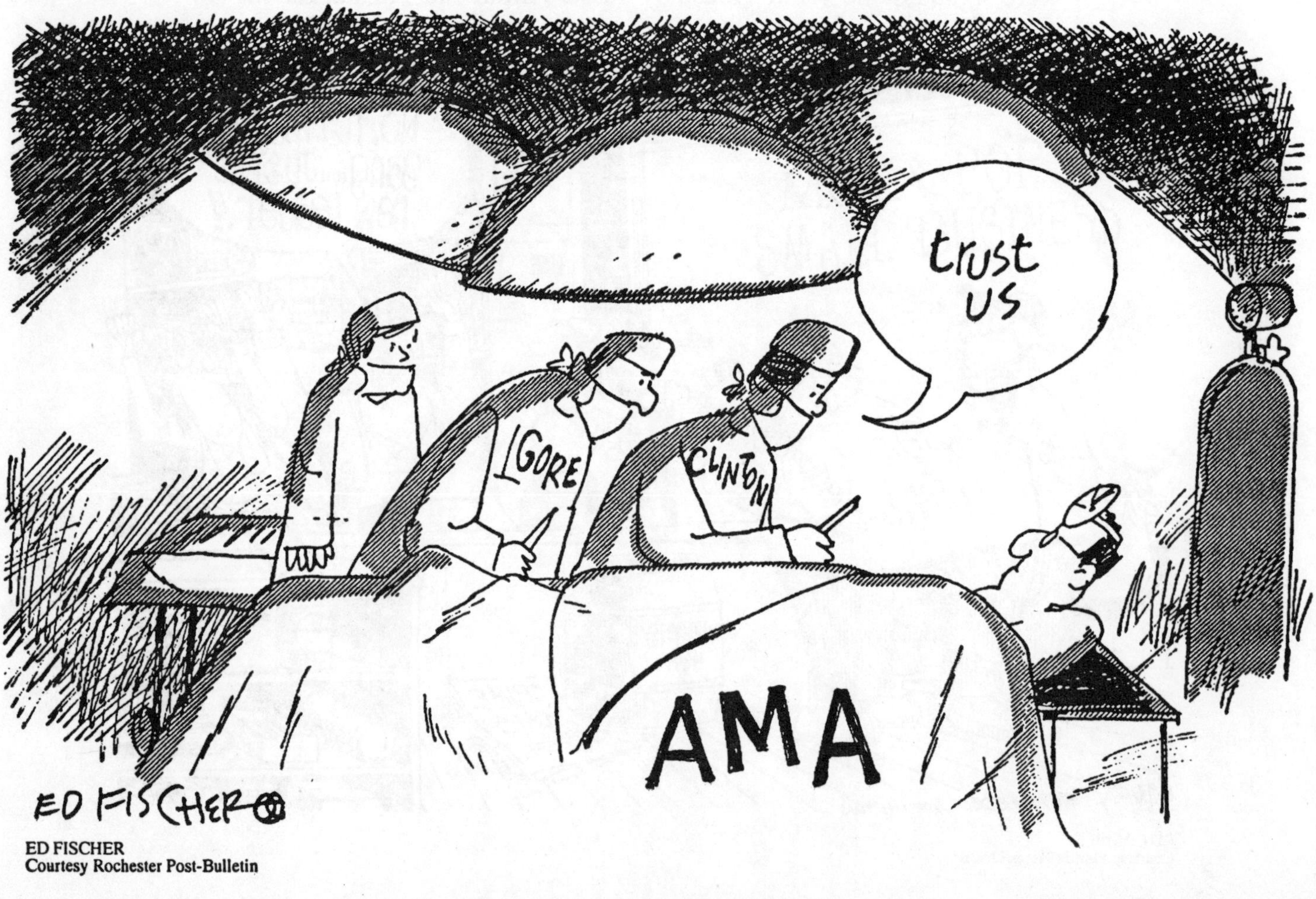
trust us
GORE
CLINTON
AMA
ED FISCHER

ED FISCHER
Courtesy Rochester Post-Bulletin

JEFF MACNELLY
Courtesy Chicago Tribune and
Tribune Media Services

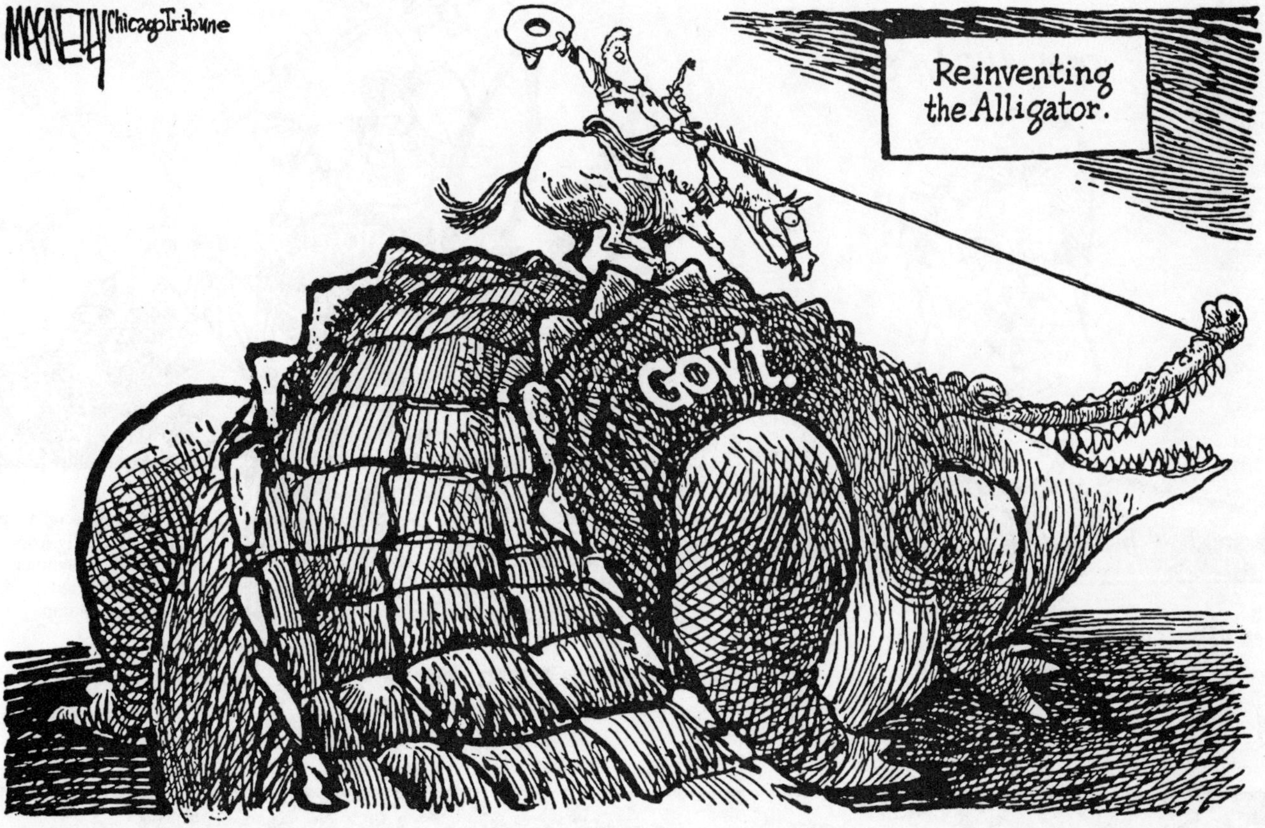
MACNELLY Chicago Tribune
Reinventing the Alligator.
GOV'T.

JOHN DEERING
Courtesy Arkansas Democrat Gazette

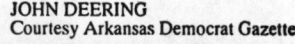

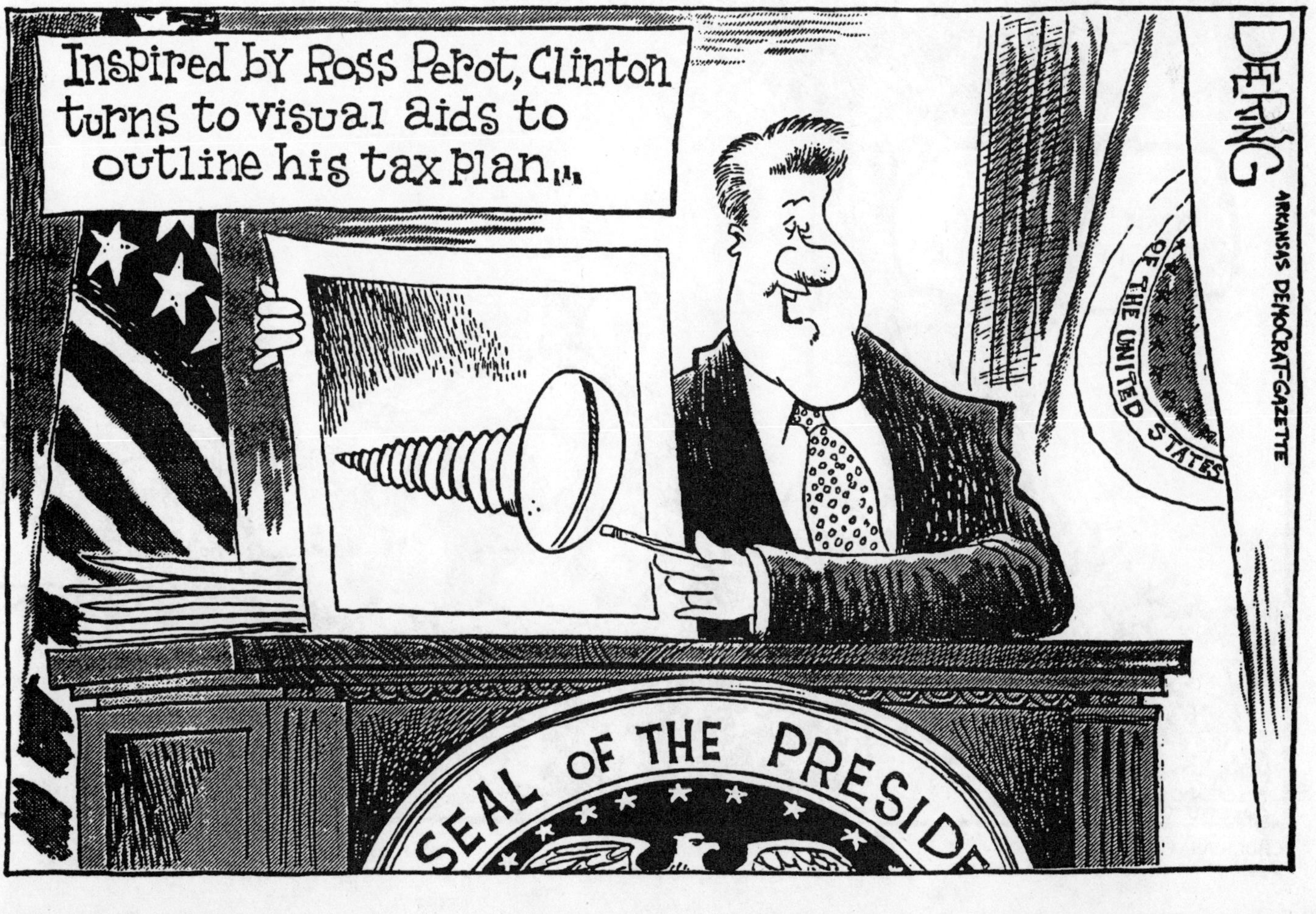
Inspired by Ross Perot, Clinton turns to visual aids to outline his tax plan...
DEERING
ARKANSAS DEMOCRAT-GAZETTE
OF THE UNITED STATES
SEAL OF THE PRESIDE

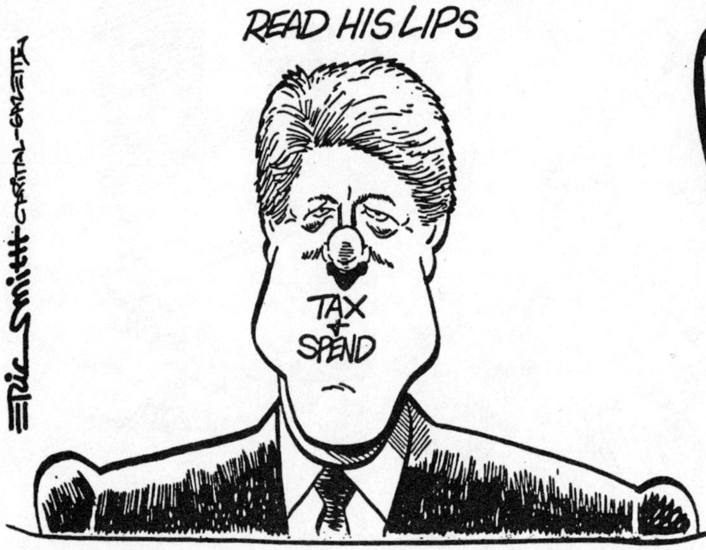
READ HIS LIPS
TAX + SPEND
Eric Smith CAPITAL-GAZETTE

ERIC SMITH
Courtesy Capital Gazette Newspapers

HUGH HAYNIE
Courtesy Louisville Courier Journal

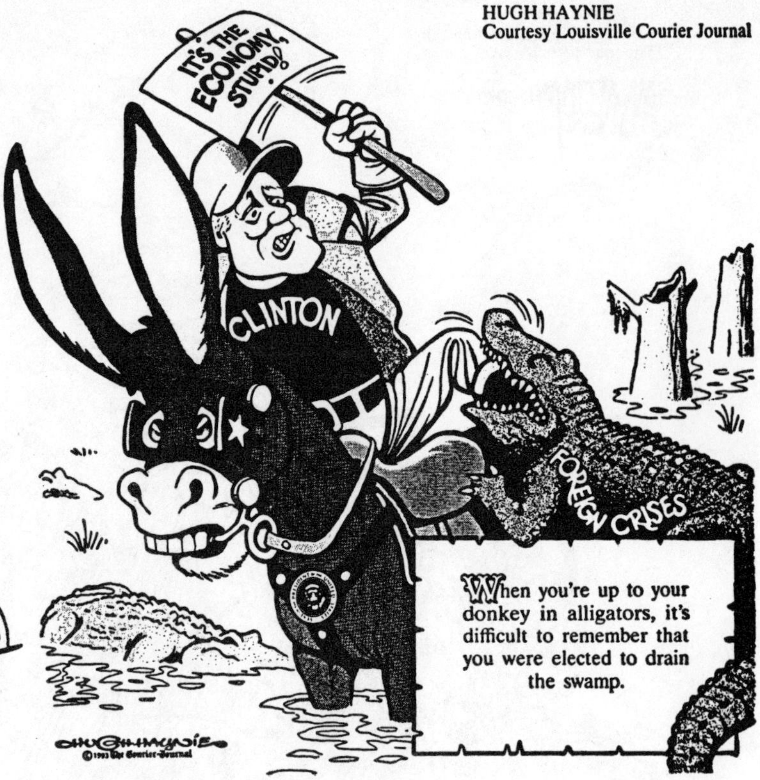
IT'S THE ECONOMY, STUPID!
CLINTON
FOREIGN CRISES
When you're up to your donkey in alligators, it's difficult to remember that you were elected to drain the swamp.

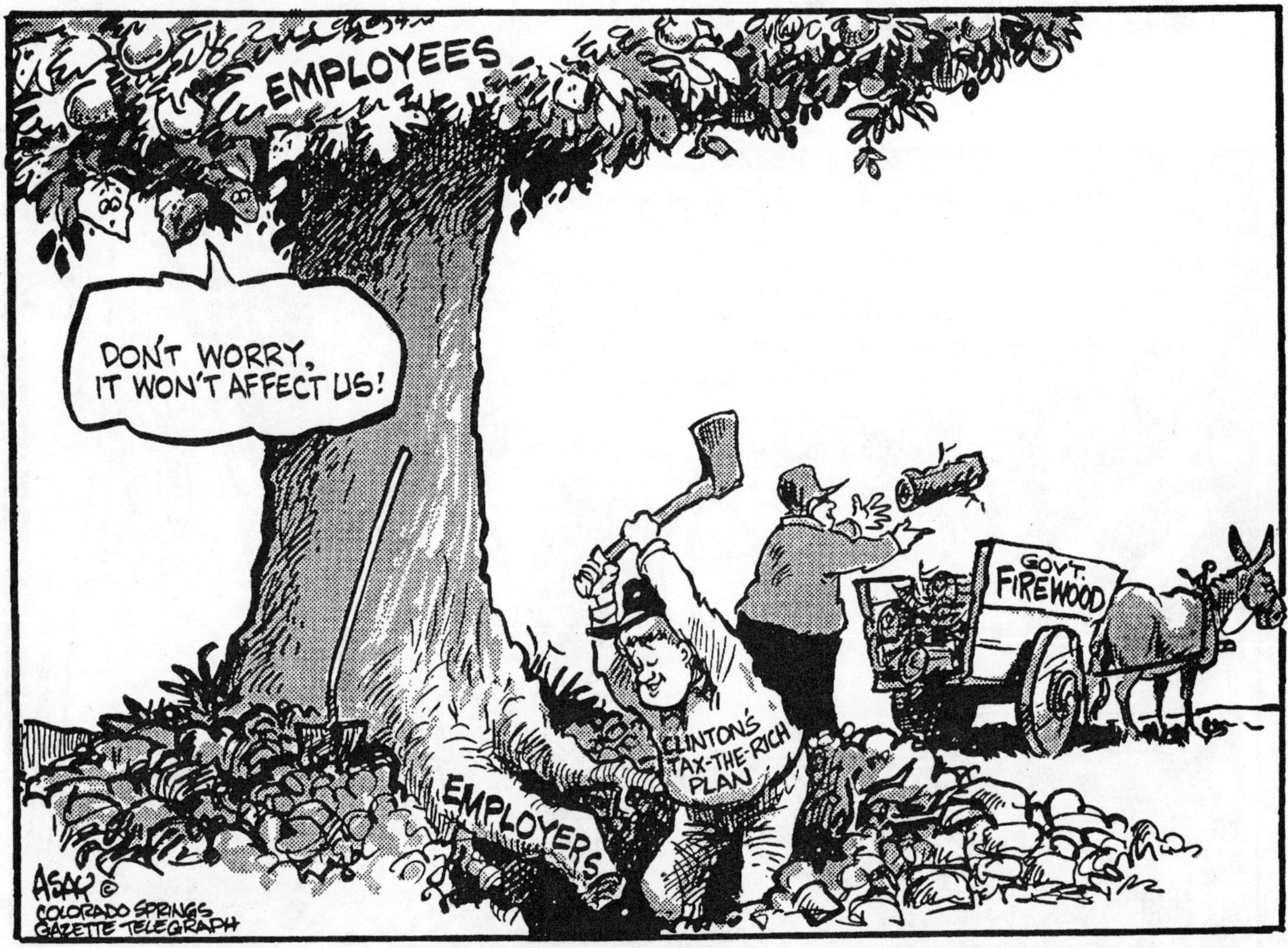
EMPLOYEES
DON'T WORRY, IT WON'T AFFECT US!
GOV'T. FIREWOOD
CLINTON'S TAX-THE-RICH PLAN
EMPLOYERS
ASAY © COLORADO SPRINGS GAZETTE TELEGRAPH

CHUCK ASAY
Courtesy Colorado Springs Gazette Telegraph

ED GAMBLE
Courtesy Florida Times-Union

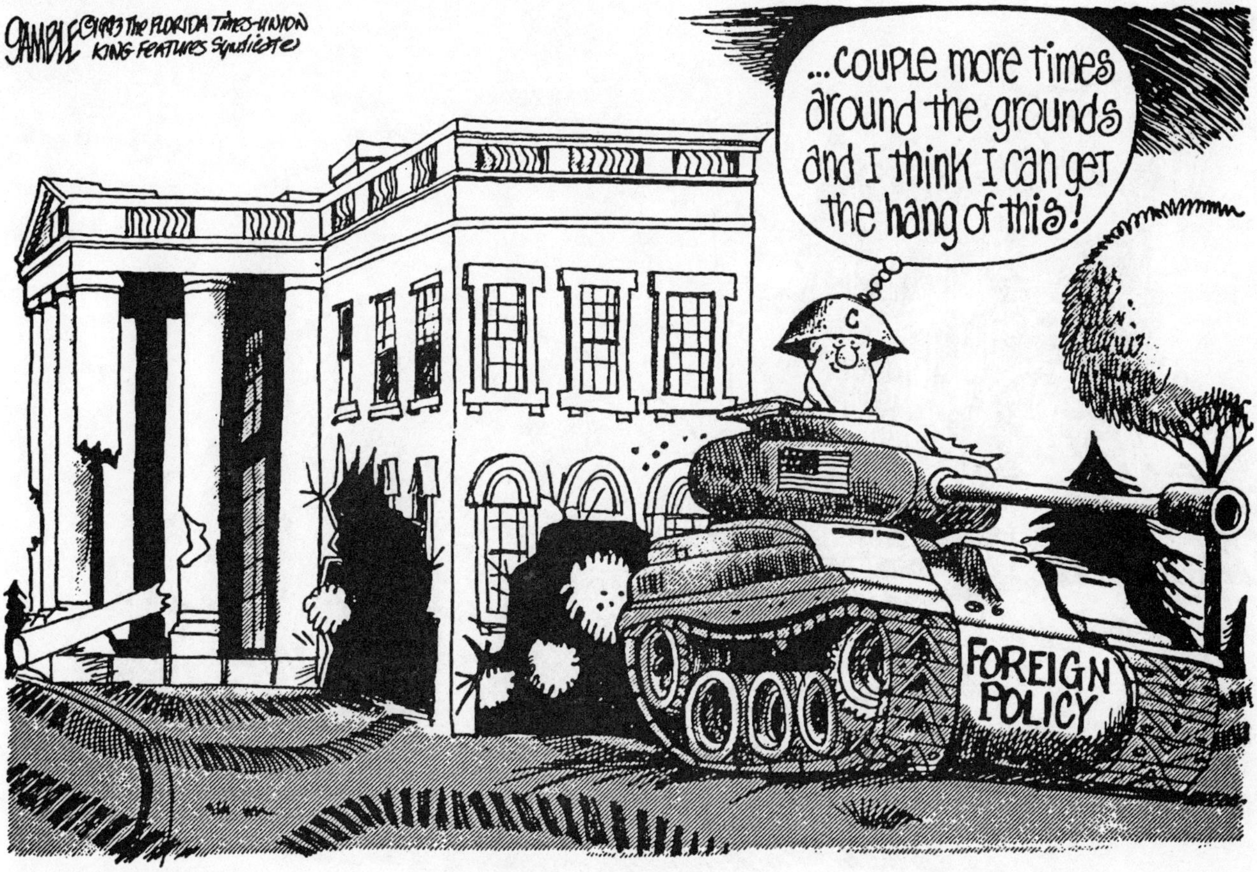
GAMBLE ©1993 The FLORIDA TIMES-UNION KING FEATURES Syndicate
...couple more times around the grounds and I think I can get the hang of this!
C
FOREIGN POLICY

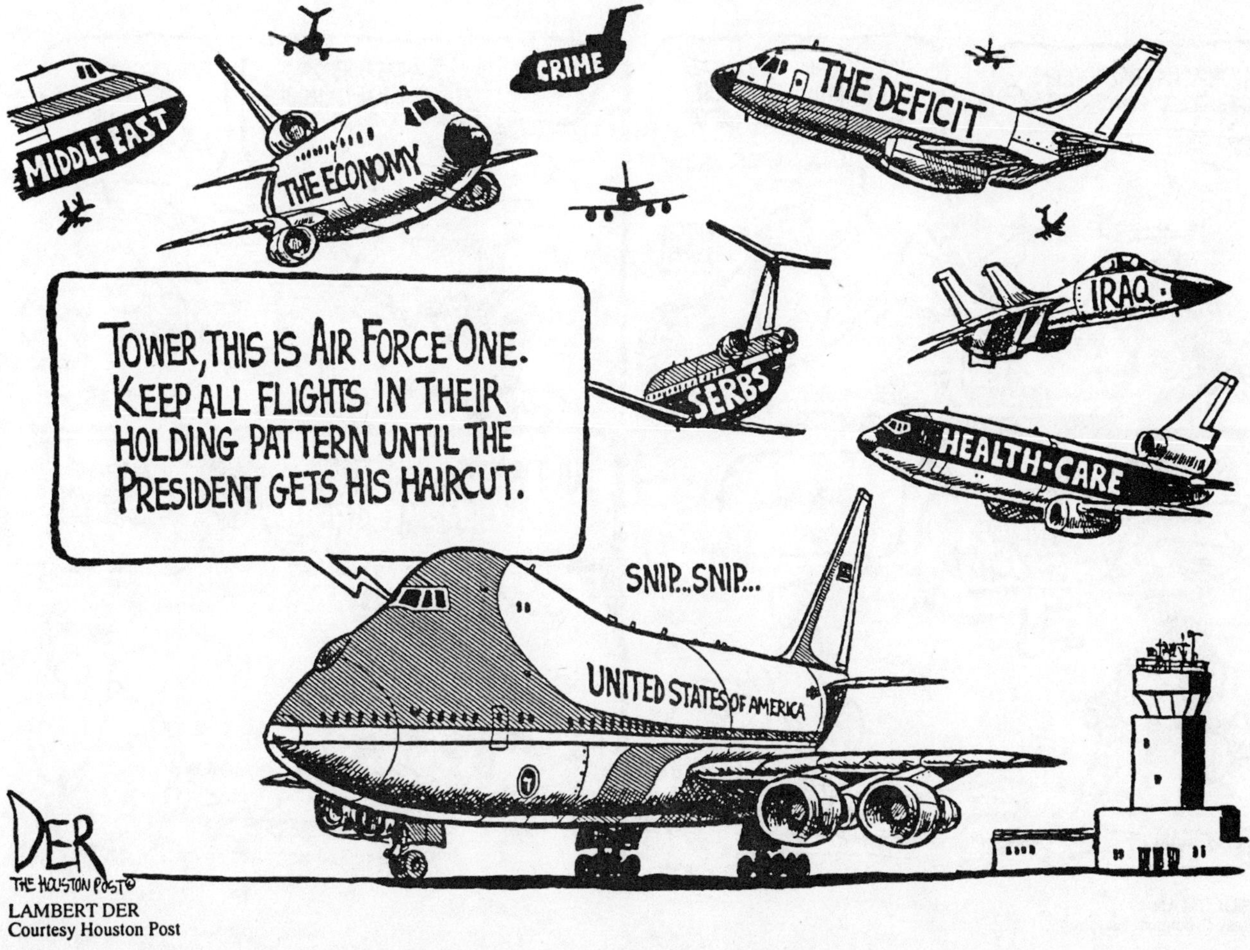
MIDDLE EAST
THE ECONOMY
CRIME
THE DEFICIT
TOWER, THIS IS AIR FORCE ONE. KEEP ALL FLIGHTS IN THEIR HOLDING PATTERN UNTIL THE PRESIDENT GETS HIS HAIRCUT.
SERBS
IRAQ
HEALTH-CARE
SNIP...SNIP...
UNITED STATES OF AMERICA
DER THE HOUSTON POST©

LAMBERT DER
Courtesy Houston Post

JEFF MACNELLY
Courtesy Chicago Tribune and
Tribune Media Services

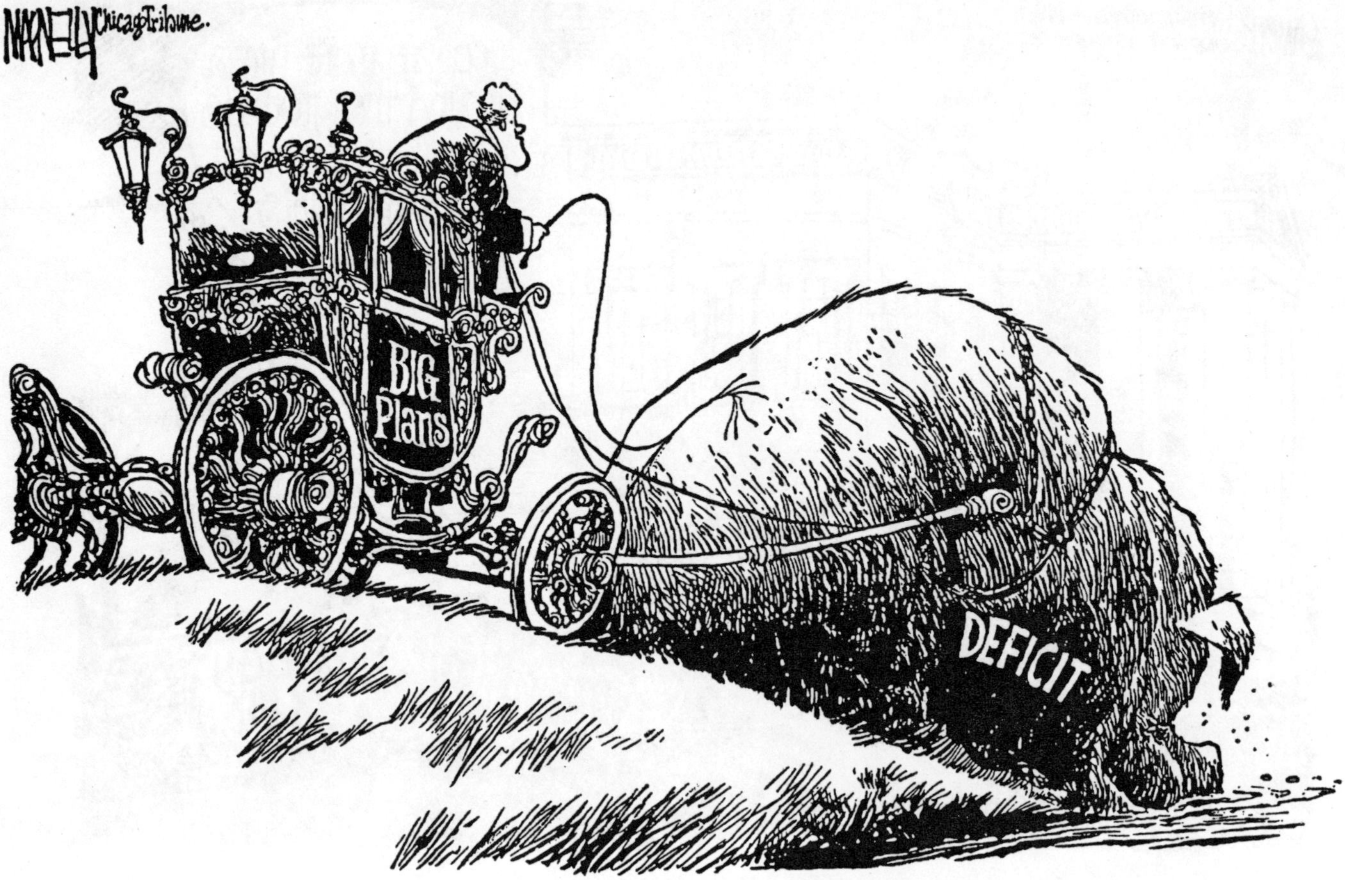
MACNELLY Chicago Tribune.
BIG Plans
DEFICIT

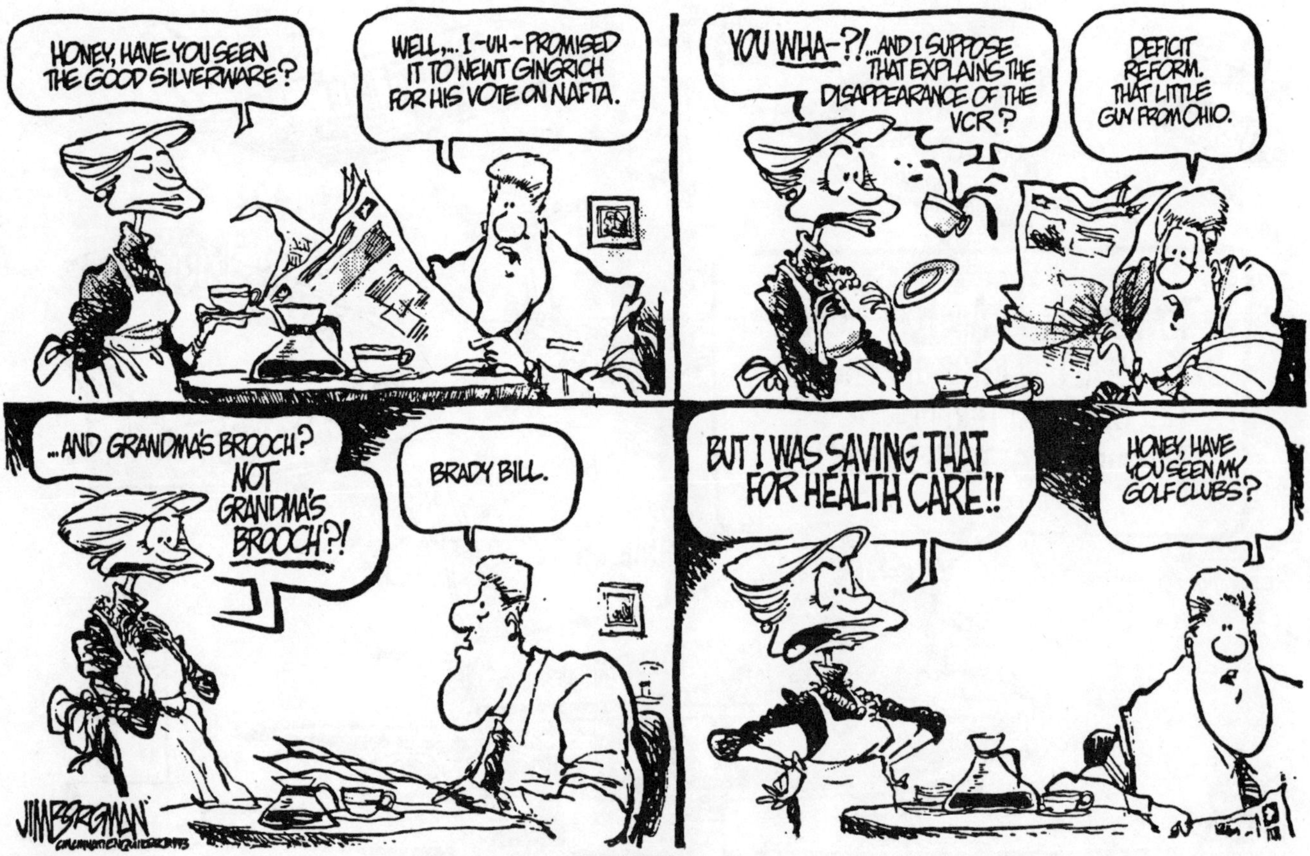
HONEY, HAVE YOU SEEN THE GOOD SILVERWARE?
WELL,... I-UH-PROMISED IT TO NEWT GINGRICH FOR HIS VOTE ON NAFTA.
YOU WHA-?!...AND I SUPPOSE THAT EXPLAINS THE DISAPPEARANCE OF THE VCR?
DEFICIT REFORM. THAT LITTLE GUY FROM OHIO.
...AND GRANDMA'S BROOCH? NOT GRANDMA'S BROOCH?!
BRADY BILL.
BUT I WAS SAVING THAT FOR HEALTH CARE!!
HONEY, HAVE YOU SEEN MY GOLF CLUBS?
JIM BORGMAN

JIM BORGMAN
Courtesy Cincinnati Enquirer

JEFF KOTERBA
Courtesy Omaha World-Herald

JONATHAN BROWN
Courtesy Clipper Publications (Utah)

FRANK CAMMUSO
Courtesy Syracuse Herald-Journal

CHAN LOWE
Courtesy The News/Sun-Sentinel (Fla.)

PAUL DUGINSKI
Courtesy McClatchy News Service

STEVE LINDSTROM
Courtesy Duluth News-Tribune

ROMAN GENN
Courtesy Easy Reader

GLENN MCCOY
Courtesy Belleville News-Democrat (Ill.)

BOB LANG
Courtesy Columbia City Post & Mail (Ind.)

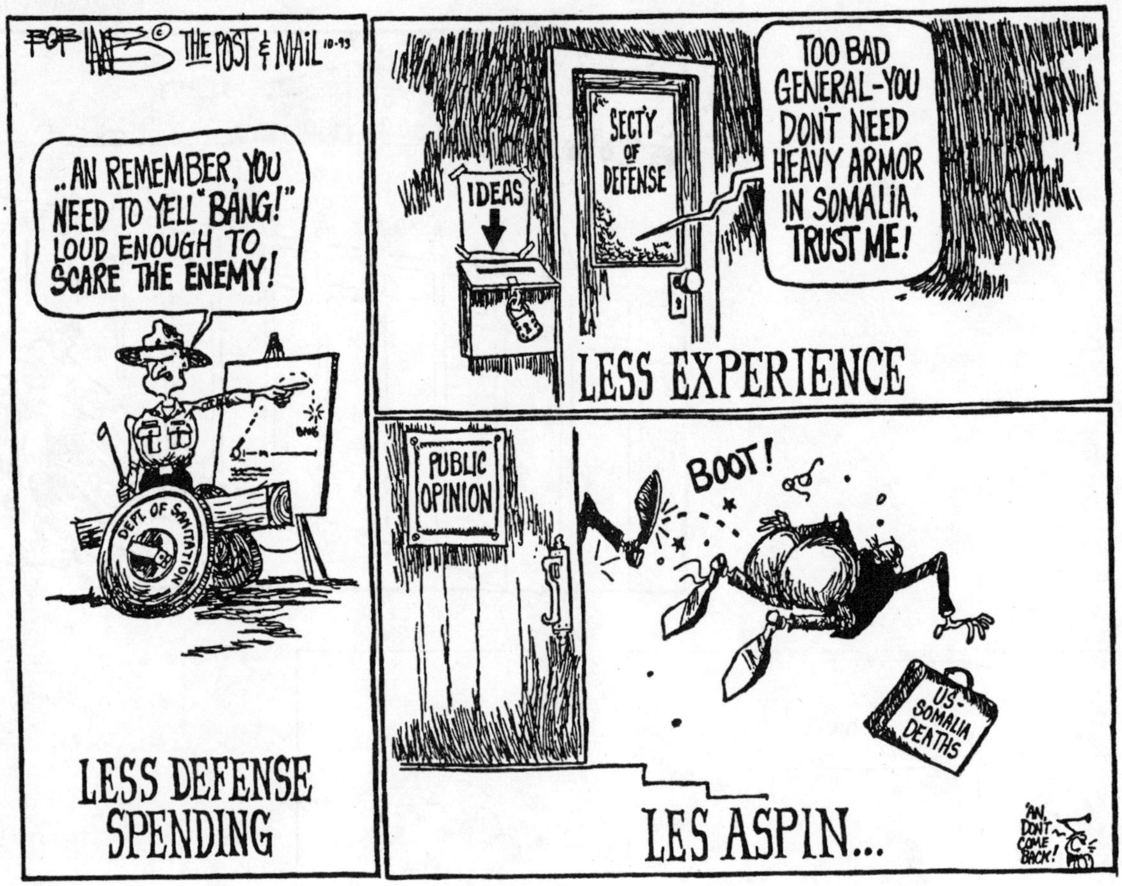
BOB LANG © THE POST & MAIL 10-93
..AN REMEMBER, YOU NEED TO YELL "BANG!" LOUD ENOUGH TO SCARE THE ENEMY!
DEPT. OF SANITATION
LESS DEFENSE SPENDING
IDEAS
SEC'TY OF DEFENSE
TOO BAD GENERAL-YOU DON'T NEED HEAVY ARMOR IN SOMALIA. TRUST ME!
LESS EXPERIENCE
PUBLIC OPINION
BOOT!
US-SOMALIA DEATHS
LES ASPIN...
'AN, DON'T COME BACK!

JOHN DEERING
Courtesy Arkansas Democrat-Gazette

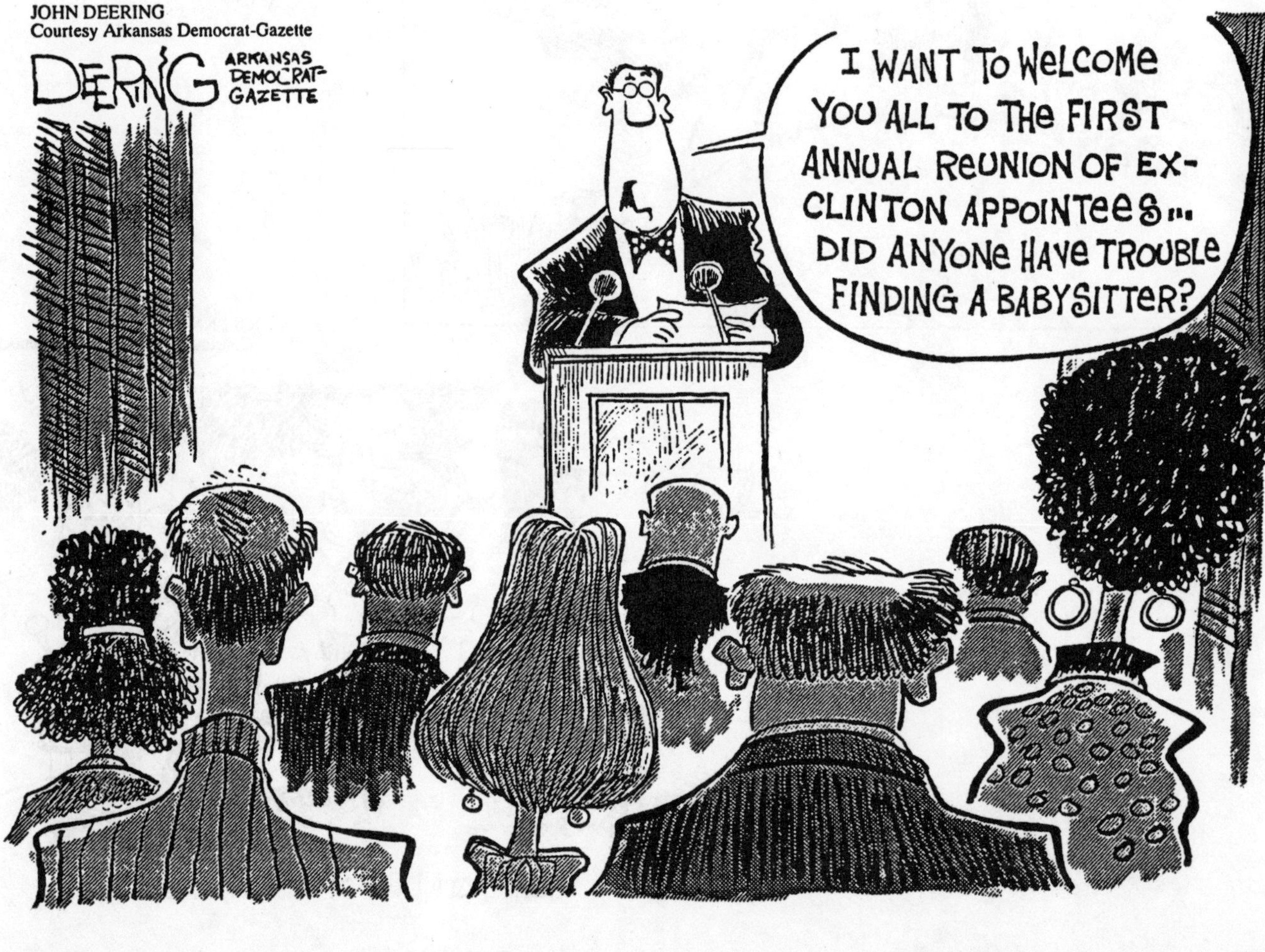
DEERING ARKANSAS DEMOCRAT-GAZETTE
I WANT TO WELCOME YOU ALL TO THE FIRST ANNUAL REUNION OF EX-CLINTON APPOINTEES... DID ANYONE HAVE TROUBLE FINDING A BABYSITTER?

WILLIAM COSTELLO
Courtesy NEA

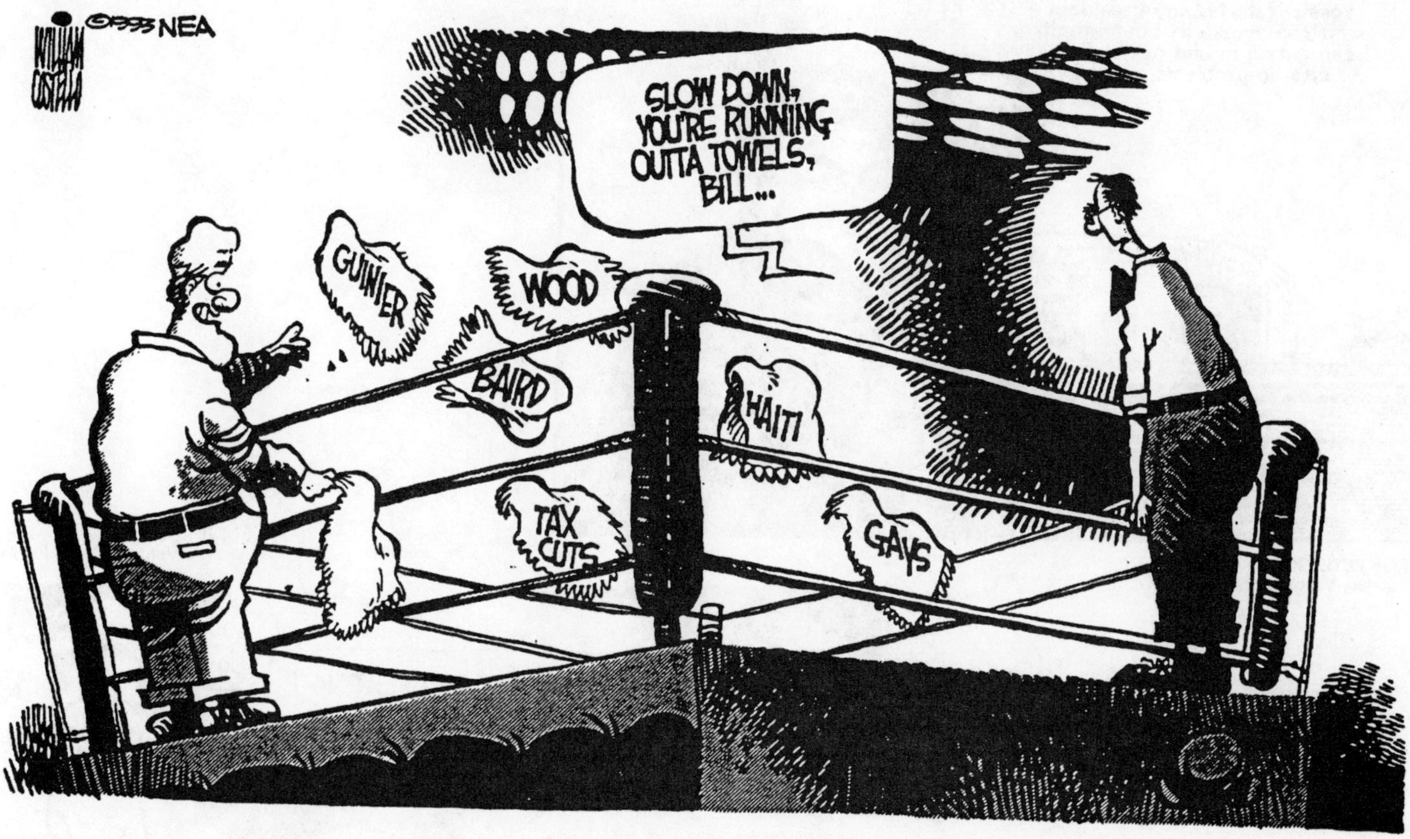
©1993 NEA
SLOW DOWN, YOU'RE RUNNING OUTTA TOWELS, BILL...
GUINIER
WOOD
BAIRD
HAITI
TAX CUTS
GAYS

JEFF MACNELLY
Courtesy Chicago Tribune and
Tribune Media Services

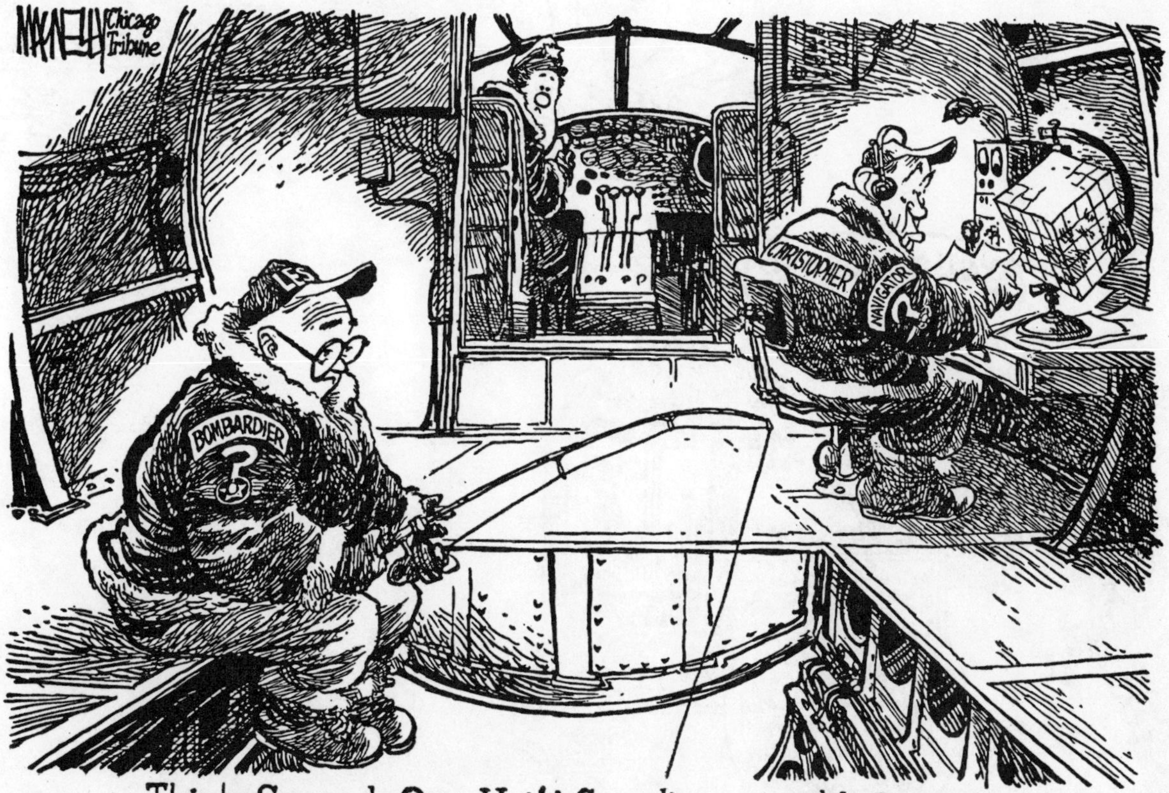
Chicago Tribune
BOMBARDIER
CHRISTOPHER
NAVIGATOR

Thirty Seconds Over Haiti, Somalia or possibly Bosnia.

ROY PETERSON
Courtesy Vancouver Sun

JACK JURDEN
Courtesy Wilmington News Journal

CHIP BECK
Courtesy Northern Virginia Sun
and Associated Features

ART WOOD
Courtesy Farm Bureau News

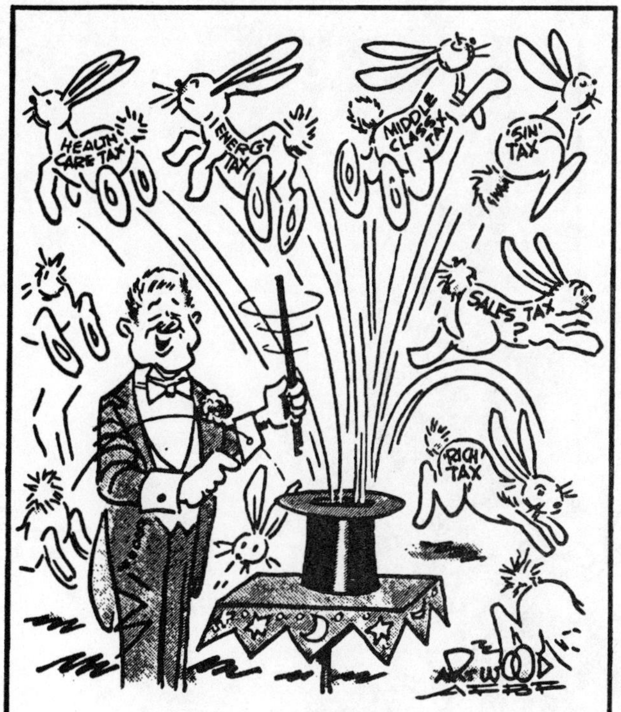
HEALTH CARE TAX
ENERGY TAX
MIDDLE CLASS TAX
'SIN' TAX
SALES TAX?
RICH TAX

'Now for my next trick...'

CHARLES BISSELL
Courtesy The Tennessean

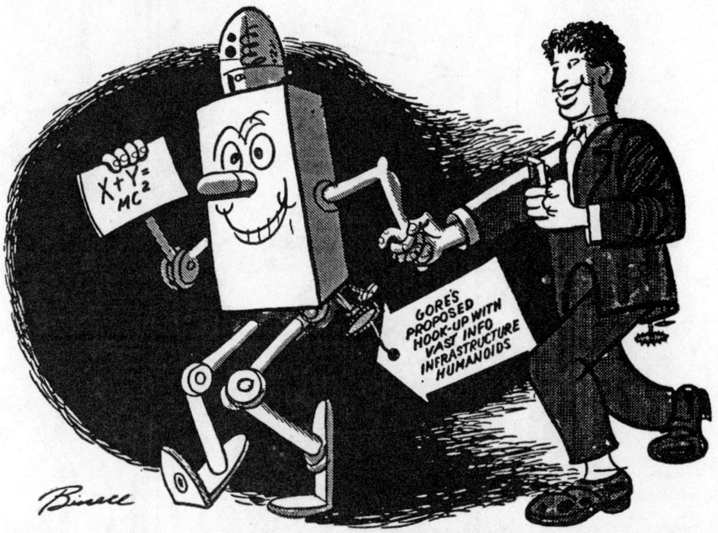
X+Y= MC²
GORE'S PROPOSED HOOK-UP WITH VAST INFO INFRASTRUCTURE HUMANOIDS
Bissell

"NOW LOOSEN THAT LEFT, NOW RIGHT! FINE! REMEMBER I'VE BEEN ACCUSED OF BEING A LITTLE BIT STIFF MYSELF."

JEFF STAHLER
Courtesy Cincinnati Post

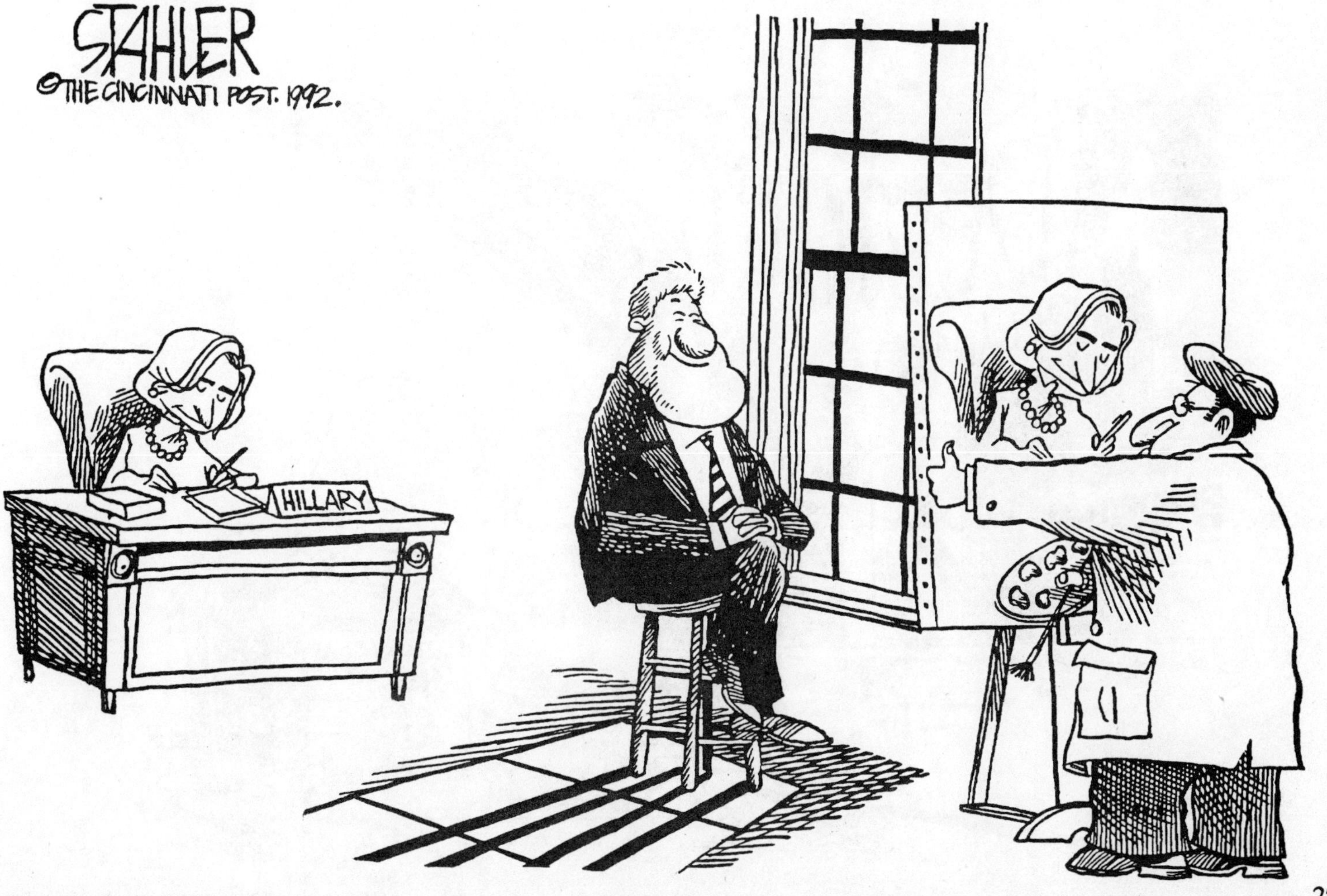
STAHLER
©THE CINCINNATI POST. 1992.
HILLARY

BEN SARGENT
Courtesy Austin American Statesman

BUBBA FLINT
Courtesy Ft. Worth Star-Telegram

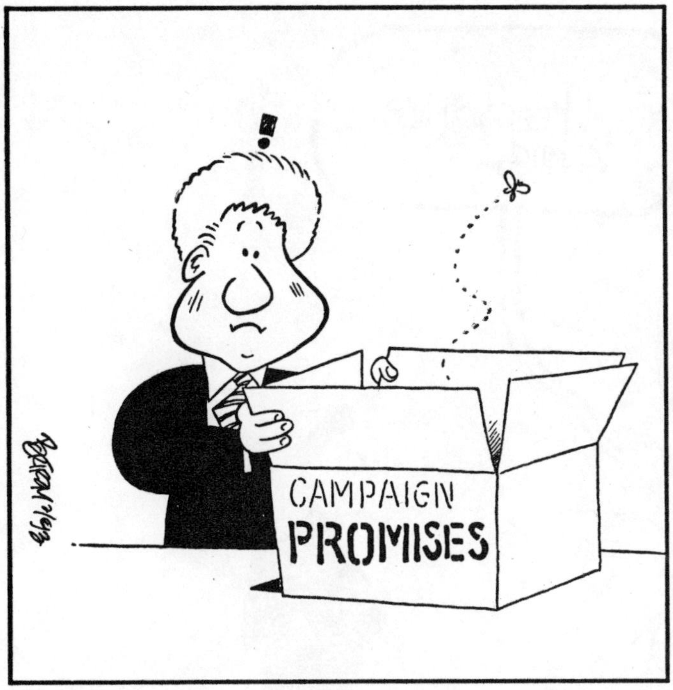
CAMPAIGN
PROMISES

JIM BERTRAM
Courtesy St. Cloud Times

PAUL SZEP
Courtesy Boston Globe

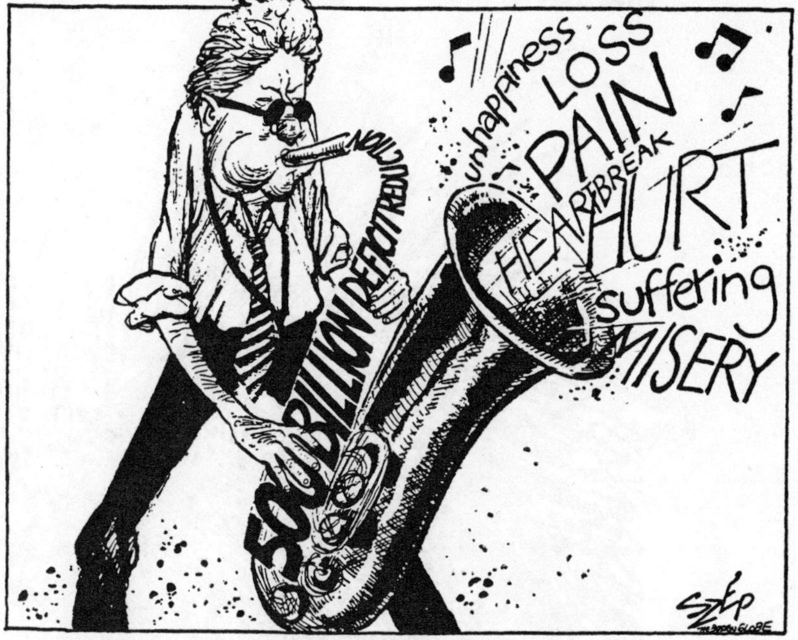
500 BILLION DEFICIT REDUCTION
unhappiness
LOSS
PAIN
HEARTBREAK
HURT
suffering
MISERY

The Blues Player

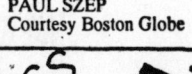

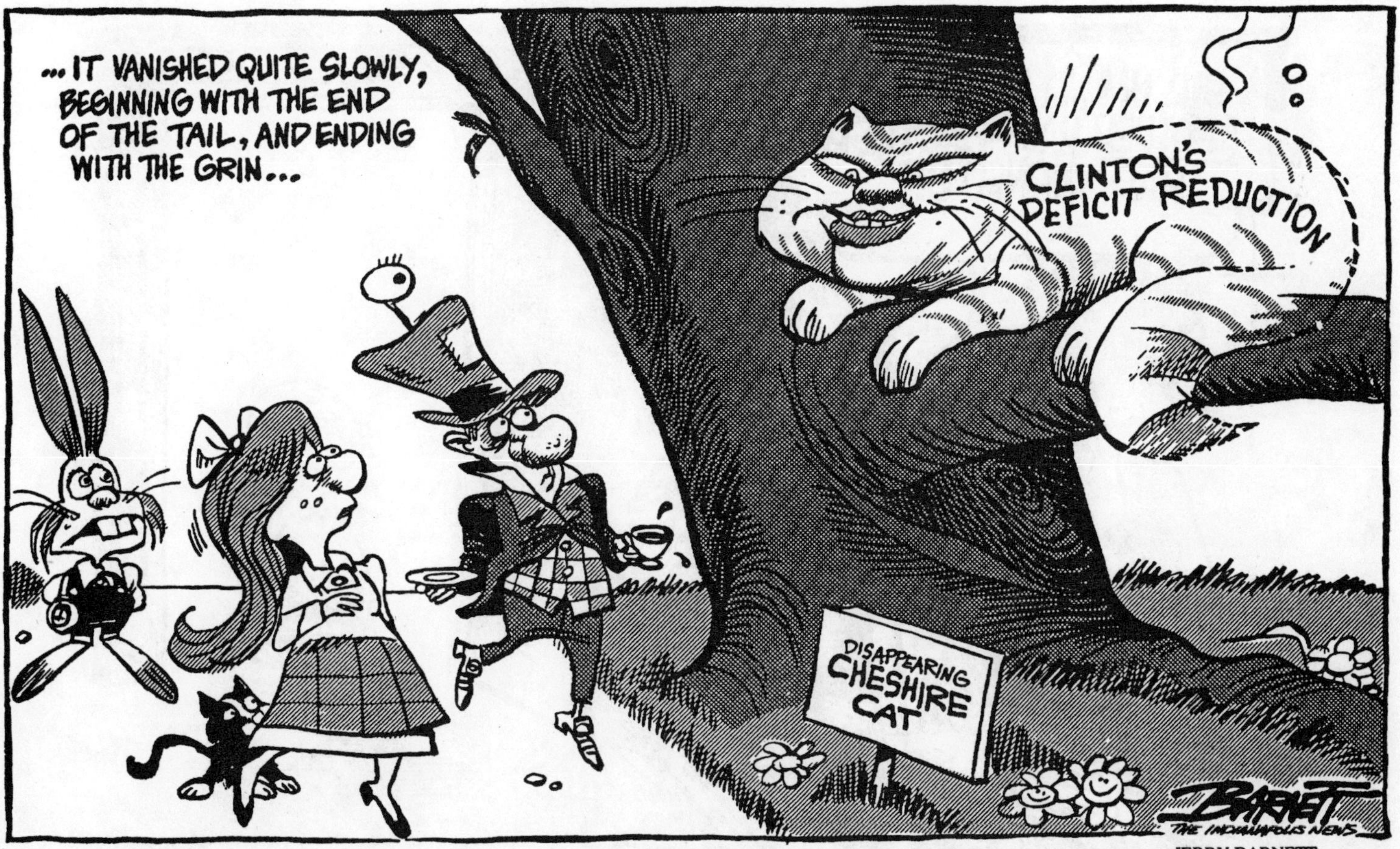
... IT VANISHED QUITE SLOWLY, BEGINNING WITH THE END OF THE TAIL, AND ENDING WITH THE GRIN...
CLINTON'S DEFICIT REDUCTION
DISAPPEARING CHESHIRE CAT

JERRY BARNETT
Courtesy Indianapolis News

MIKE LUCKOVICH
Courtesy Atlanta Constitution

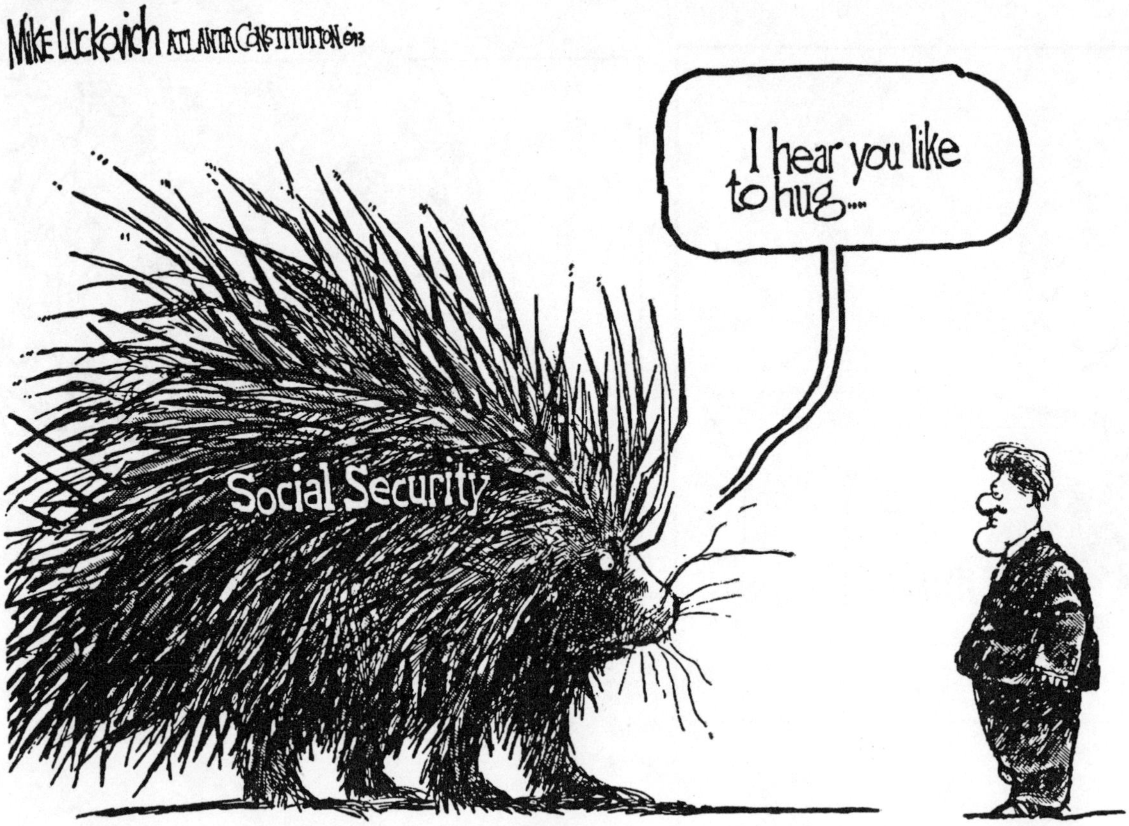
MIKE LUCKOVICH ATLANTA CONSTITUTION ©93
I hear you like to hug....
Social Security

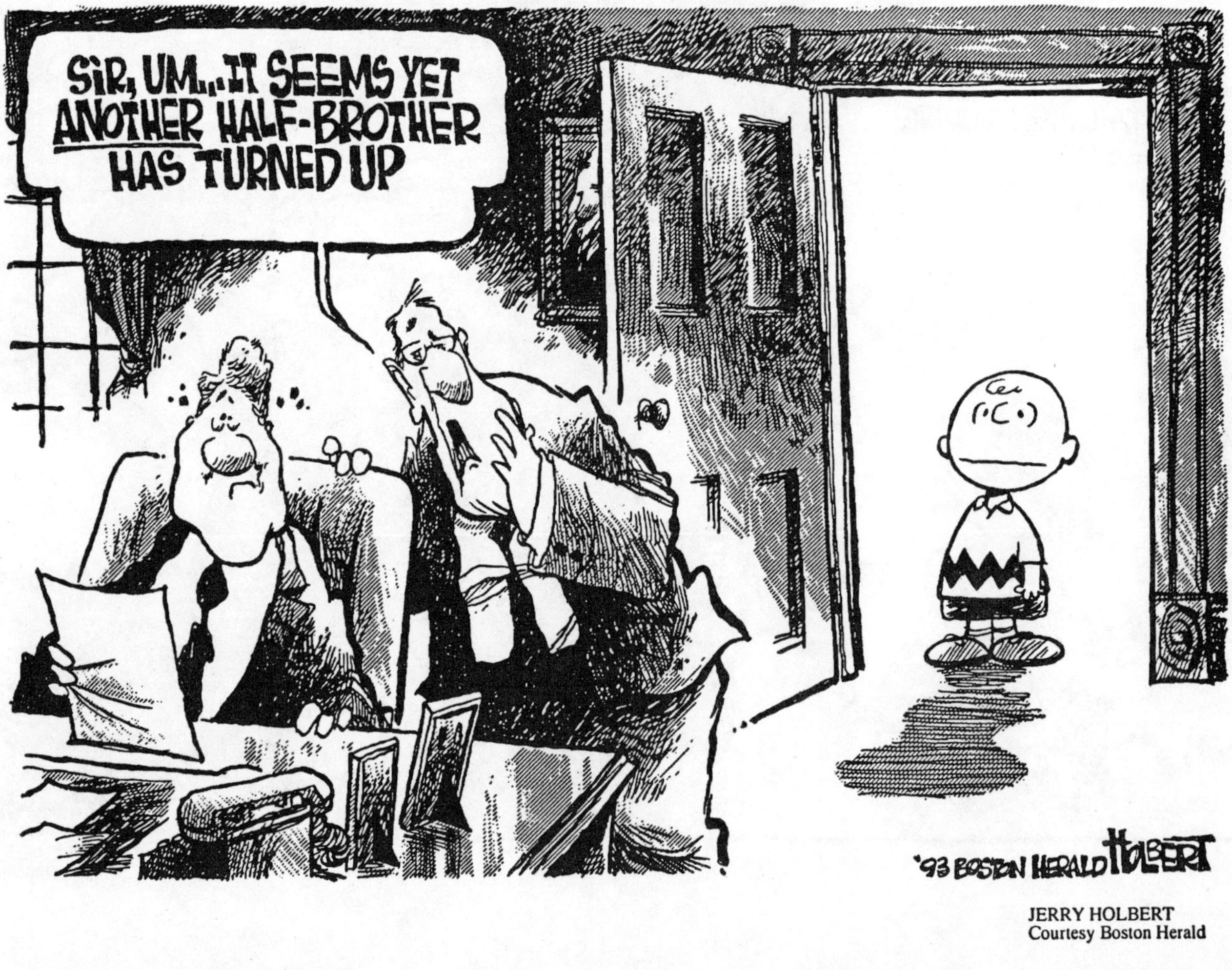
SIR, UM... IT SEEMS YET ANOTHER HALF-BROTHER HAS TURNED UP
'93 BOSTON HERALD HOLBERT

JERRY HOLBERT
Courtesy Boston Herald

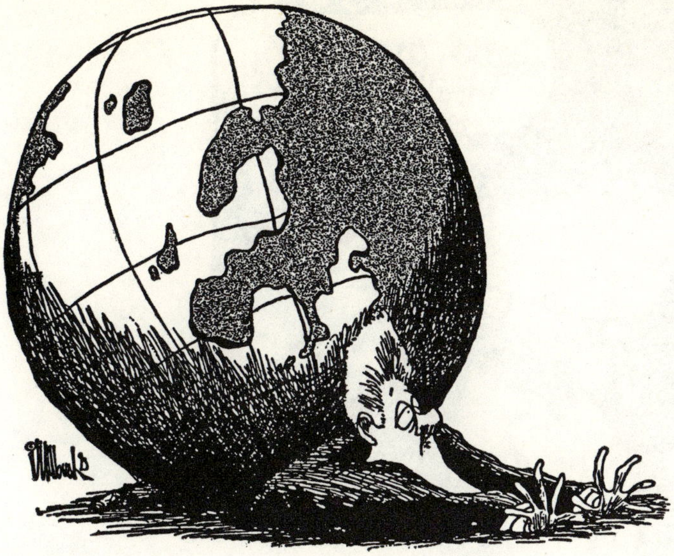

JIM BUSH
Courtesy Washington Post

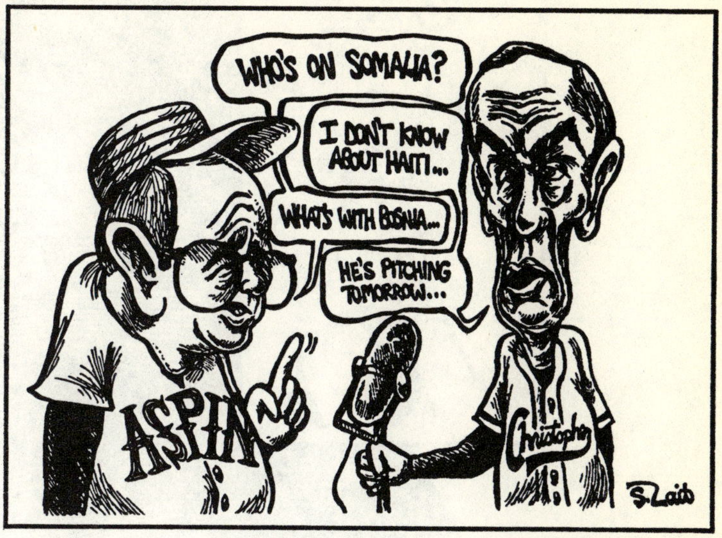
WHO'S ON SOMALIA?
I DON'T KNOW ABOUT HAITI...
WHAT'S WITH BOSNIA...
HE'S PITCHING TOMORROW...
ASPIN
Christopher
S. Lait

STEVEN LAIT
Courtesy Oakland Tribune

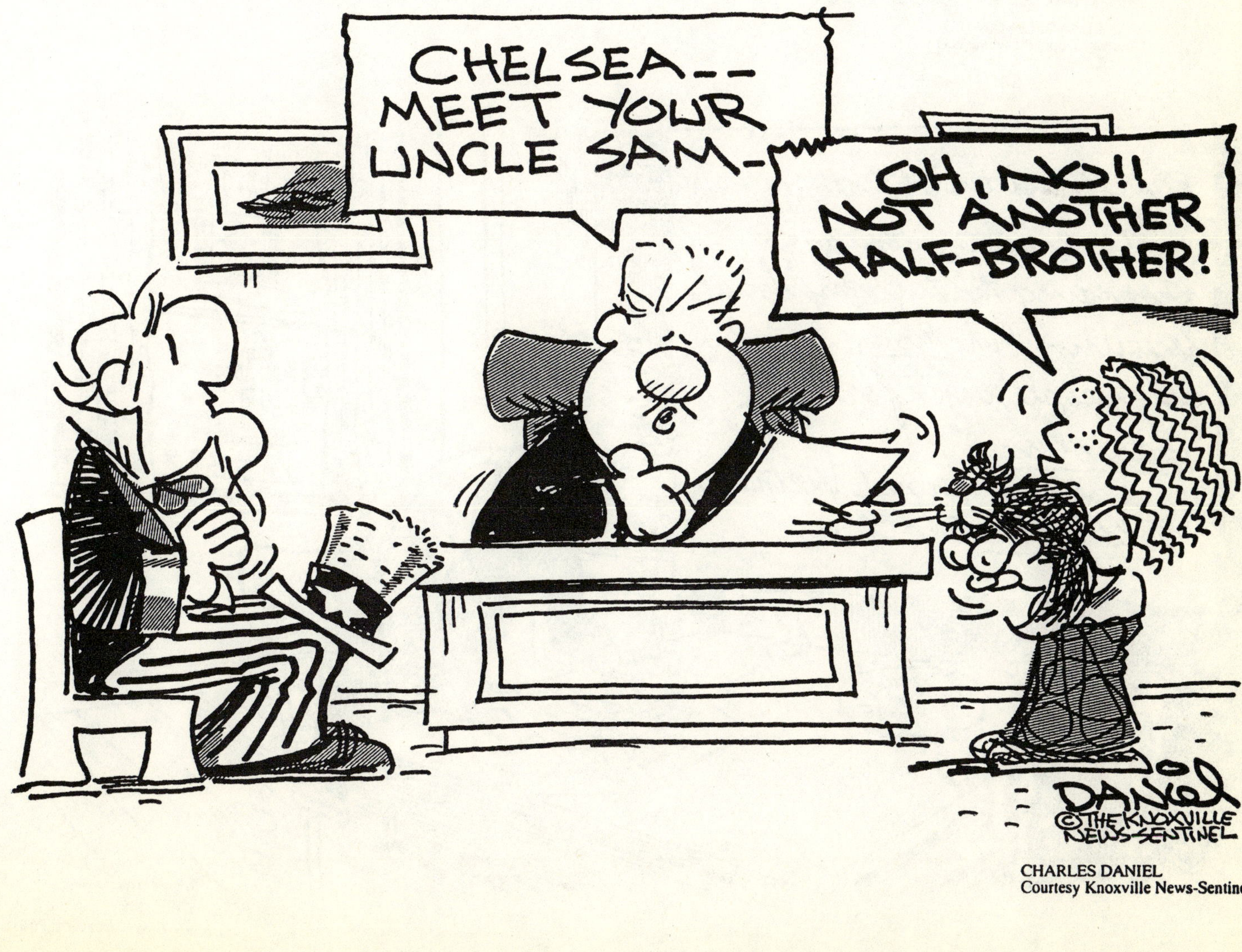
CHELSEA-- MEET YOUR UNCLE SAM-
OH, NO!! NOT ANOTHER HALF-BROTHER!
DANIEL
©THE KNOXVILLE NEWS-SENTINEL

CHARLES DANIEL
Courtesy Knoxville News-Sentinel

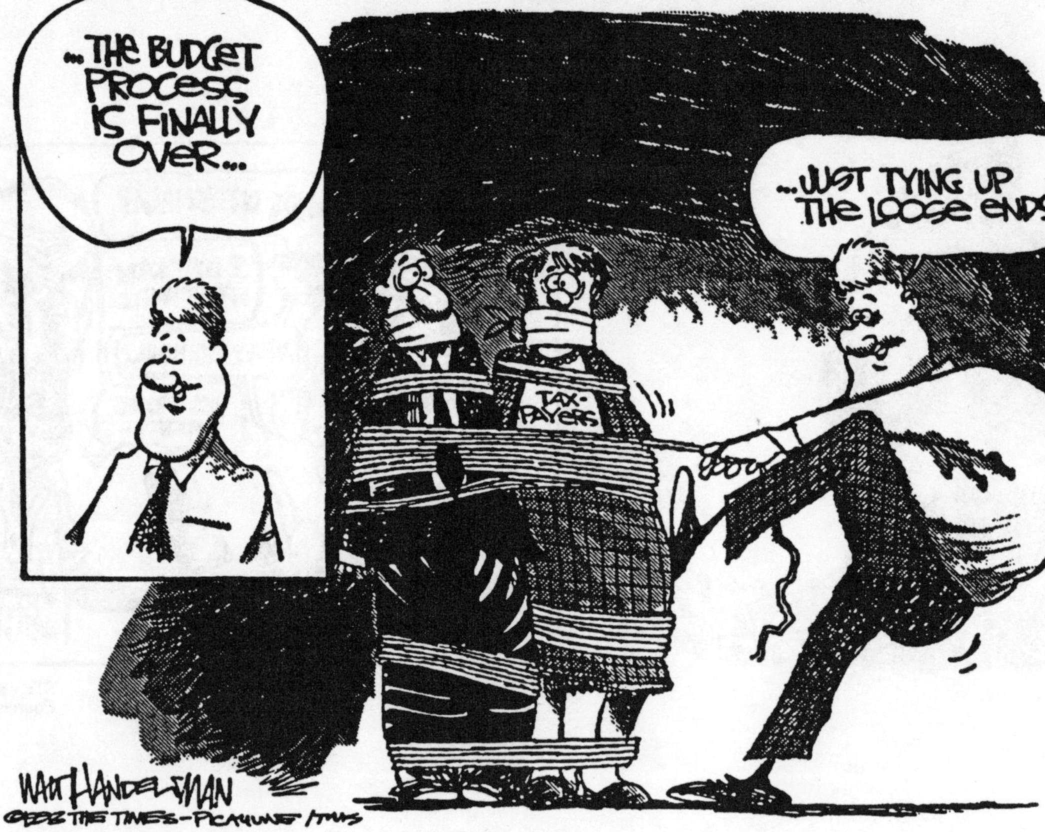
...THE BUDGET PROCESS IS FINALLY OVER...
...JUST TYING UP THE LOOSE ENDS.
TAX-PAYERS
WALT HANDELSMAN

WALT HANDELSMAN
Courtesy Times-Picayune (N.O.)

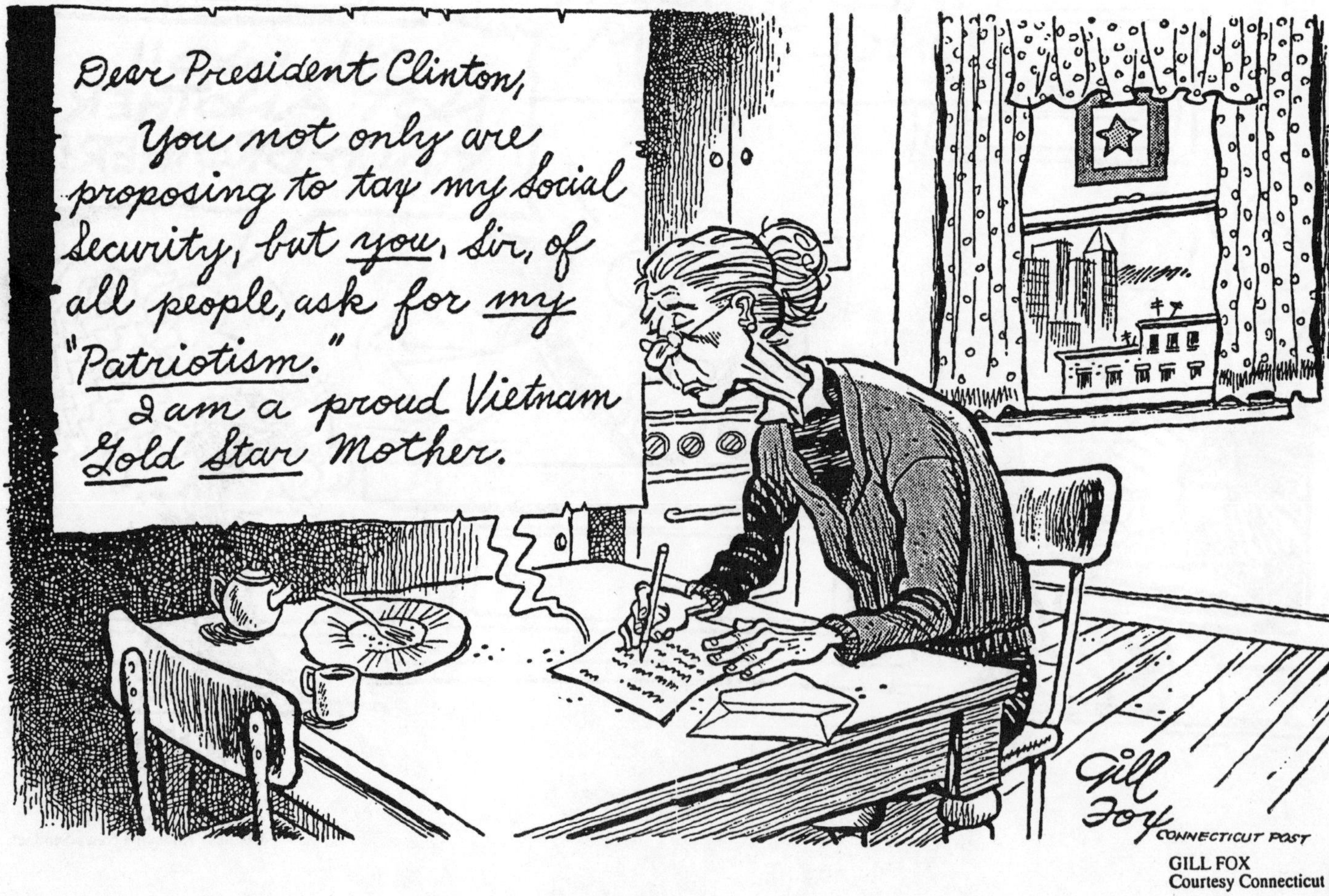
Dear President Clinton,
You not only are proposing to tax my Social Security, but you, Sir, of all people, ask for my "Patriotism."
I am a proud Vietnam Gold Star Mother.
GILL FOX
CONNECTICUT POST

GILL FOX
Courtesy Connecticut Post

LARRY WRIGHT
Courtesy Detroit News

JOE HOFFECKER
Courtesy Cincinnati Business Courier

MIKE THOMPSON
Courtesy State Journal-Register (Ill.)

31

GEORGE DANBY
Courtesy Bangor Daily News

STEVE KELLEY
Courtesy San Diego Union

ED STEIN
Courtesy Rocky Mountain News and NEA

WALT HANDELSMAN
Courtesy Times-Picayune (N.O.)

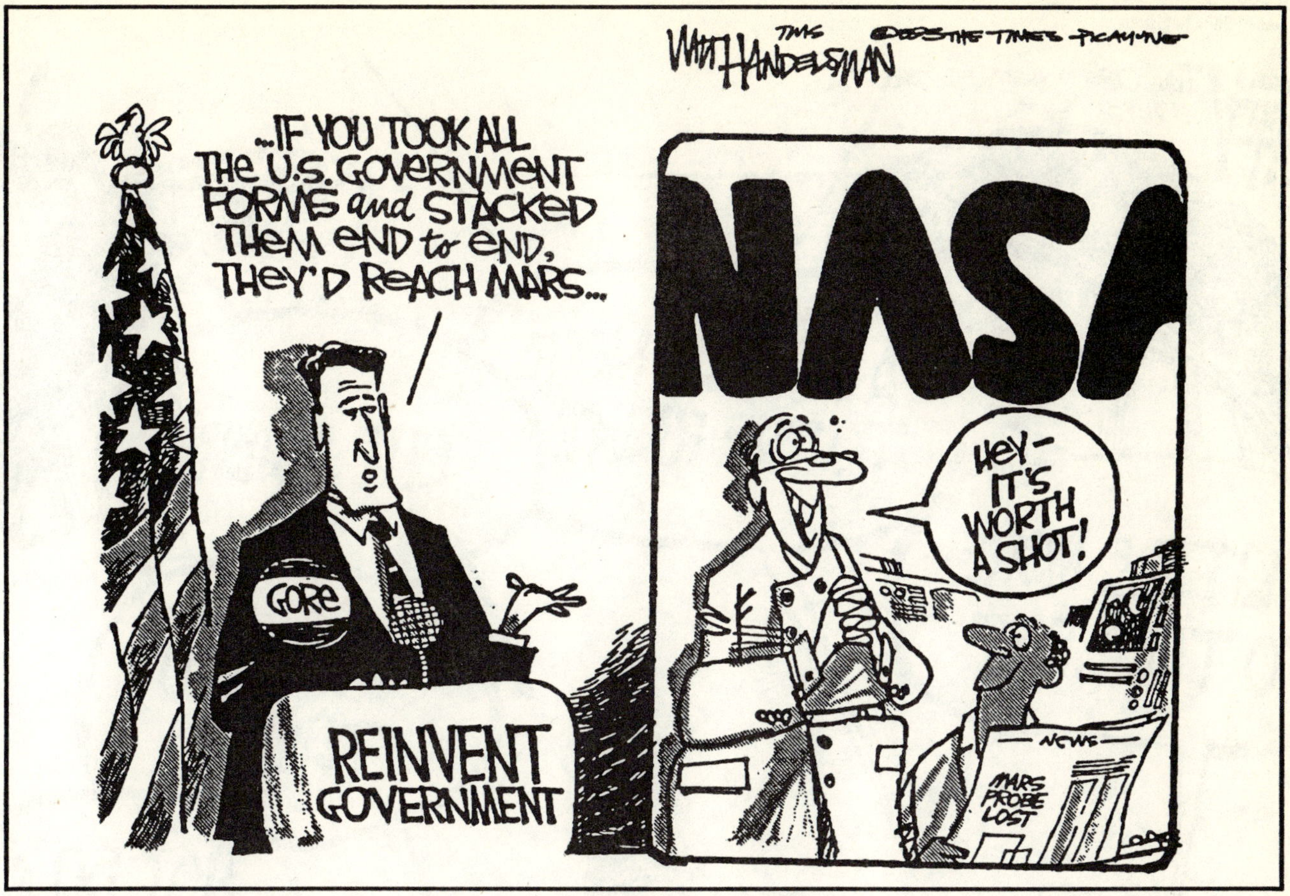
WALT HANDELSMAN
©1993 THE TIMES-PICAYUNE
...IF YOU TOOK ALL THE U.S. GOVERNMENT FORMS and STACKED THEM END to END, THEY'D REACH MARS...
GORE
REINVENT GOVERNMENT
NASA
HEY- IT'S WORTH A SHOT!
NEWS
MARS PROBE LOST

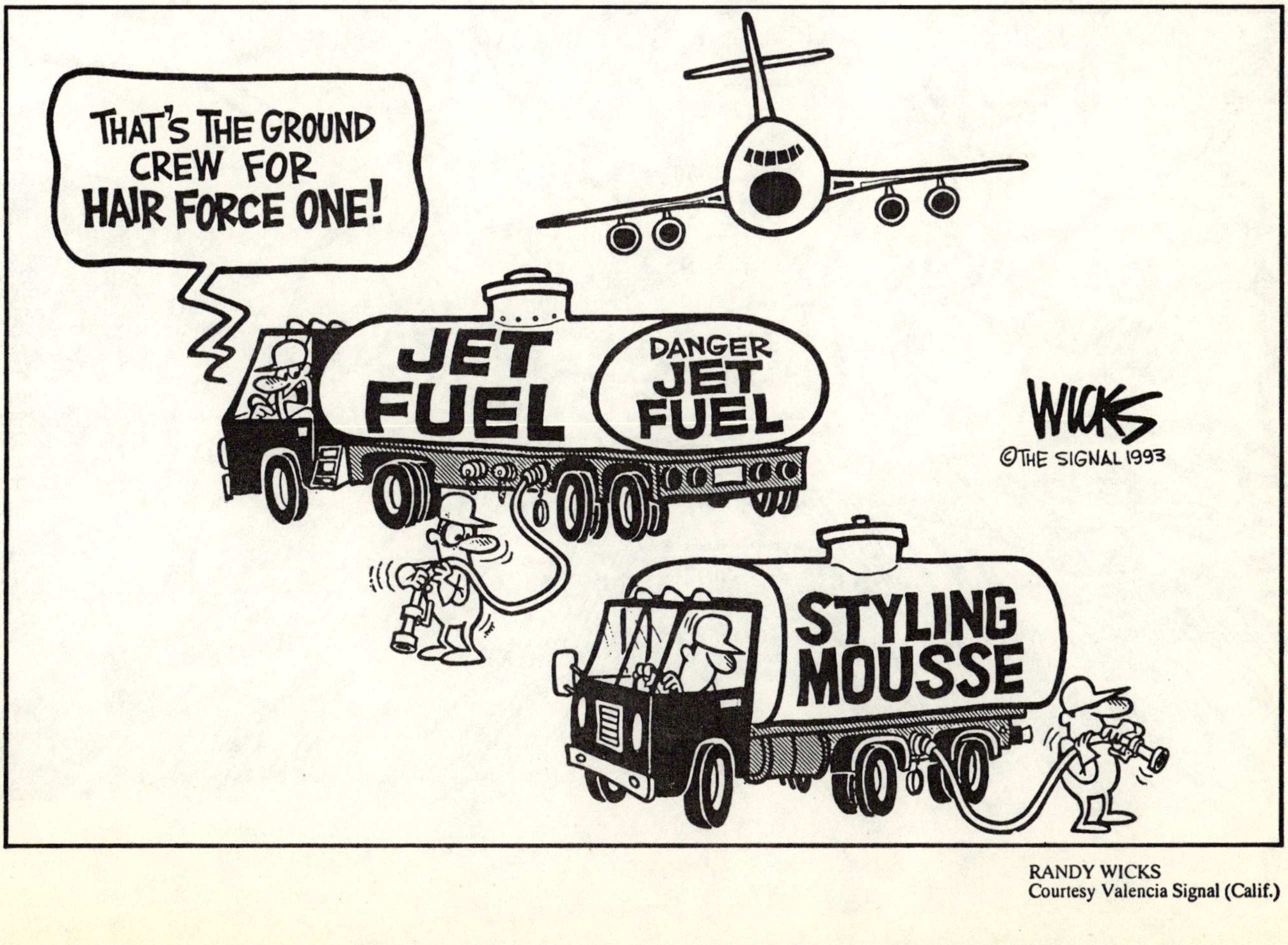
THAT'S THE GROUND CREW FOR HAIR FORCE ONE!
JET FUEL
DANGER JET FUEL
STYLING MOUSSE
WICKS
©THE SIGNAL 1993

RANDY WICKS
Courtesy Valencia Signal (Calif.)

BRIAN DUFFY
Courtesy Des Moines Register

Health Care

After eight months of generally secretive work, Hillary Rodham Clinton and the president unveiled their new health care plan on September 22. The far-reaching reform package is intended to make adequate health care available to every American. It proposes that some 70 percent of the population be required to obtain health insurance through regional health alliances. The alliances would be controlled by the federal government and charged with ensuring that every citizen—whether rich or poor—gets the same health care.

The Clinton Administration could only guess at the ultimate cost of the plan. The president acknowledges that it could cost private business at least $200 billion over the next seven years, and many small businesses fear they may not be able to survive. Heavy new sin taxes, including an additional seventy-five cents per pack on cigarettes and higher levies on alcohol, have been proposed to help pay for the costly program.

Under the rules of the proposed plan, consulting a specialist would be difficult and price controls might make private practice for doctors unfeasible. One part of the president's package that is sure to generate widespread opposition is the planned cutback in expenditures for Medicare and Medicaid.

The task of transforming this sweeping 245-page draft into legislation that can pass a nervous Congress could extend beyond 1994.

GARY BROOKINS
Courtesy Richmond Times-Dispatch

LAMBERT DER
Courtesy Houston Post

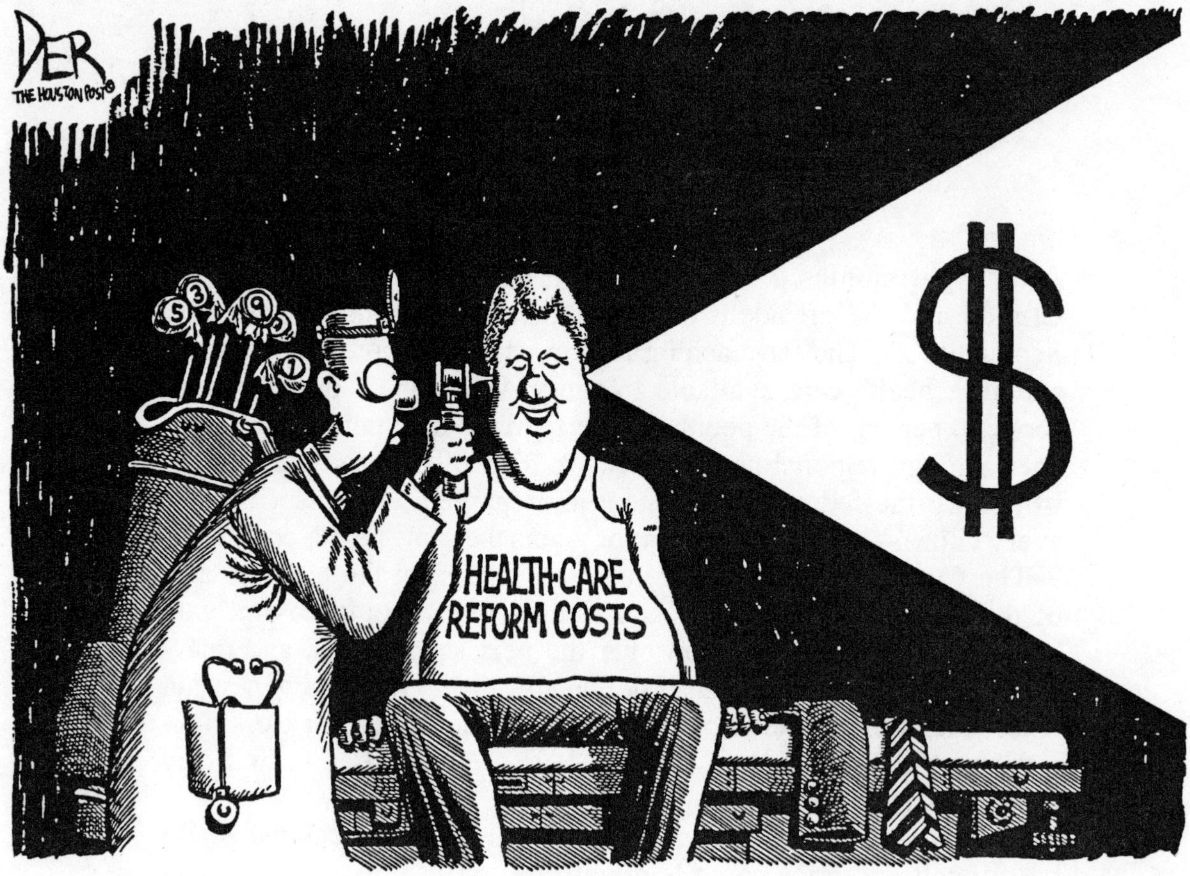
DER
THE HOUSTON POST
HEALTH-CARE
REFORM COSTS
$

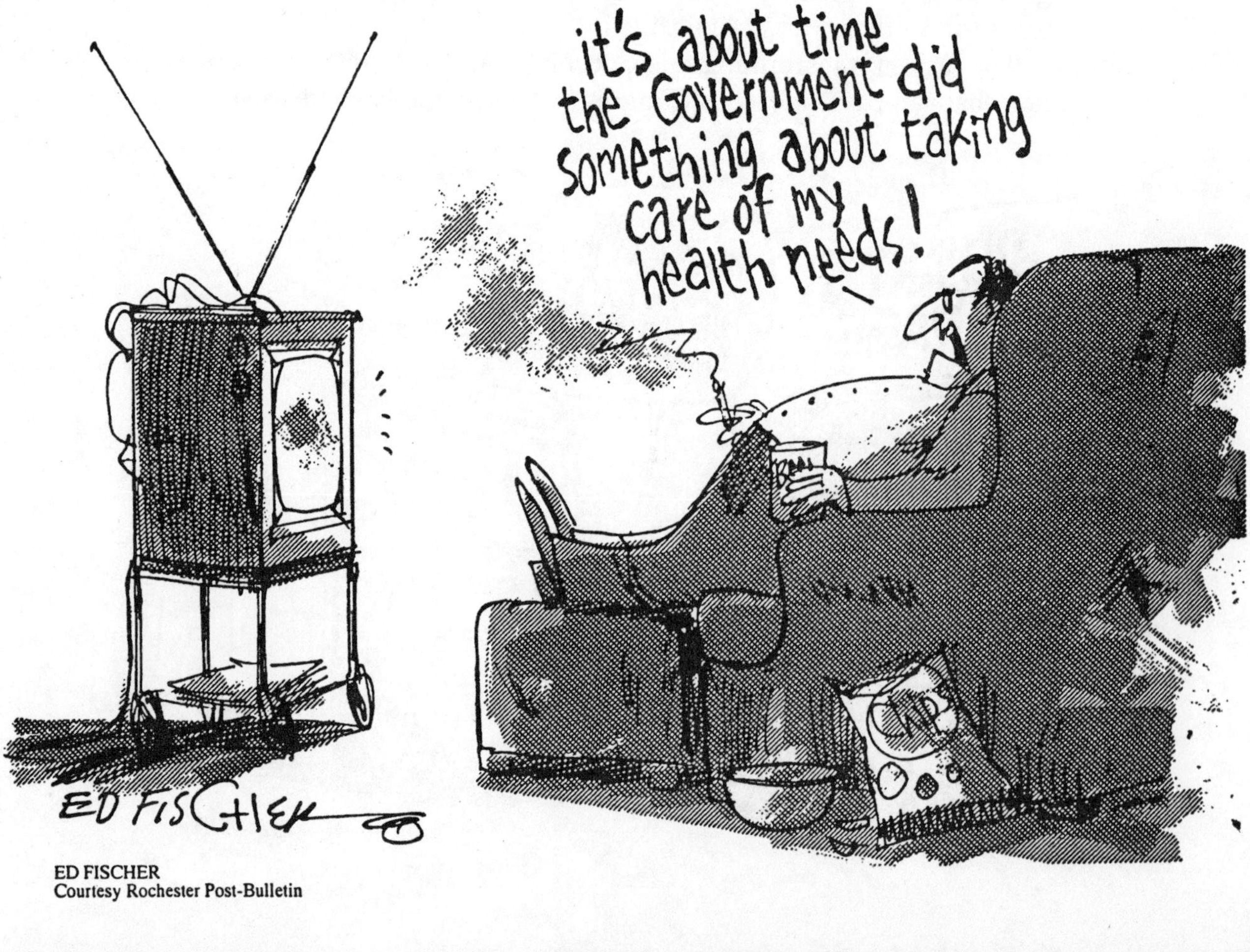
it's about time the Government did something about taking care of my health needs!
ED FISCHER

ED FISCHER
Courtesy Rochester Post-Bulletin

GARY VARVEL
Courtesy Indianapolis News

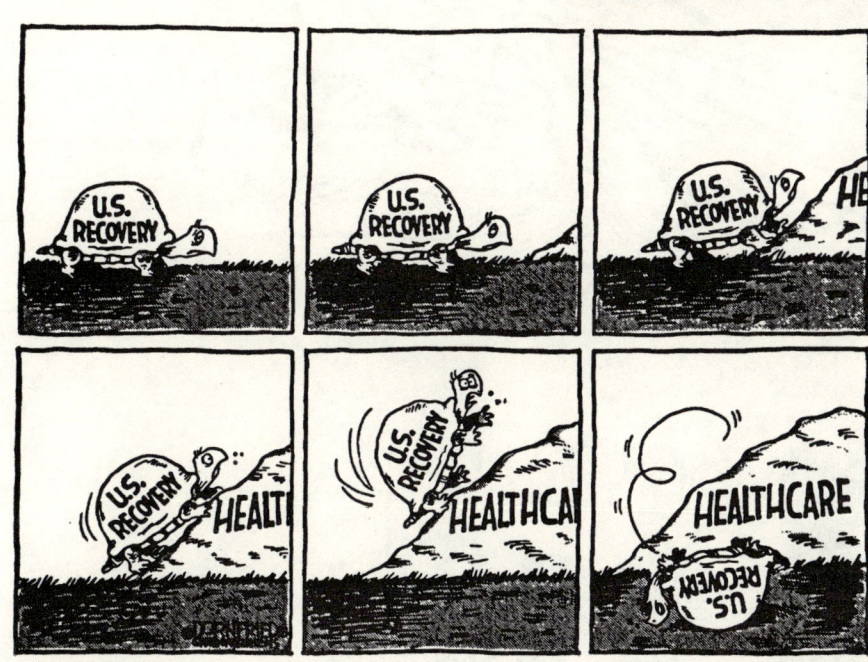

BOB DORNFRIED
Courtesy Greenwich News

STEVE KELLEY
Courtesy San Diego Union

MIKE PETERS
Courtesy Dayton Daily News

BEN SARGENT
Courtesy Austin American Statesman

WALT HANDELSMAN
Courtesy Times-Picayune (N.O.)

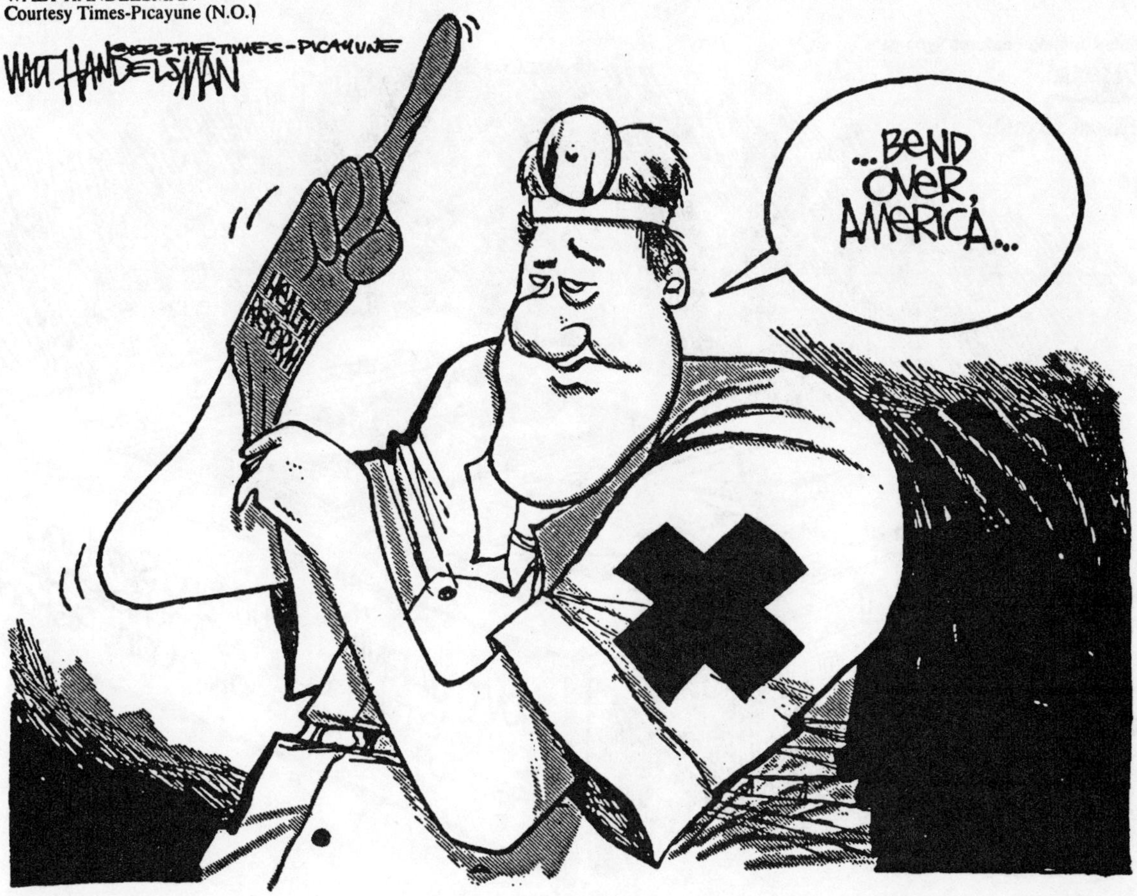
WALT HANDELSMAN ©1993 THE TIMES-PICAYUNE
HEALTH REFORM
...BEND OVER, AMERICA...

DON LEE
Courtesy Sandusky Register

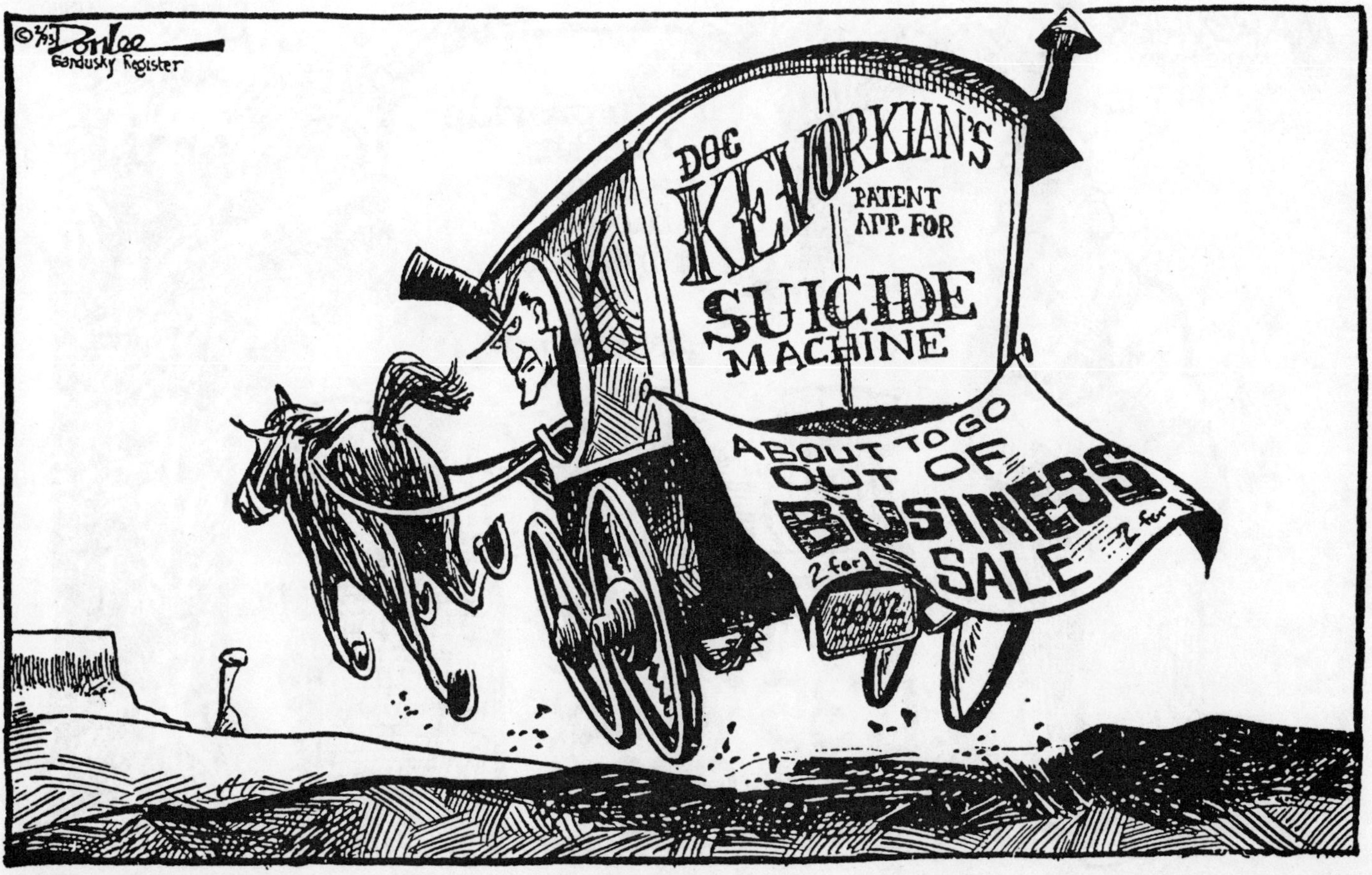
DonLee Sandusky Register
DOC KEVORKIAN'S
PATENT APP. FOR
SUICIDE MACHINE
ABOUT TO GO OUT OF BUSINESS
SALE
2 for 1
2 for

JIM MORIN
Courtesy Miami Herald

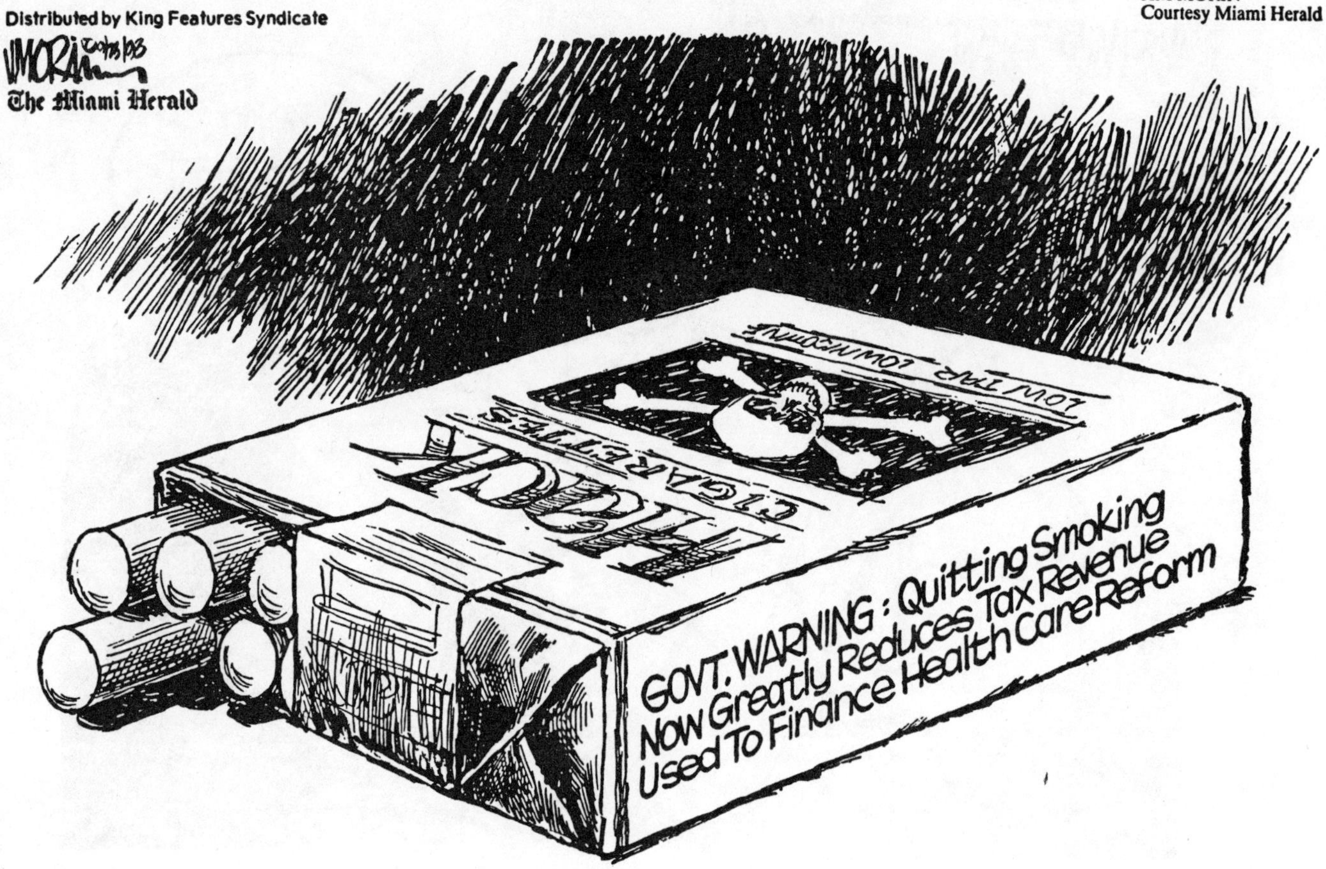
Distributed by King Features Syndicate
The Miami Herald
LOW TAR LOW NICOTINE
CIGARETTES
GOVT. WARNING : Quitting Smoking
Now Greatly Reduces Tax Revenue
Used To Finance Health Care Reform

JIMMY MARGULIES
Courtesy The Record (N.J.)

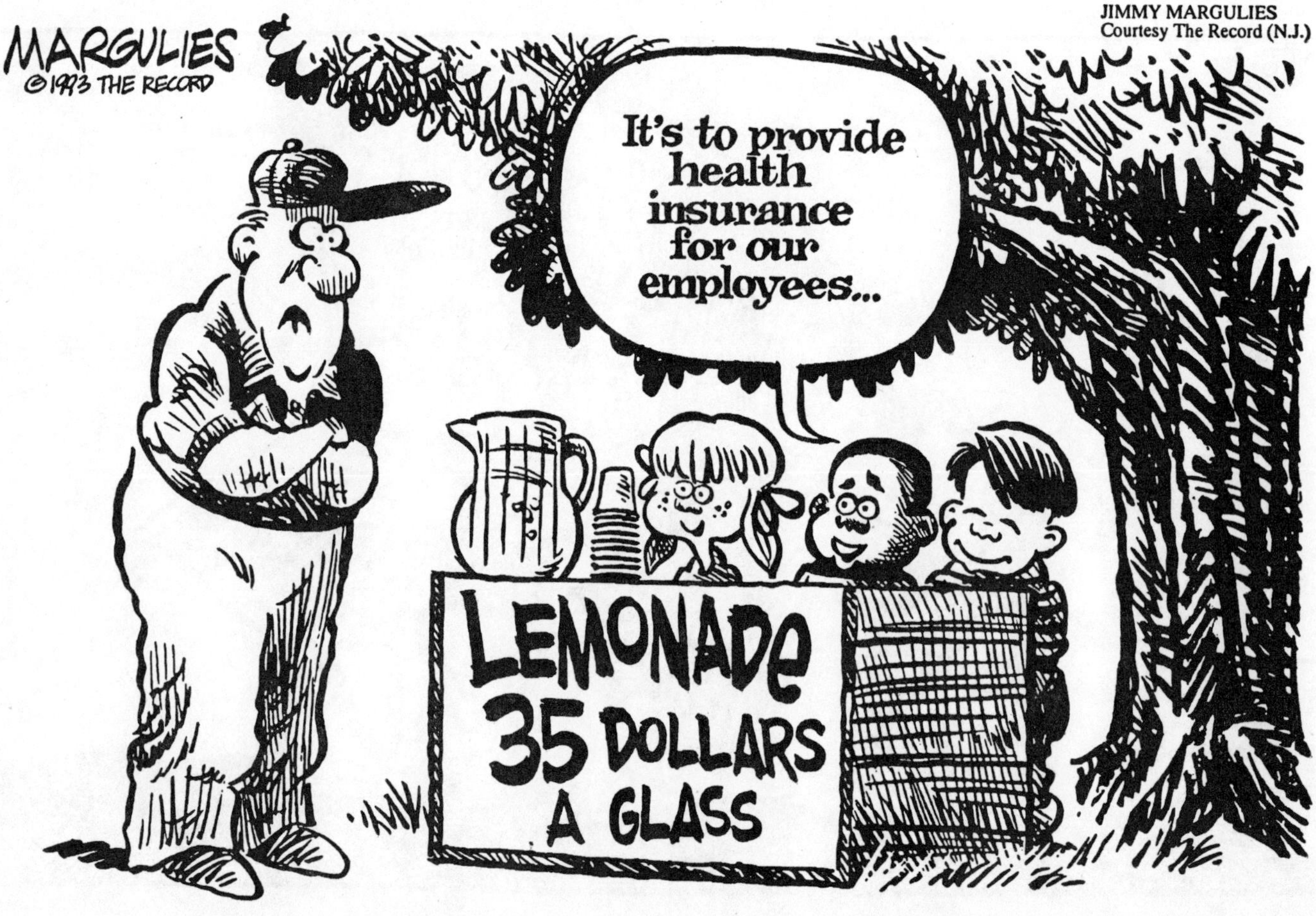
MARGULIES
©1993 THE RECORD
It's to provide health insurance for our employees...
LEMONADE
35 DOLLARS
A GLASS

JIM BUSH
Courtesy Washington Post

NICK ANDERSON
Courtesy Louisville Courier Journal

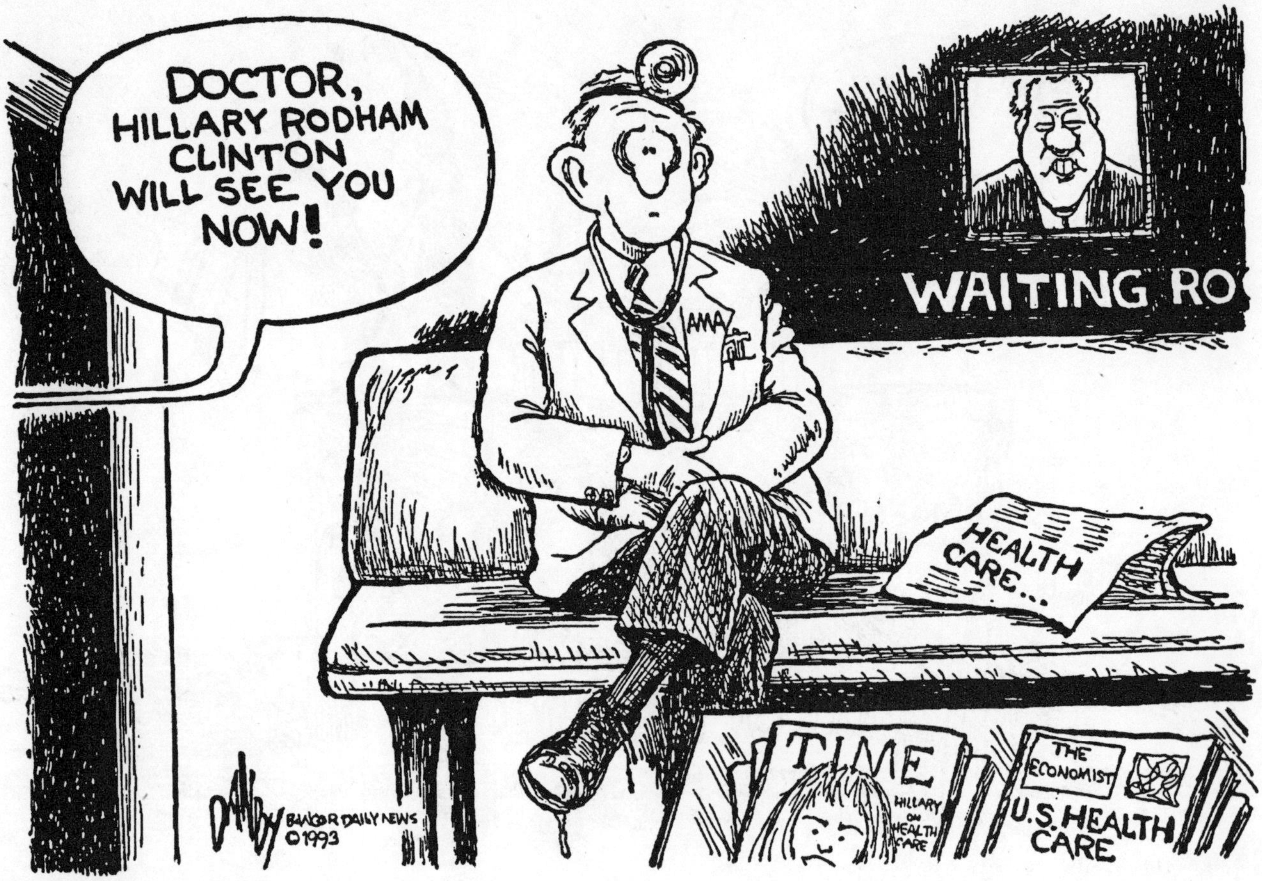
DOCTOR, HILLARY RODHAM CLINTON WILL SEE YOU NOW!
WAITING RO
AMA
HEALTH CARE...
TIME
HILLARY ON HEALTH CARE
THE ECONOMIST
U.S. HEALTH CARE
DANBY BANGOR DAILY NEWS ©1993

GEORGE DANBY
Courtesy Bangor Daily News

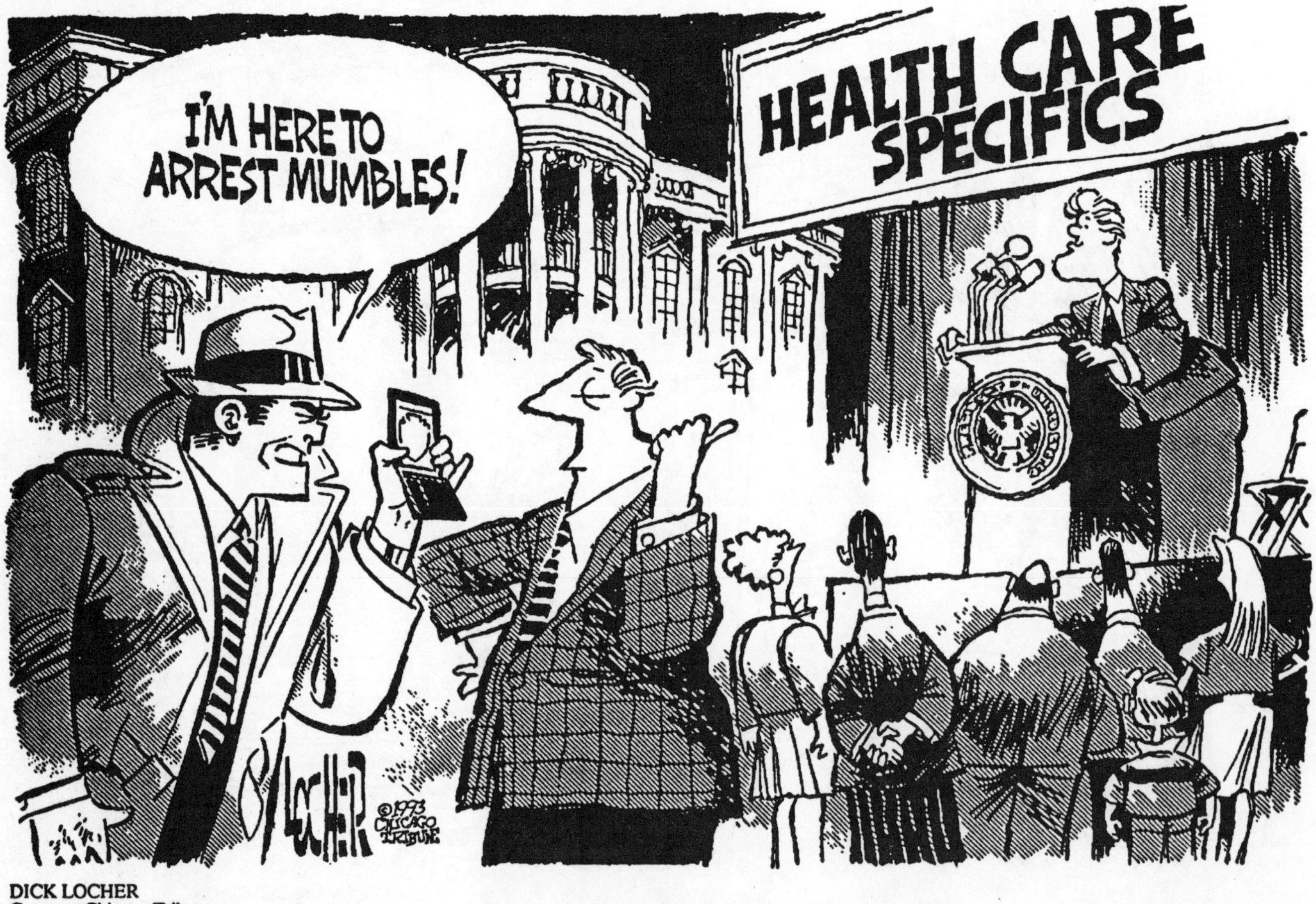
I'M HERE TO ARREST MUMBLES!
HEALTH CARE SPECIFICS
LOCHER ©1993 CHICAGO TRIBUNE

DICK LOCHER
Courtesy Chicago Tribune

WAYNE STAYSKAL
Courtesy Tampa Tribune

"IT'S GOT SOMETHING TO DO WITH HEALTH CARE REFORM!"

WILLIAM COSTELLO
Courtesy NEA

DANA SUMMERS
Courtesy Orlando Sentinel

PAUL SZEP
Courtesy Boston Globe

CHUCK ASAY
Courtesy Colorado Springs Gazette Telegraph

JACK HIGGINS
Courtesy Chicago Sun-Times

VIC CANTONE
Courtesy Rothco

DICK WRIGHT
Courtesy Providence Journal-Bulletin

TOM DARCY
Courtesy Newsday

Sticky Business

BRUCE MACKINNON
Courtesy Halifax Chronicle-Herald

JIM BERRY
Courtesy NEA

DAVID DONAR
Courtesy Macomb Daily (Miss.)

NICK ANDERSON
Courtesy Louisville Courier-Journal

47

JOHN KNUDSEN
Courtesy The Tidings (Calif.)

MIKE THOMPSON
Courtesy State Journal-Register (Ill.)

Gary Brookins
Courtesy Ritchmond Times-Dispatch

BRUCE BEATTIE
Courtesy Daytona Beach News-Journal

"We're trying to provide access to national health care without bankrupting the government. Here's your application for Canadian citizenship!"

JERRY ROBINSON
Courtesy Cartoonists & Writers Syndicate

EDDIE GERMANO
Courtesy the Enterprise (Mass.)

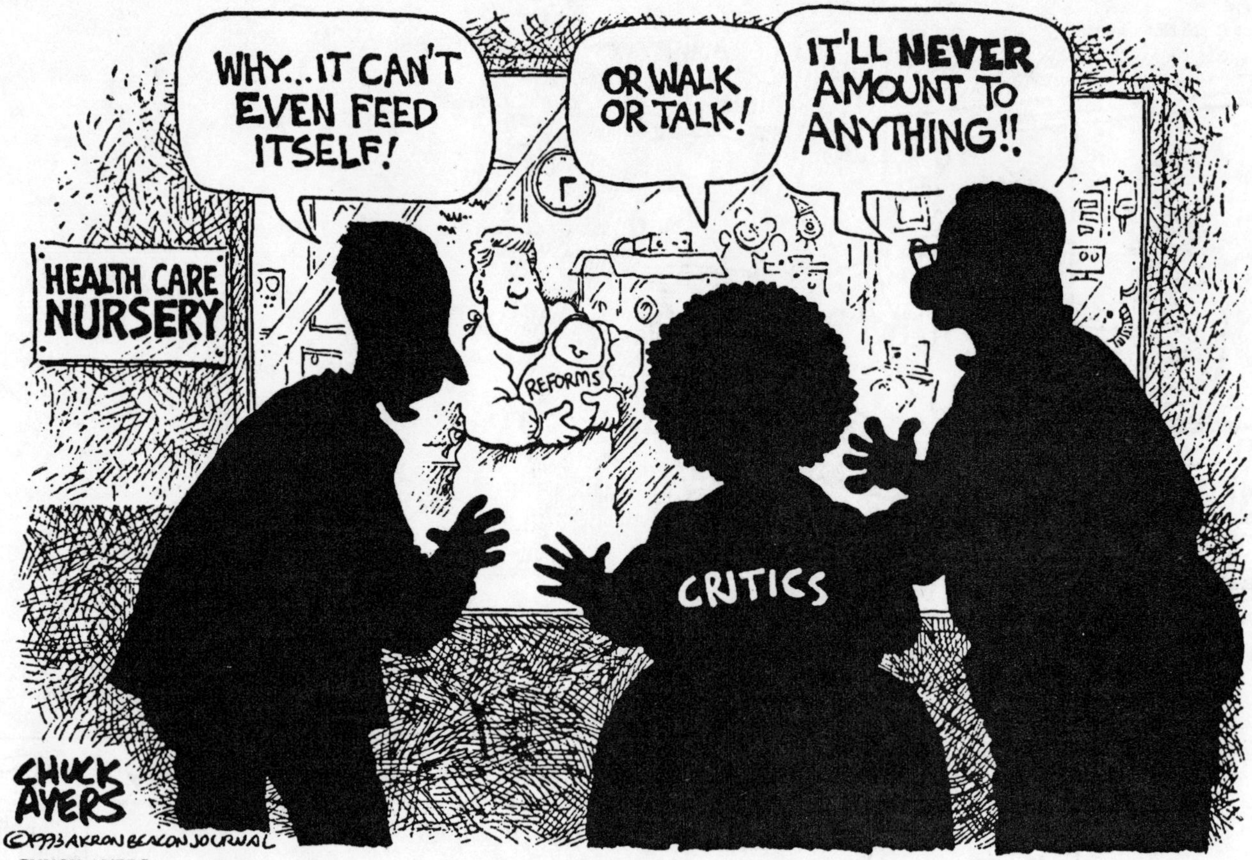
WHY... IT CAN'T EVEN FEED ITSELF!
OR WALK OR TALK!
IT'LL NEVER AMOUNT TO ANYTHING!!
HEALTH CARE NURSERY
REFORMS
CRITICS
CHUCK AYERS
©1993 AKRON BEACON JOURNAL

CHUCK AYERS
Courtesy Akron Beacon Journal

JEFF STAHLER
Courtesy Cincinnati Post

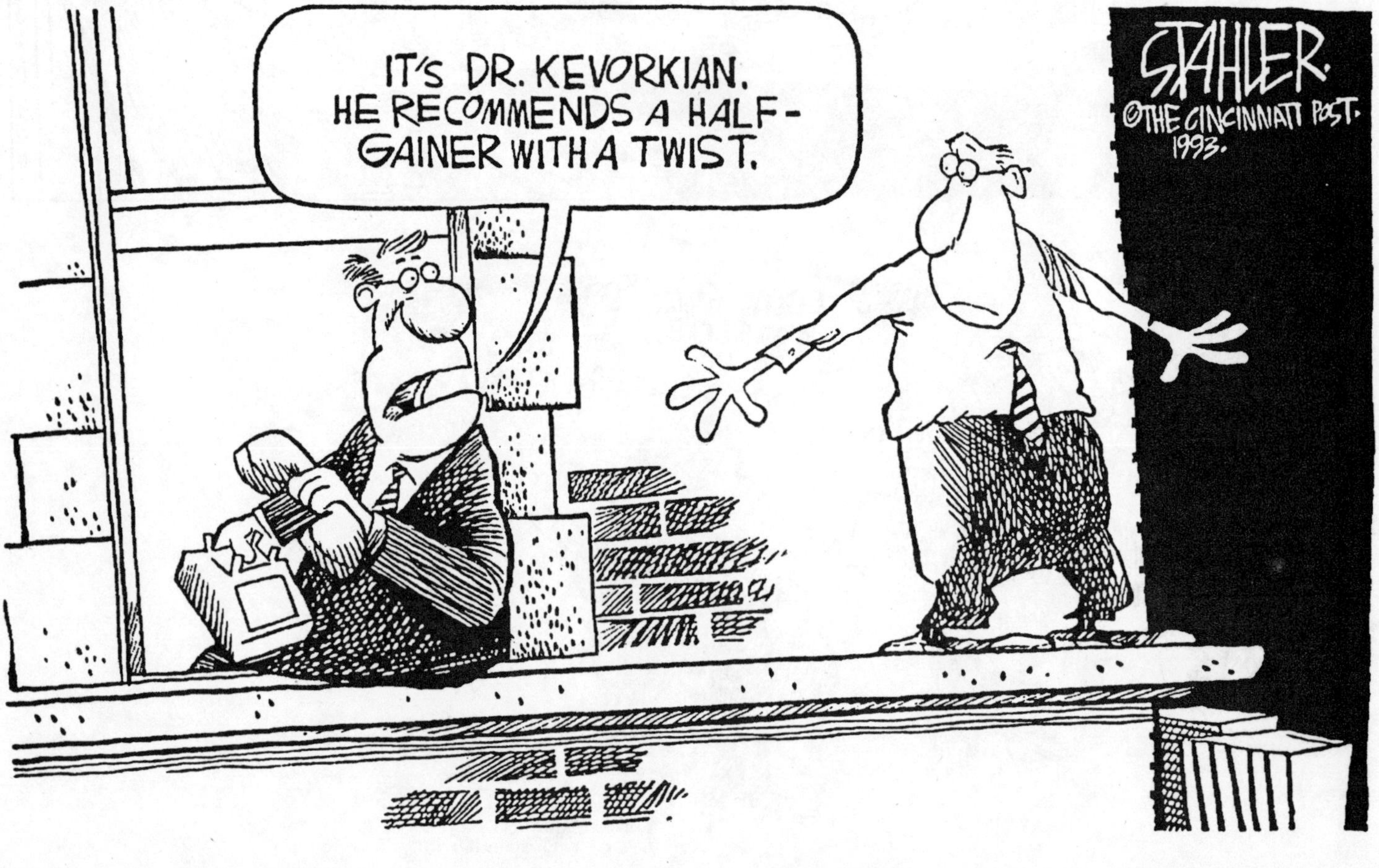
IT'S DR. KEVORKIAN. HE RECOMMENDS A HALF-GAINER WITH A TWIST.
STAHLER
©THE CINCINNATI POST. 1993.

Russia

Russia continued to struggle with democratic reforms set in place by Boris Yeltsin. In March, as the economy worsened, more than 30,000 protesters marched to the walls of the Kremlin and demanded Yeltsin's resignation. Inflation was running at 30 percent a month, and severe shortages of food and medicine led many citizens to wonder if they might have been better off under communism.

Yeltsin met with President Clinton in April as the U.S. showed strong support for the Russian government. Clinton called for additional aid for Russia and the other former Soviet republics, and Secretary of State Warren Christopher announced to the world that it was "of the utmost importance to the U.S., and indeed to the world, that President Yeltsin's reform efforts succeed."

In October, hardliners began stocking the huge Russian White House, which also housed parliament, with arms and anti-reform combat veterans led by Vice-President Alexander Rutskoi and parliament chairman Ruslan Khasbulatov. After shooting broke out, tanks began shelling the White House. The two rebel leaders surrendered after a ten-hour battle that left almost 200 dead.

Yeltsin then disbanded parliament and called for December elections, hoping for a new body more favorable to reform. Ultranationalists made a surprisingly strong showing, however, signaling that Yeltsin is not yet out of trouble—not by a long shot.

BEN SARGENT
Courtesy Austin American Statesman

CHUCK ASAY
Courtesy Colorado Springs Gazette Telegraph

JOHN TREVER
Courtesy Albuquerque

ROBERT ARIAIL
Courtesy The State (S.C.)

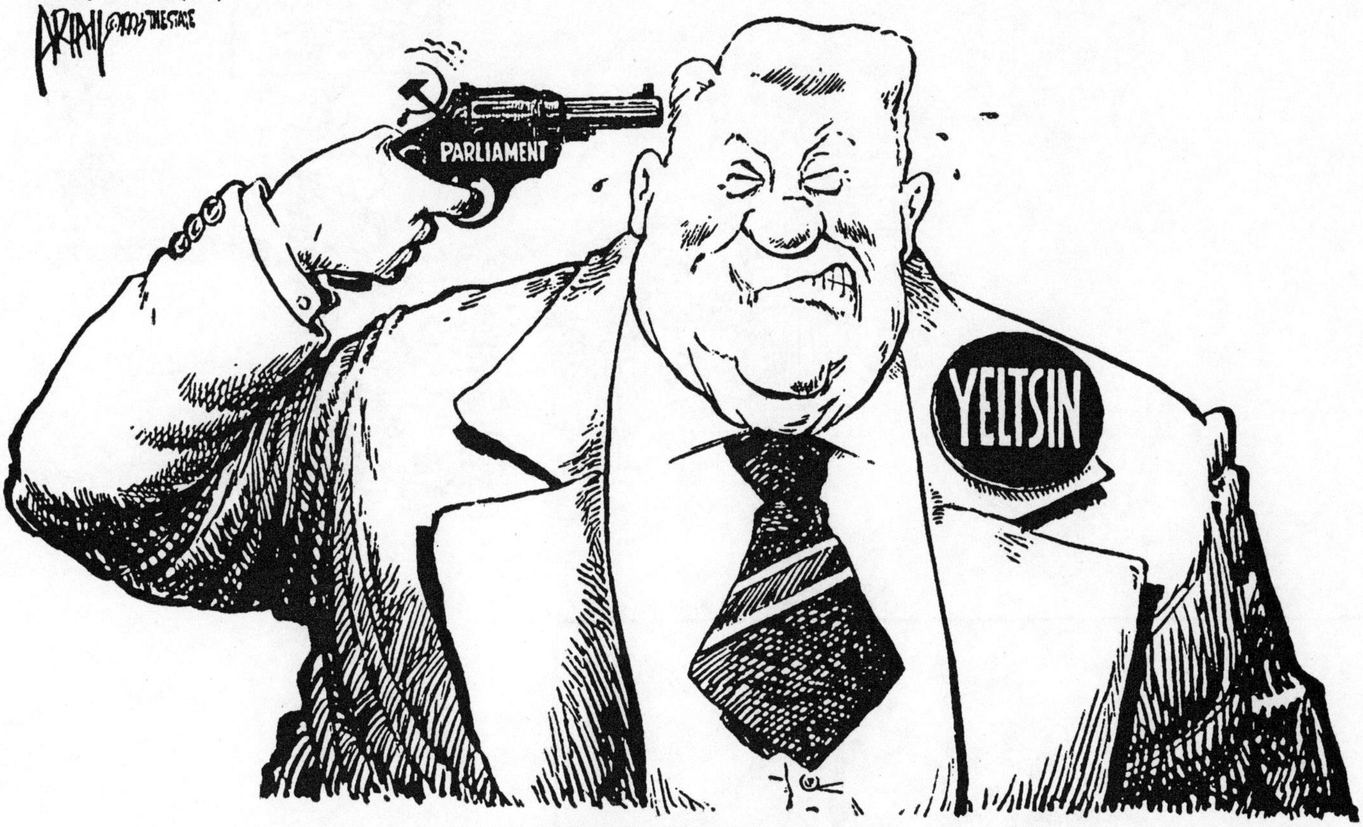
PARLIAMENT
YELTSIN

"RUSSIAN RULE-ETTE"

JAMES GRASDAL
Courtesy Edmonton Journal

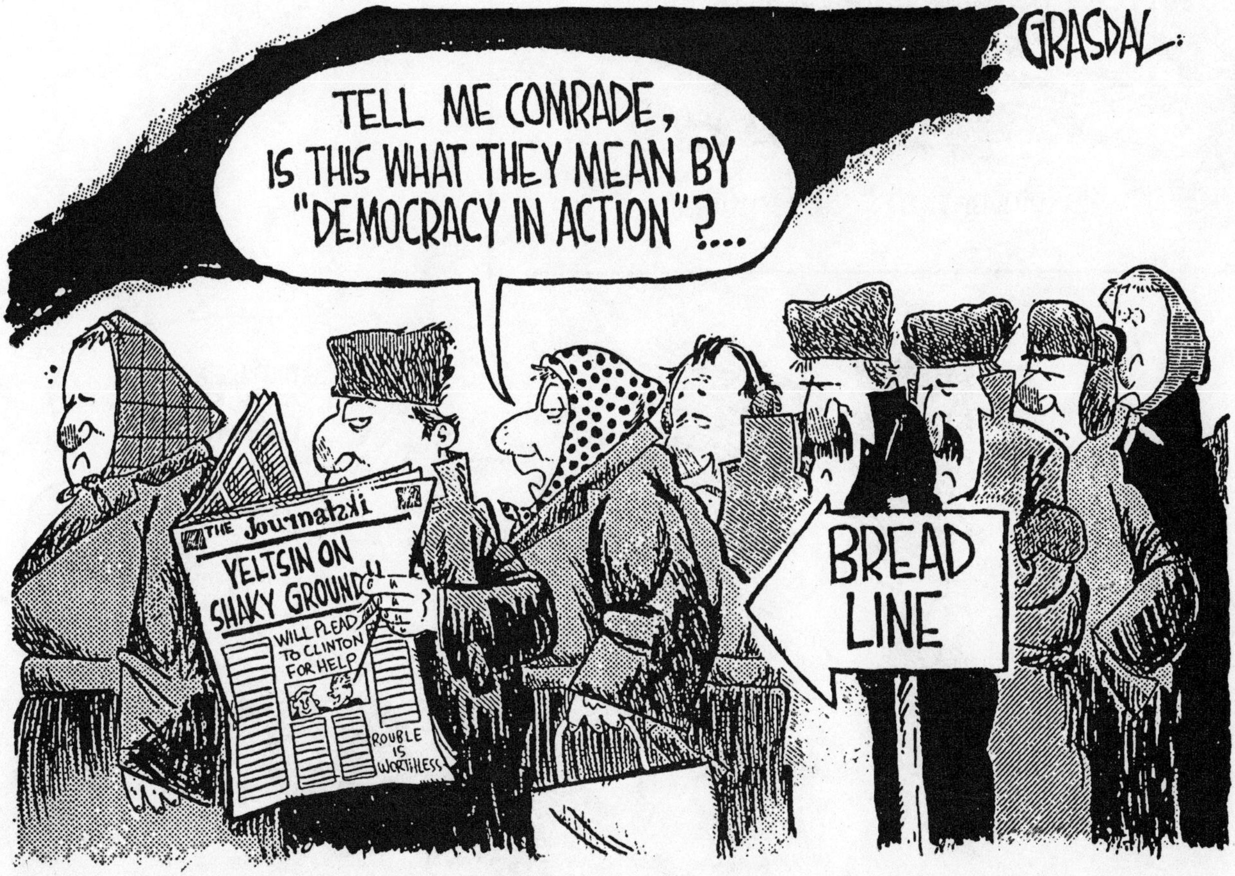
GRASDAL
TELL ME COMRADE, IS THIS WHAT THEY MEAN BY "DEMOCRACY IN ACTION"?...
YELTSIN ON SHAKY GROUND
WILL PLEAD TO CLINTON FOR HELP
ROUBLE IS WORTHLESS
BREAD LINE

CHARLES DANIEL
Courtesy Knoxville News-Sentinel

CHARLES FAGAN
Courtesy Associated Features Syndicate

PAT BAGLEY
Courtesy Salt Lake Tribune

FRED CURATOLO
Courtesy Edmonton Sun

DICK WALLMEYER
Courtesy Long Beach Press-Telegram

JERRY ROBINSON
Courtesy Cartoonists & Writers Syndicate

TOM ENGELHARDT
Courtesy St. Louis Post-Dispatch

GEORGE DANBY
Courtesy Bangor Daily News

BRUCE BEATTIE
Courtesy Daytona Beach News-Journal

JIM McCLOSKEY
Courtesy Staunton Daily News Leader

DENNIS DRAUGHON
Courtesy Scranton Times

57

EDMUND VALTMAN
Courtesy Rothco

TIM MENEES
Courtesy Pittsburgh Post-Gazette

DAVID GRANLUND
Courtesy Middlesex News

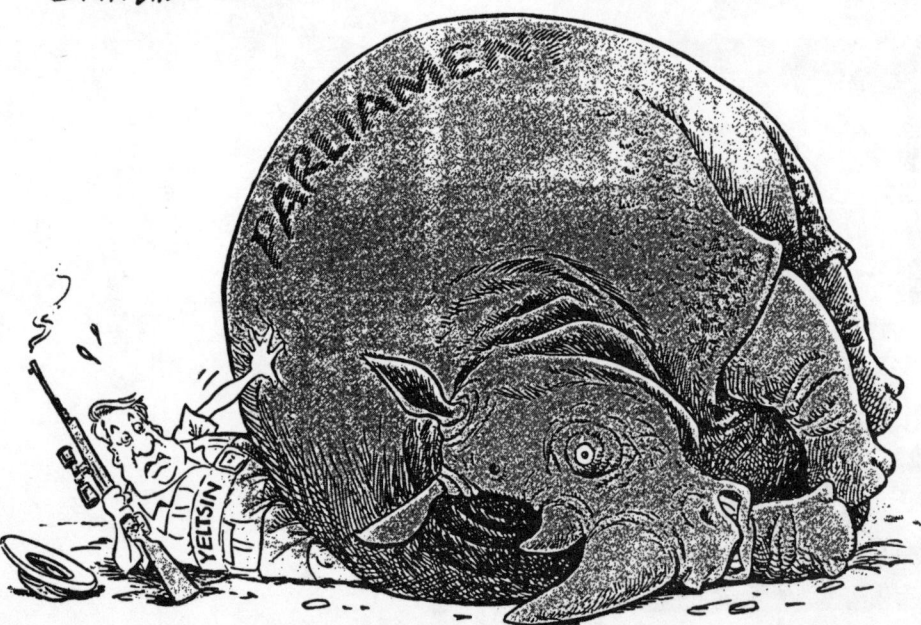

The Middle East

In September, a remarkable event was beamed to the world on television. At the White House, Israeli Prime Minister Yitzhak Rabin and P.L.O. Chairman Yasser Arafat grasped each other's hand, sealing the accord that will give Palestine self-rule and oversee Israel's withdrawal from the turbulent West Bank and Gaza. Israeli soldiers watched in amazement at Jerusalem's ancient Damascus Gate, and in Jerico crowds in the main square broke into a joyous dance. Shock waves from the historic agreement were felt around the world. Morocco's King Hassan publicly welcomed Rabin to his palace and wished the Israeli people a happy new year. Representatives from Jordan signed a blueprint for peace talks to come.

The two principals began hammering out the details of the accord in December. It is uncertain whether Arafat will be able to convince his followers that the agreement is in their best interests, and Rabin faces a similar problem with his fellow citizens. As the year ended, protests against the agreement popped up in various places. Arafat appeared to be backpedaling somewhat as he felt pressure from his followers. But Mideast watchers generally felt that Arafat and Rabin had come too far along the road to peace to allow a complete breakdown in the accords.

JIMMY MARGULIES
Courtesy The Record (N.J.)

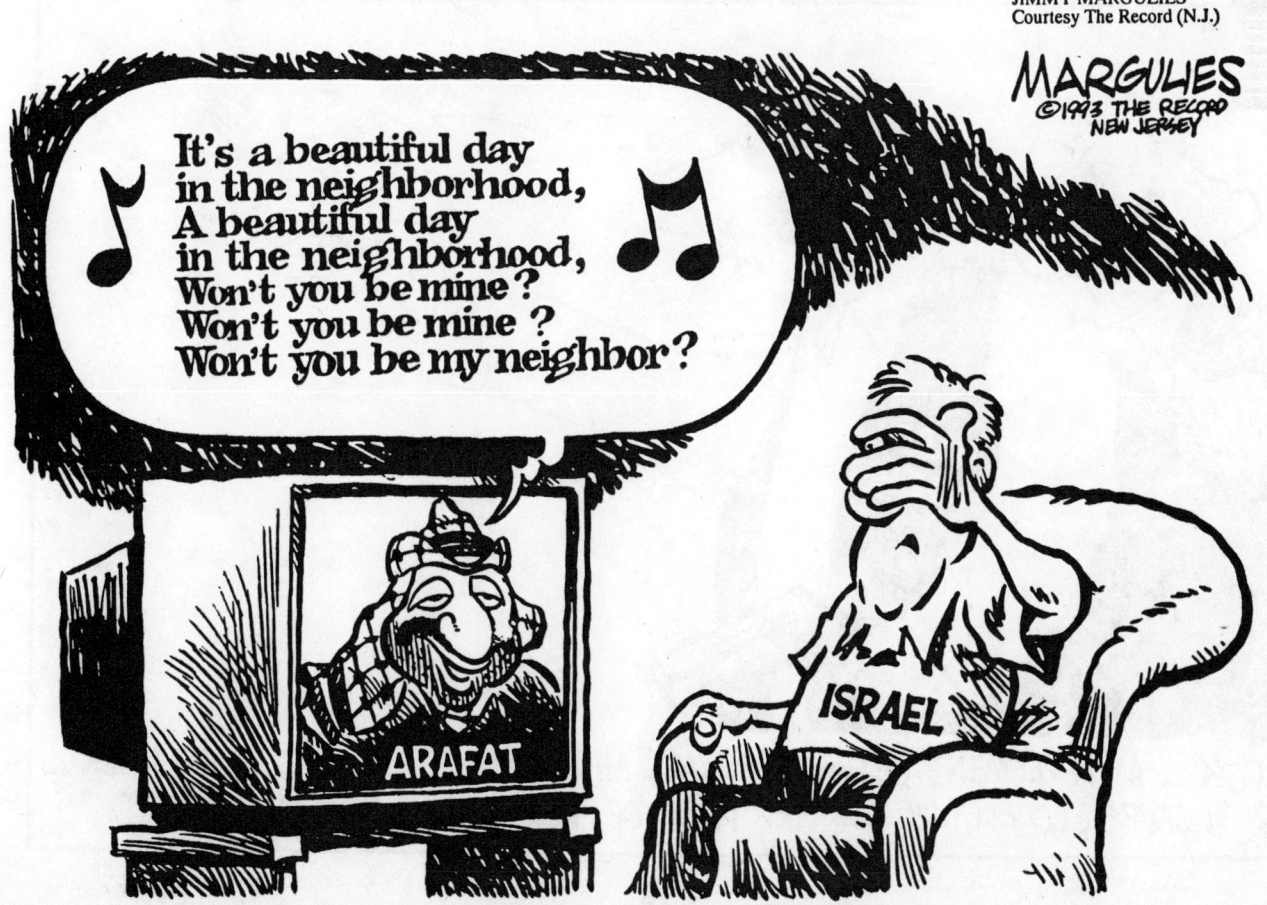

DAVID HITCH
Courtesy Worcester Telegram & Gazette

"GO AHEAD... KNOCK IT OFF AGAIN.... I DARE YOU!"

"LOOK ... AN AGREEMENT BETWEEN ISRAEL AND THE P.L.O. ... SO SOUGHT AFTER ... FOR DECADES, SO ELUSIVE ... SO FULL OF PROMISE ... LET'S KILL IT."

TOM GIBB
Courtesy Rothco

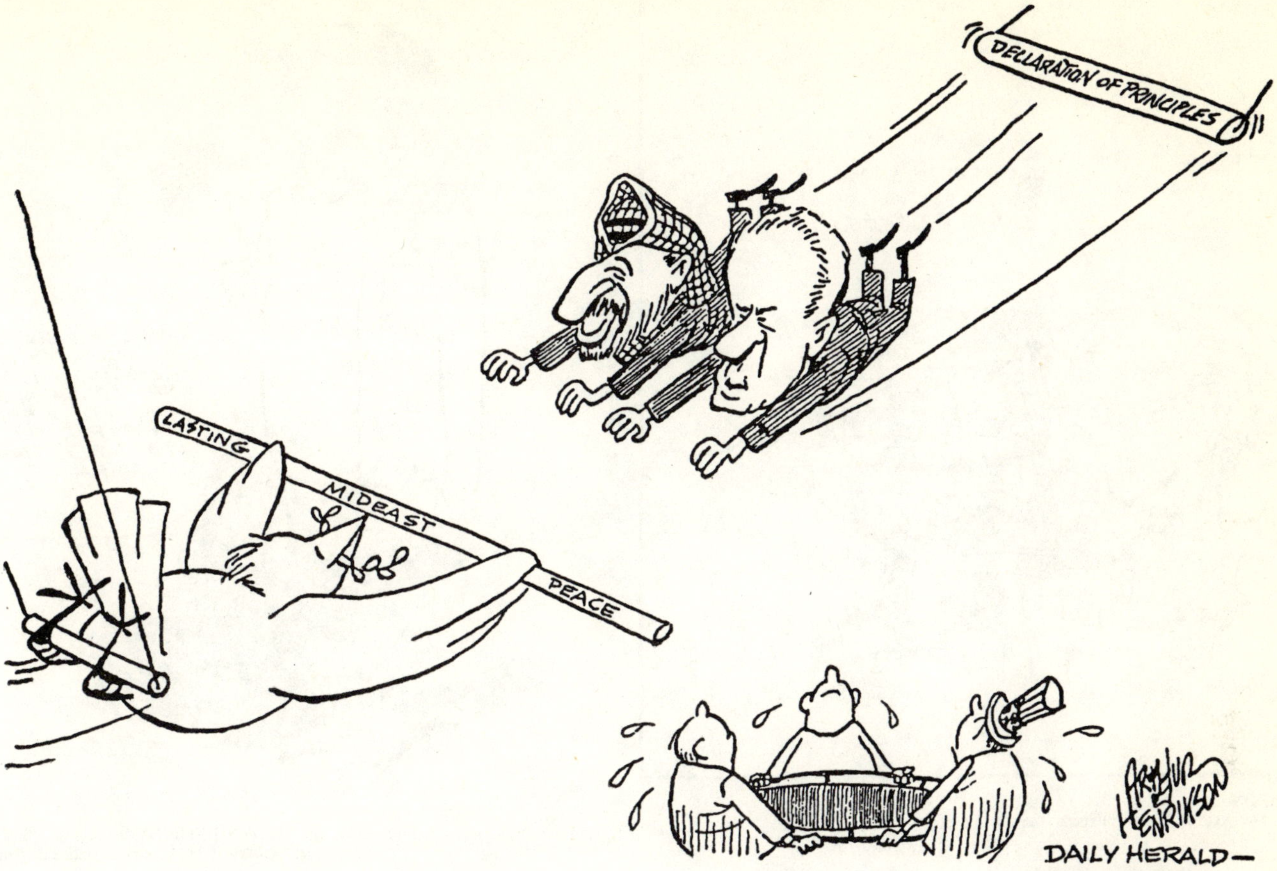
DECLARATION OF PRINCIPLES
LASTING MIDEAST PEACE
ARTHUR HENRIKSON
DAILY HERALD—

ART HENRIKSON
Courtesy Daily Herald (Ill.)

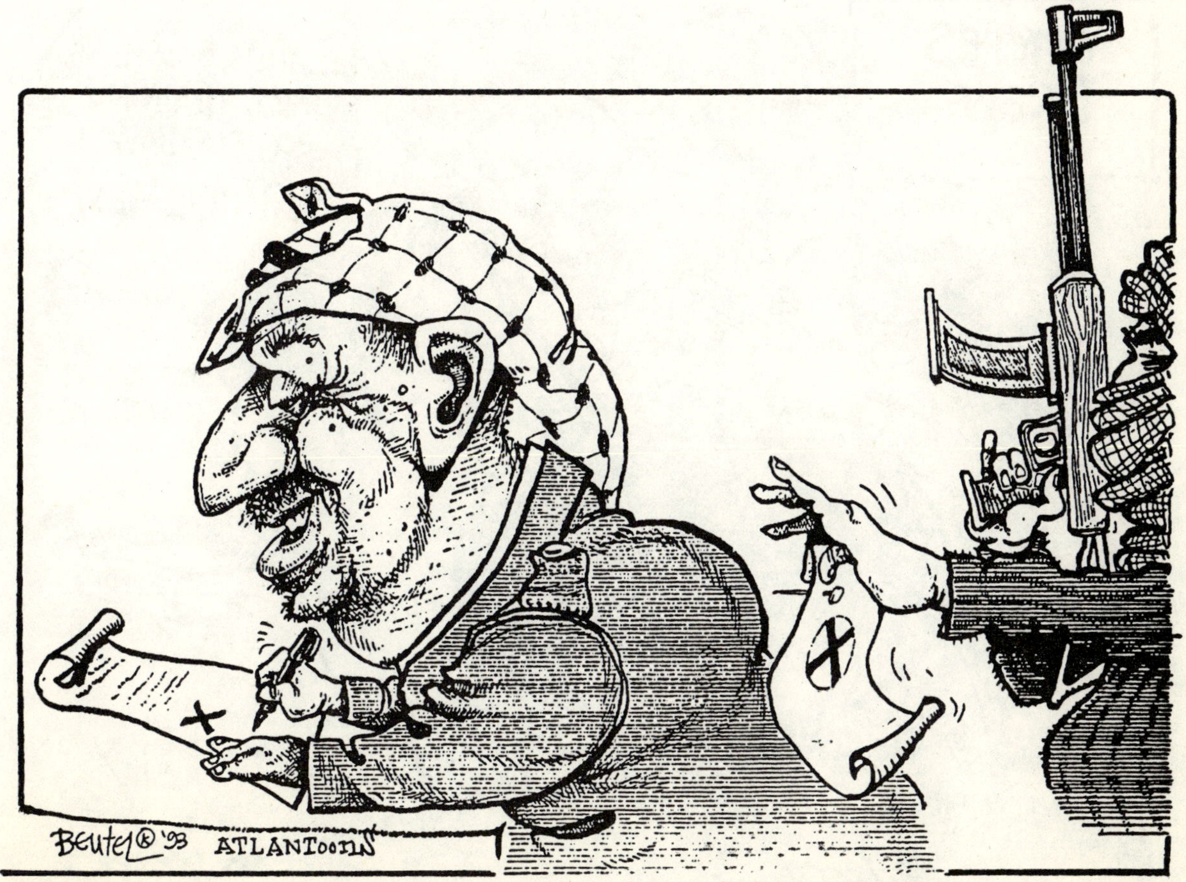
BEUTEL © '93 ATLANTOONS

JOSH BEUTEL
Courtesy St. John's Evening Telegram

DAN O'BREN
Courtesy Youngstown Daily Buisness Journal

J. R. SHINGLETON
Courtesy Waterbury Republican-American

HY ROSEN
Courtesy Albany Times-Union

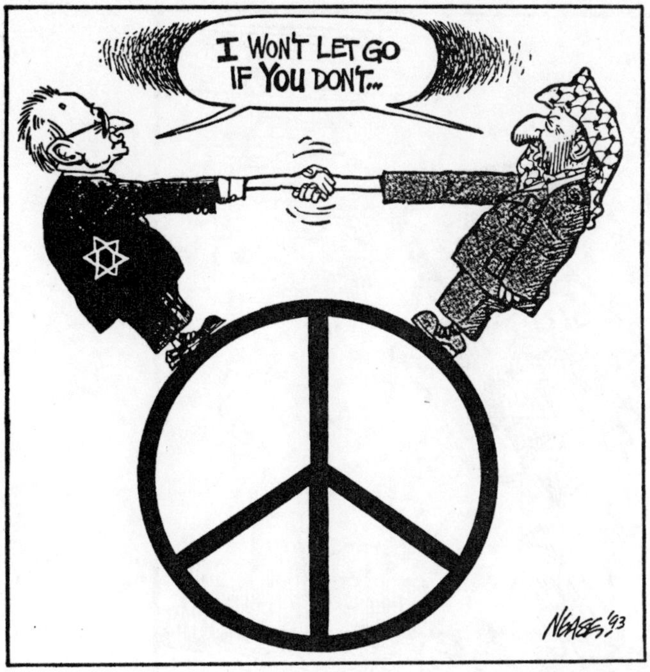
I WON'T LET GO IF YOU DON'T...
NEASE '93

STEVE NEASE
Courtesy Toronto Star

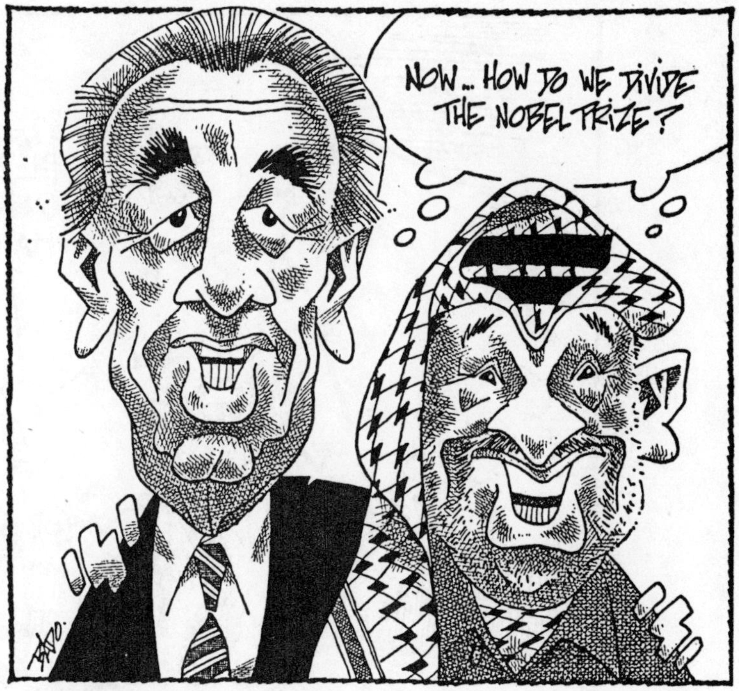
NOW... HOW DO WE DIVIDE THE NOBEL PRIZE?

GUY BADEAUX
Courtesy Le Droit (Ottawa)

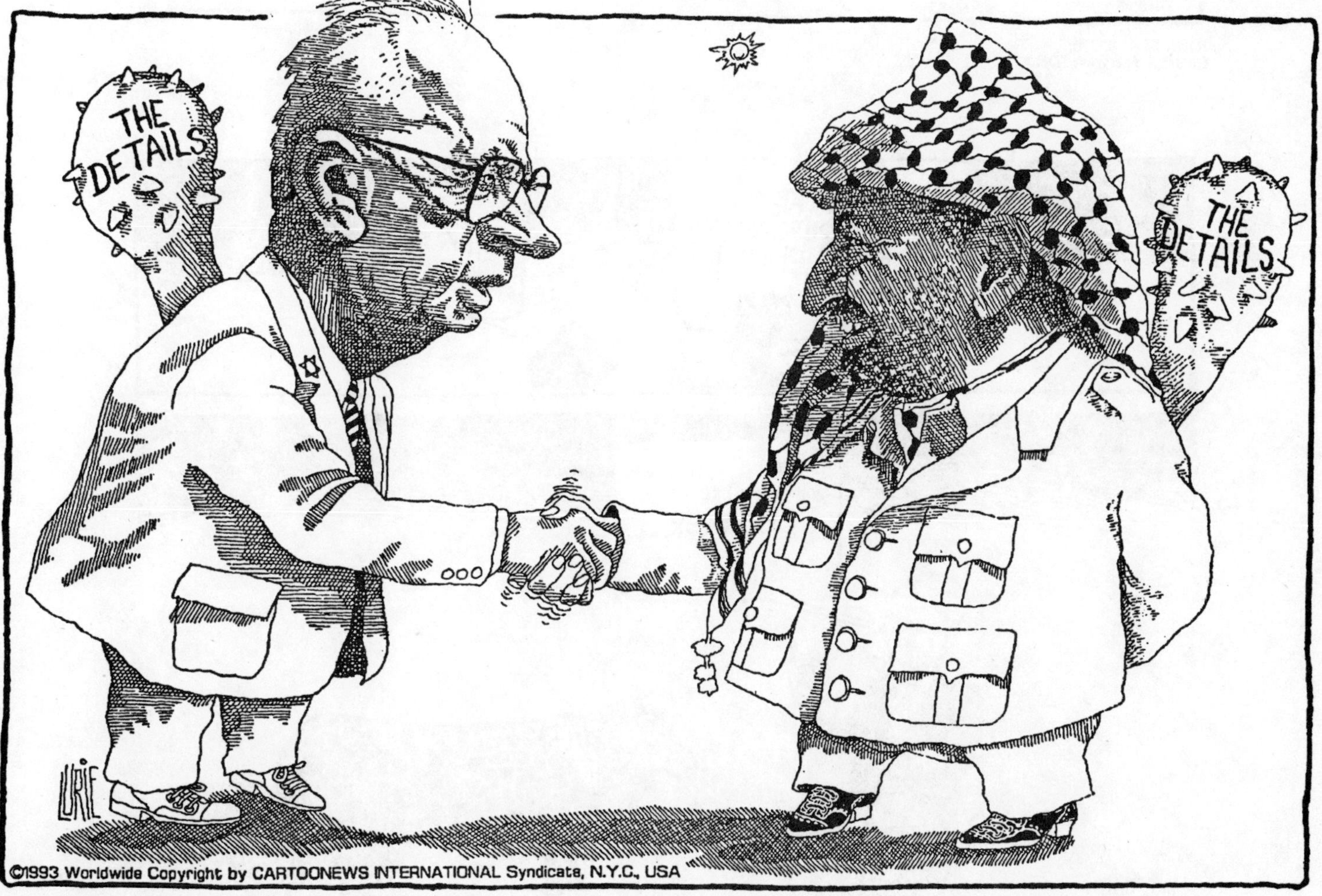
THE DETAILS
THE DETAILS
LURIE
©1993 Worldwide Copyright by CARTOONEWS INTERNATIONAL Syndicate, N.Y.C., USA

RANAN LURIE
Courtesy Cartoonews International

JOHN STAMPONE
Courtesy The Wave (Del.)

MIKE SMITH
Courtesy Las Vegas Sun

NAFTA

As did his predecessors George Bush and Jimmy Carter, President Clinton worked hard to pass the North American Free Trade Agreement. This controversial treaty would eventually remove most trade barriers between the United States and its neighbors, Canada and Mexico. The sometimes bitter debate, whose most outspoken opponent was Ross Perot, cut across political lines and created unusual alliances. Clinton was supported by all five living past presidents, as well as most of the leadership of the Republican party. Many rank-and-file Democrats in Congress opposed the proposal, as did labor unions.

Proponents said NAFTA would create jobs by opening new markets in Mexico and Canada, while opponents declared it would encourage American businesses to move factories—and jobs—out of the U.S. Clinton received a big boost in his fight for NAFTA when Vice-President Gore out-debated Perot before a nationwide television audience. During the final days before the measure came up for consideration, Clinton was charged with buying votes from lawmakers by promising them whatever they wanted in exchange for their votes. Such is the power of the presidency. On November 17, the House of Representatives passed NAFTA by a vote of 234 to 200.

The White House had argued that a NAFTA victory would "strengthen the president's hand" in dealing with Asian leaders later in the year.

MIKE PETERS
Courtesy Dayton Daily News

ED GAMBLE
Courtesy Florida Times-Union

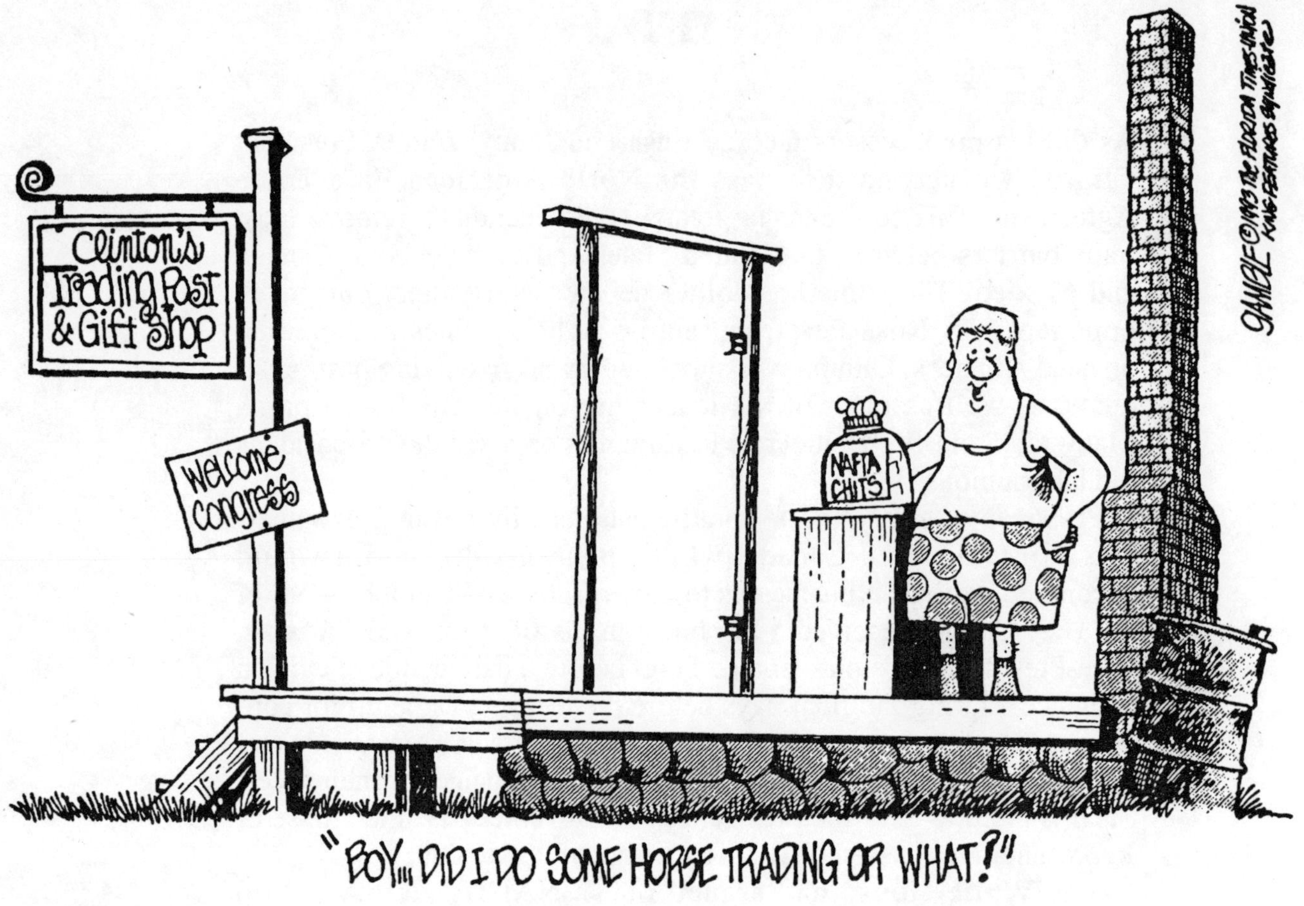
Clinton's Trading Post & Gift Shop
Welcome Congress
NAFTA CHITS
GAMBLE ©1993 The Florida Times-Union King Features Syndicate
"BOY... DID I DO SOME HORSE TRADING OR WHAT?"

ROGER SCHILLERSTROM
Courtesy Crain Communications

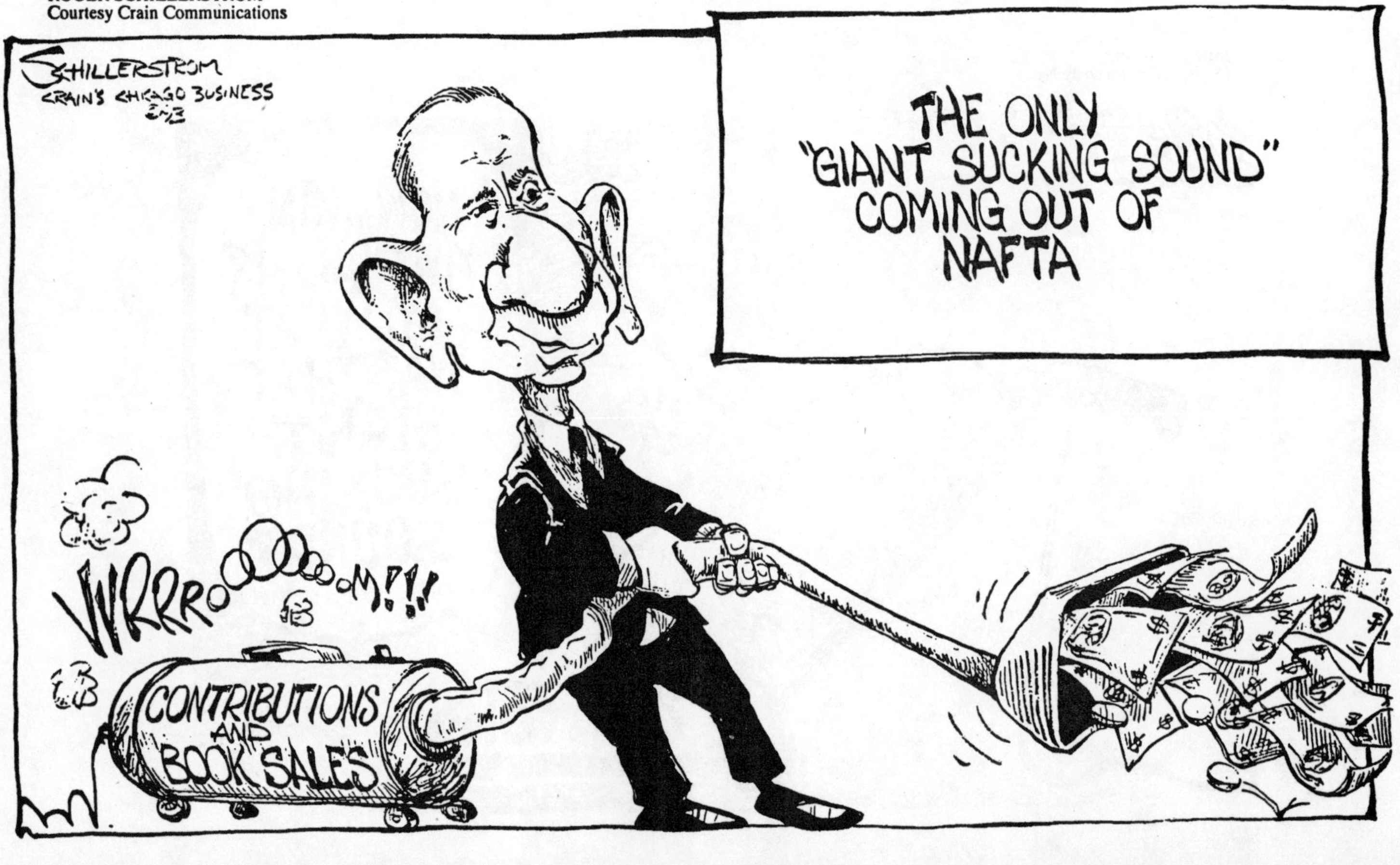
SCHILLERSTROM
CRAIN'S CHICAGO BUSINESS
THE ONLY "GIANT SUCKING SOUND" COMING OUT OF NAFTA
VVRRROOOOOOM!!!
CONTRIBUTIONS AND BOOK SALES

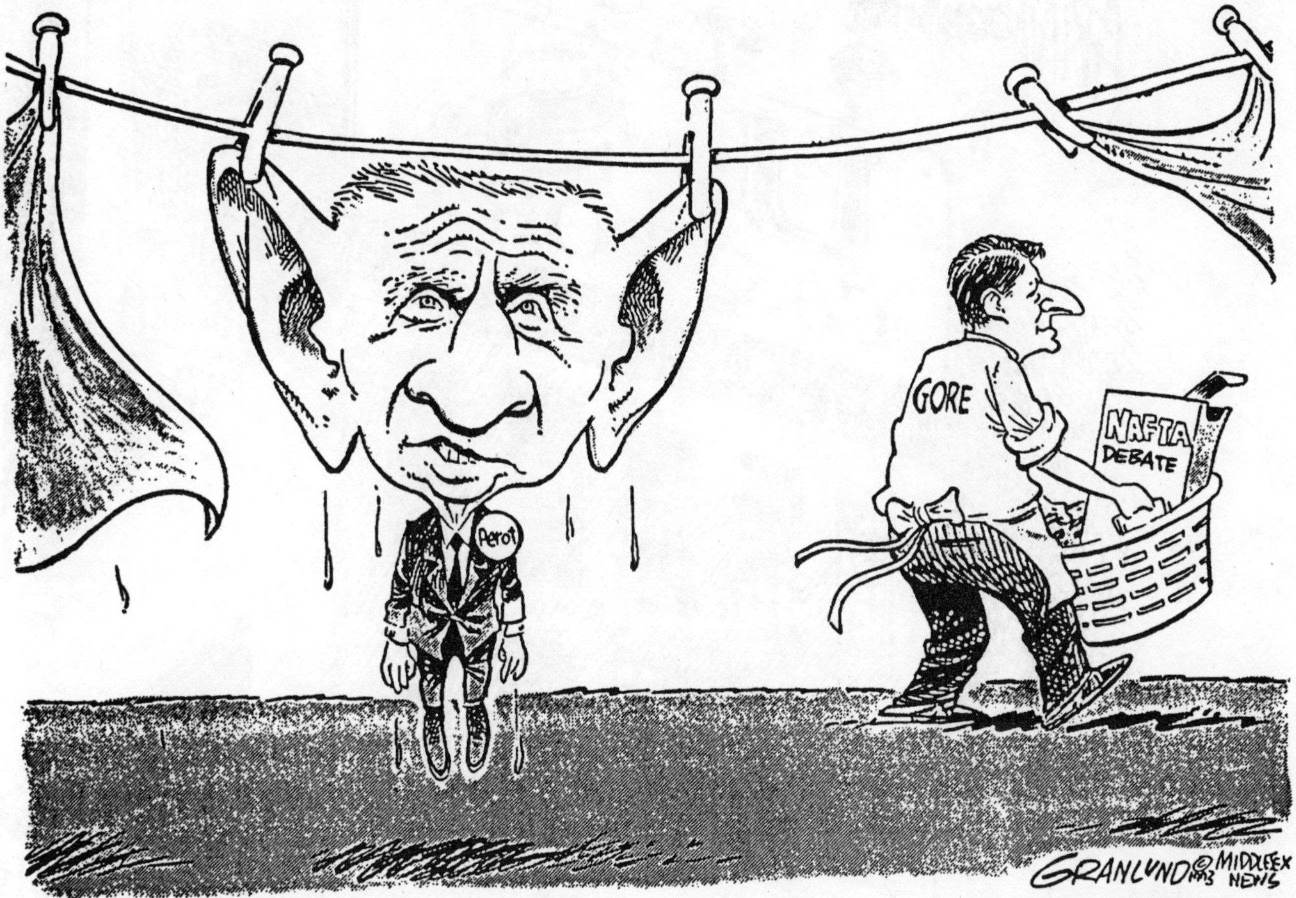
GORE
NAFTA DEBATE
Perot
GRANLUND ©1993 MIDDLESEX NEWS

DAVID GRANLUND
Courtesy Middlesex News

RICHARD CROWSON
Courtesy Wichita Eagle

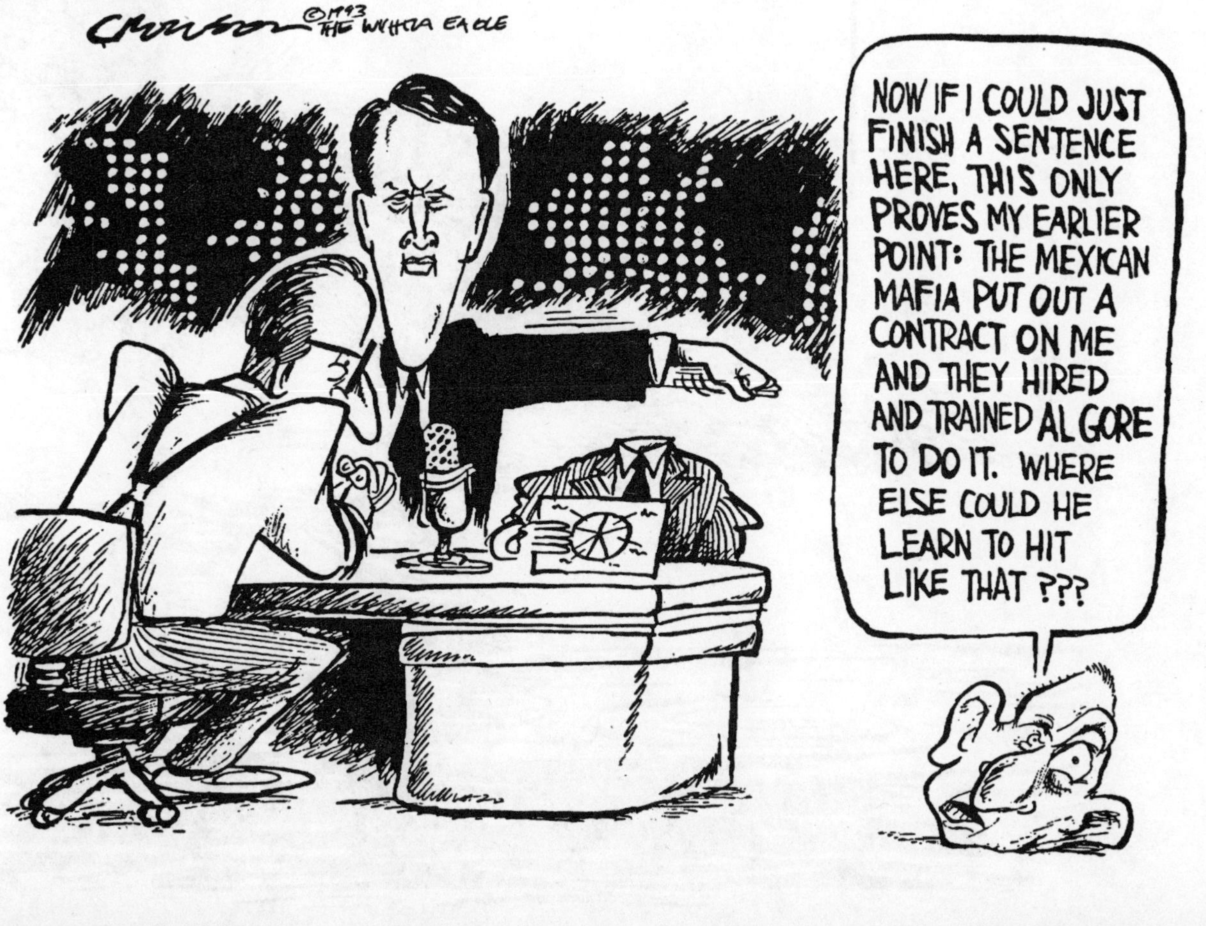
CROWSON ©1993 THE WICHITA EAGLE
NOW IF I COULD JUST FINISH A SENTENCE HERE, THIS ONLY PROVES MY EARLIER POINT: THE MEXICAN MAFIA PUT OUT A CONTRACT ON ME AND THEY HIRED AND TRAINED AL GORE TO DO IT. WHERE ELSE COULD HE LEARN TO HIT LIKE THAT ???

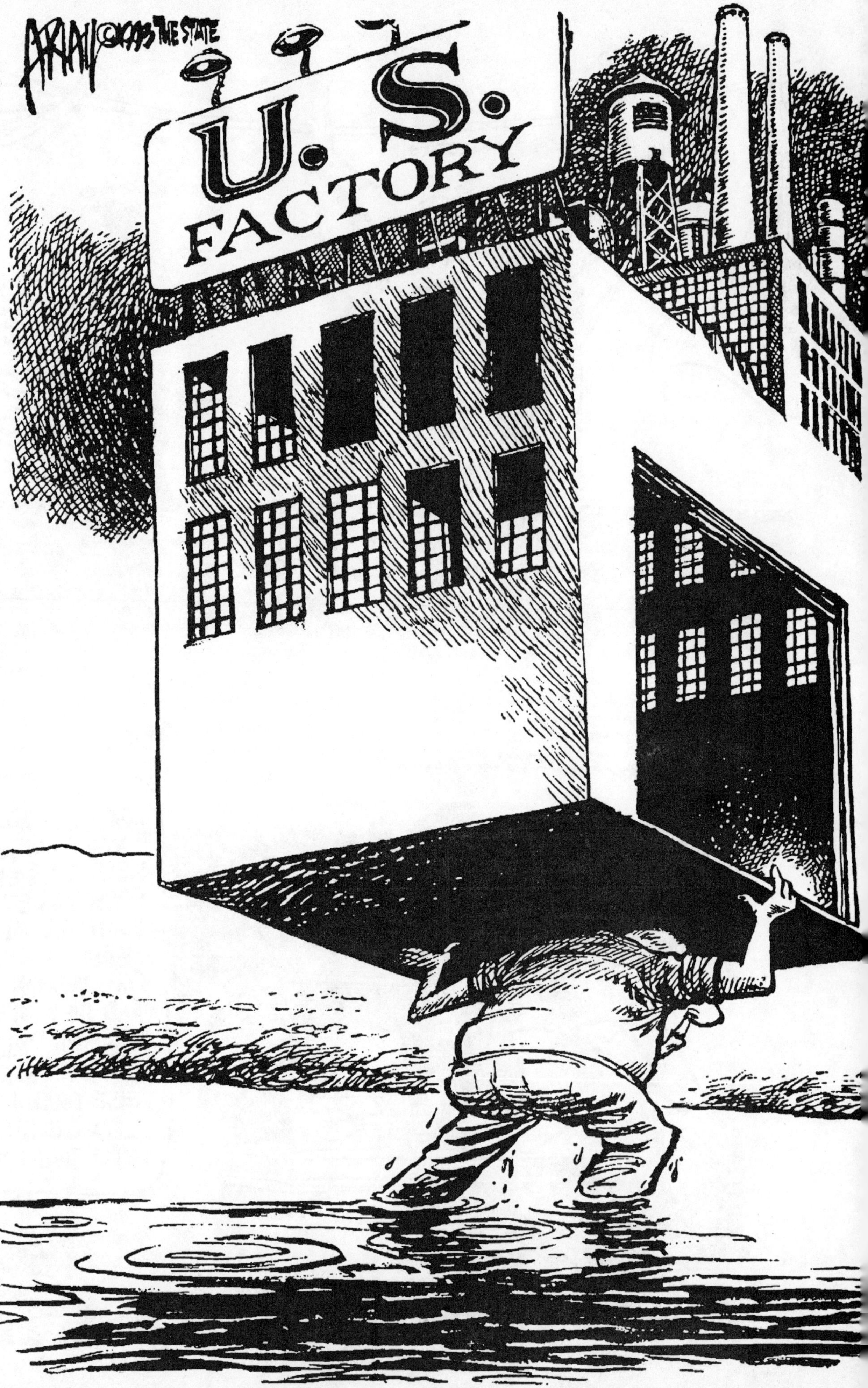
THE STATE
U. S.
FACTORY

ROBERT ARIAIL
Courtesy The State (S.C.)

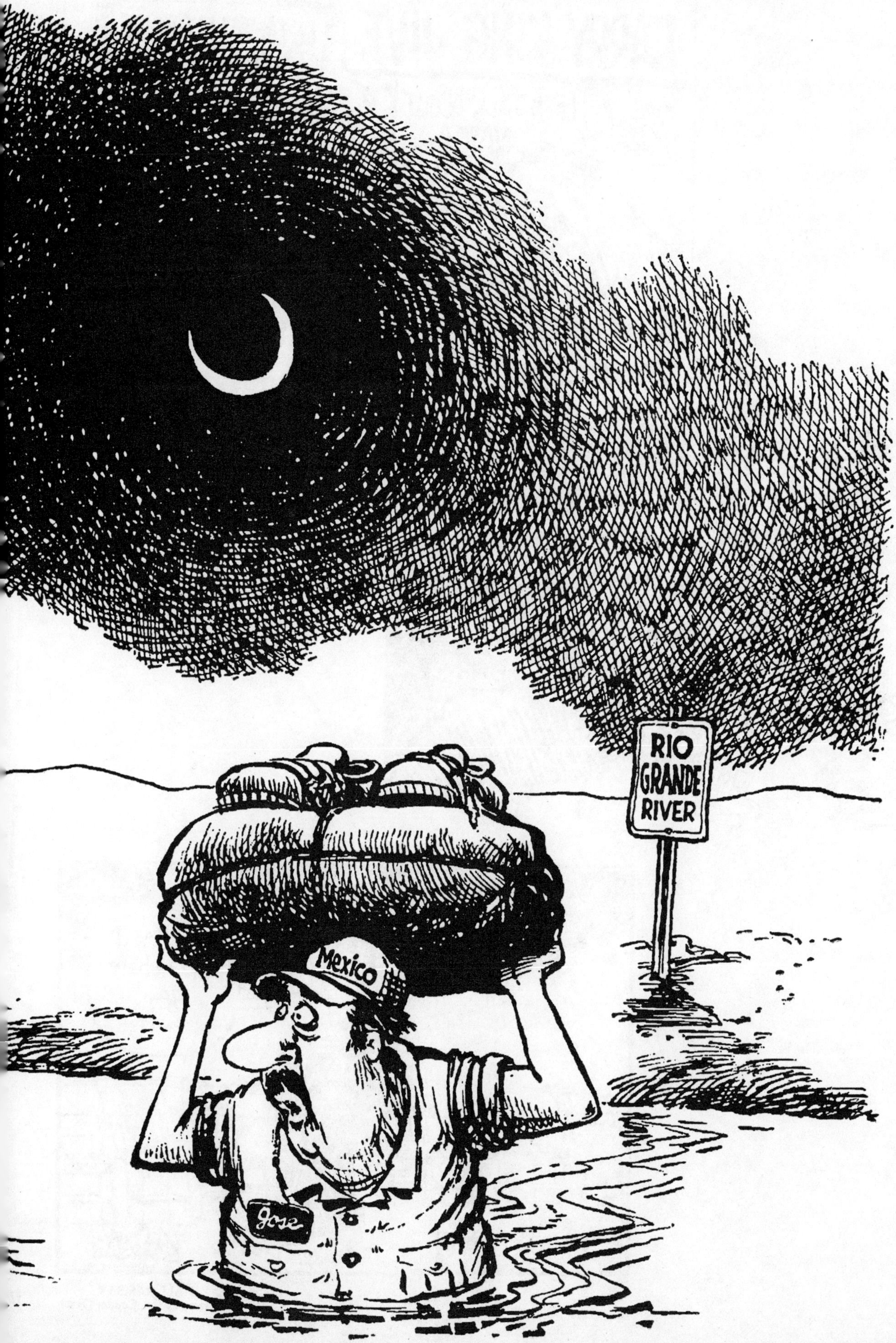
RIO GRANDE RIVER
Mexico
Jose

GARY VARVEL
Courtesy Indianapolis News

RANDY BISH
Courtesy Tribune-Review (Pa.)

MARSHALL RAMSAY
Courtesy Conroe Courier (Tex.)

JOHN SPENCER
Courtesy Philadelphia Business Journal

ART HENRIKSON
Courtesy Daily Herald (Ill.)

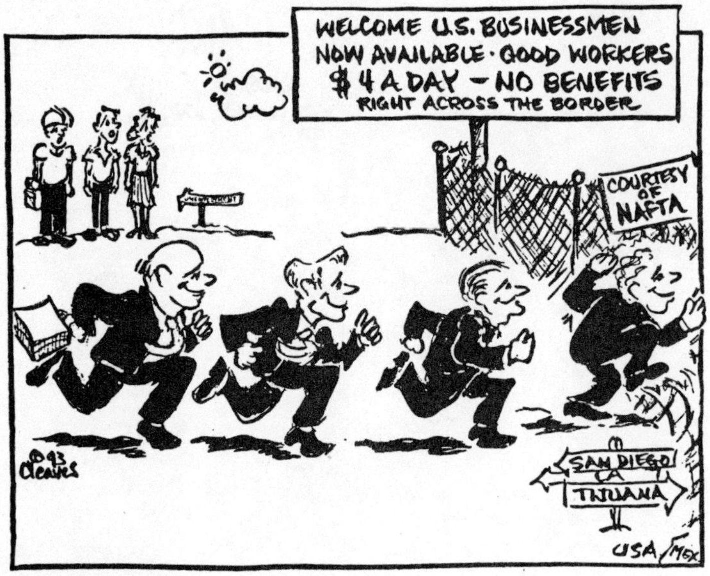
WELCOME U.S. BUSINESSMEN
NOW AVAILABLE · GOOD WORKERS
$ 4 A DAY — NO BENEFITS
RIGHT ACROSS THE BORDER
COURTESY OF NAFTA
©93 Cleaves
SAN DIEGO CA
TIJUANA
USA/MEX

ANN CLEAVES
Courtesy La Prensa (San Diego)

KIRK ANDERSON
Courtesy Madison (Wis.) Capital Times

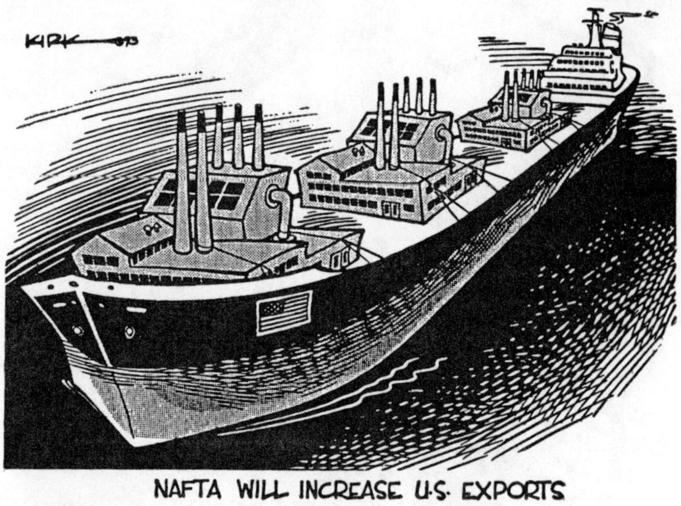
NAFTA WILL INCREASE U.S. EXPORTS

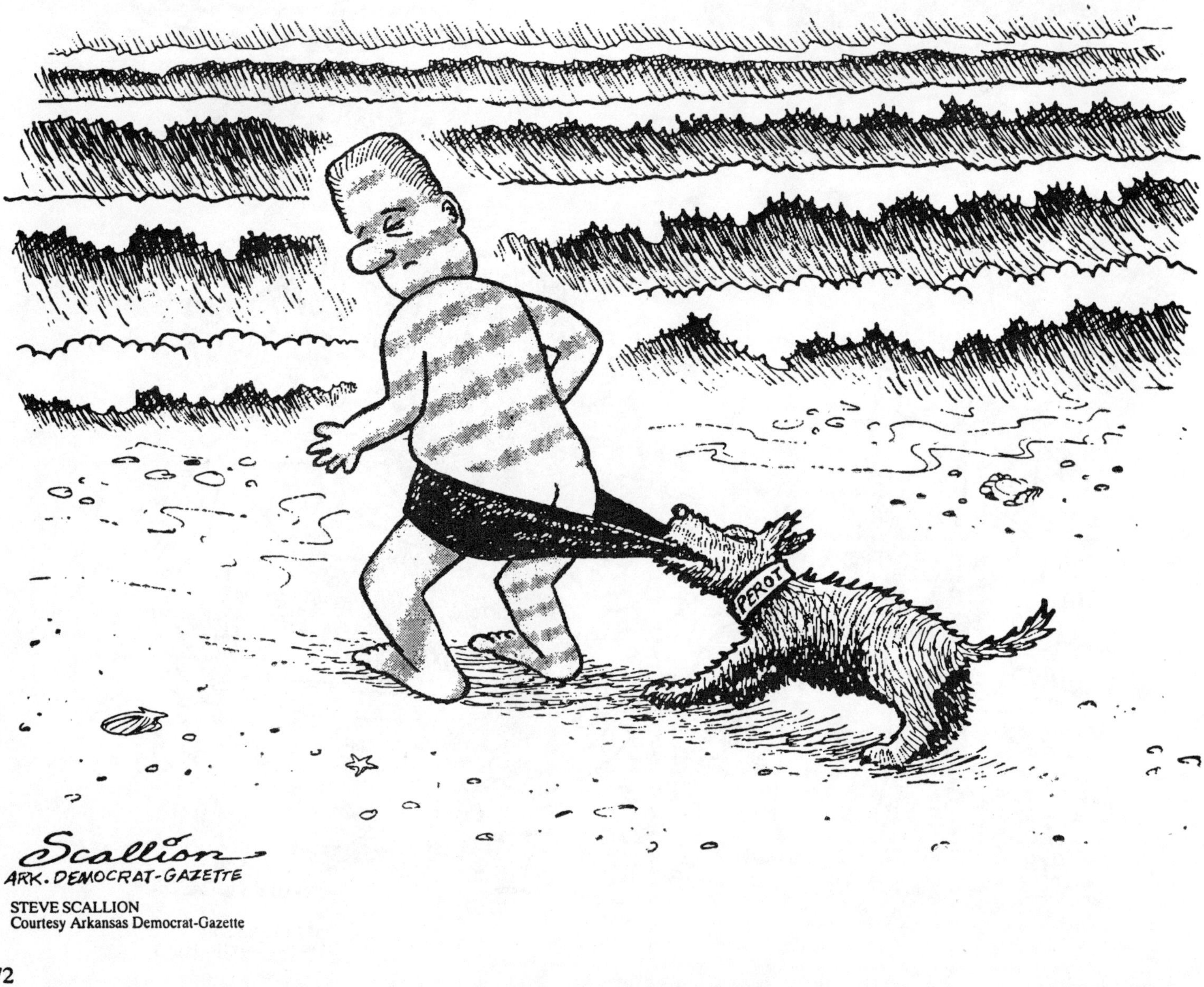
PEROT
Scallion
ARK. DEMOCRAT-GAZETTE

STEVE SCALLION
Courtesy Arkansas Democrat-Gazette

STEVE SACK
Courtesy Minneapolis Star-Tribune

With Strings Attached . . .

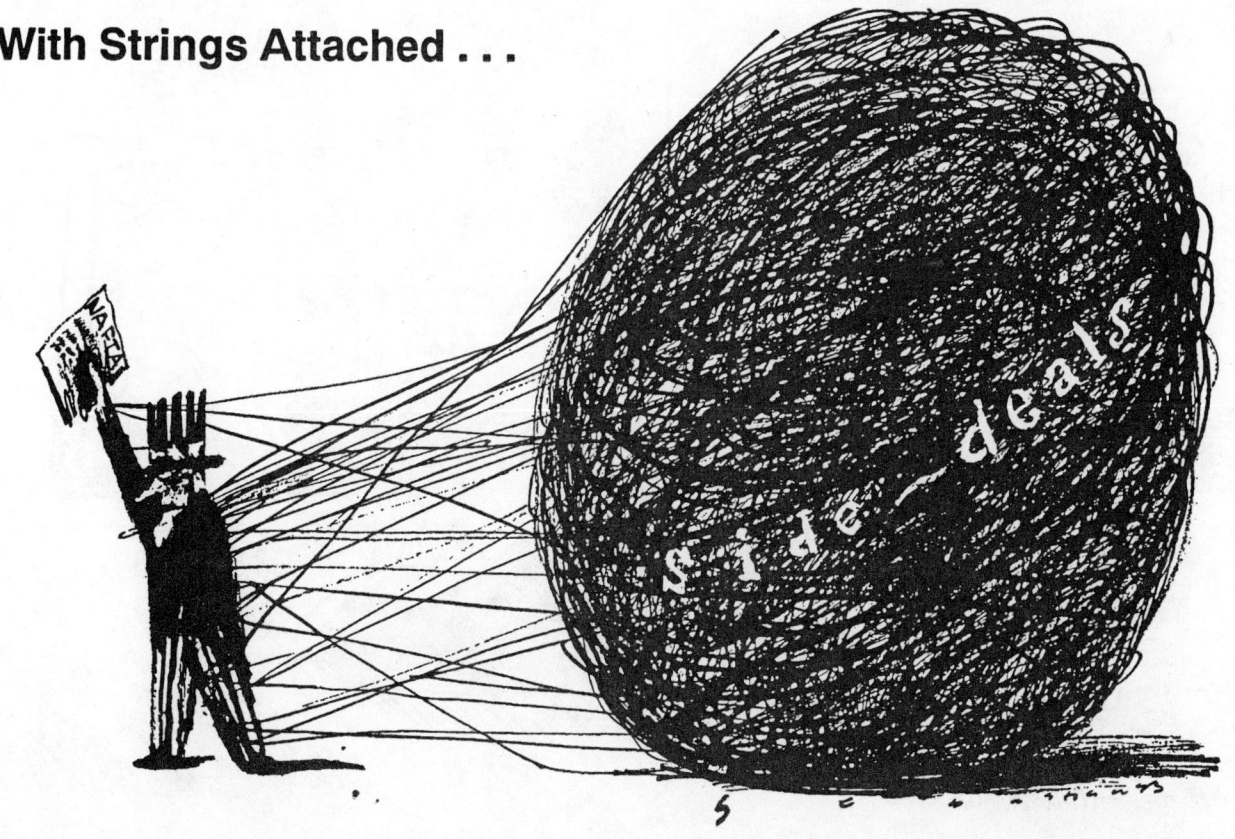

FRED SEBASTIAN
Courtesy Ottawa Citizen

MIKE LUCKOVICH
Courtesy Atlanta Constitution

PAT BAGLEY
Courtesy Salt Lake Tribune

The Family and Society

In late November the nation's Roman Catholic bishops approved a 5,000-word pastoral message that even ardent feminists could accept. It called for a return to family values, such as shared family time at mealtime and in leisure activities. It further called upon men to help their mates in the home, and encouraged women to express their ideas and feelings more fully.

Catholic liberals have been pressuring for changes in the doctrines of the church, but thus far the pope has not been swayed. Many liberals, however, have begun picking up on the concept of family values and morality in society. Most of the media and leading Democrats had poked fun at Vice-President Dan Quayle when he attempted to make family values an issue in a speech a year earlier.

Crime remained an overwhelming problem for Americans during the year. More and more prisons were being built, but construction still was not keeping pace with the growing need. And the criminals were getting younger, with even nine- and ten-year-olds turning to drugs and violence.

Several allegations of sexual abuse of children by priests surfaced around the country. Some claimed that such abuses had occurred many years earlier and they had feared to discuss the incidents until they were mature adults.

JEFF MACNELLY
Courtesy Chicago Tribune and
Tribune Media Services

DAVID O'KEEFE
Courtesy Tampa Tribune

"I'M SORRY GEPPETTO, PINOCCHIO'S BIOLOGICAL PARENTS WANT CUSTODY RIGHTS."

CLAY BENNETT
Courtesy St. Petersburg Times

BOB GORRELL
Courtesy Richmond Times-Dispatch

"I FORGET.... IS THIS DELIVERY FOR THE NATURAL PARENTS, THE SURROGATE PARENTS, THE ADOPTIVE PARENTS, OR THE ATTORNEYS?!"

WAYNE STAYSKAL
Courtesy Tampa Tribune

MICHAEL RAMIREZ
Courtesy Memphis Commercial Appeal

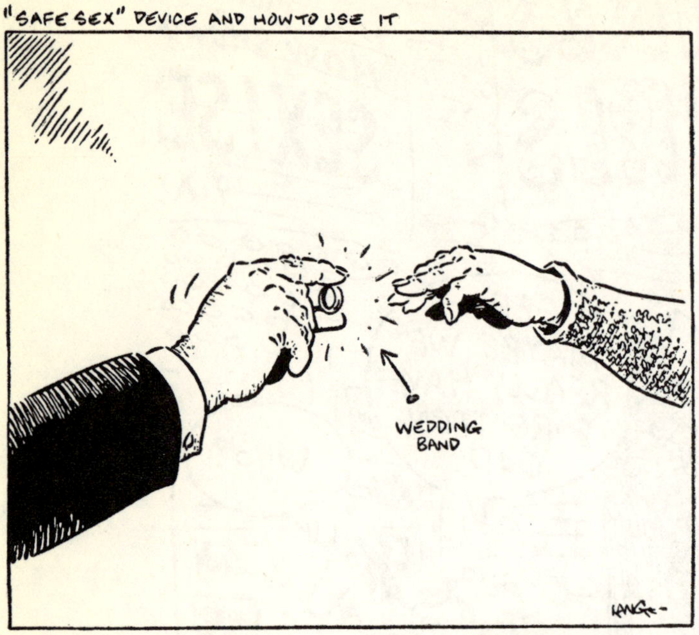

"SAFE SEX" DEVICE AND HOW TO USE IT
WEDDING BAND
LANGE

JIM LANGE
Courtesy Daily Oklahoman

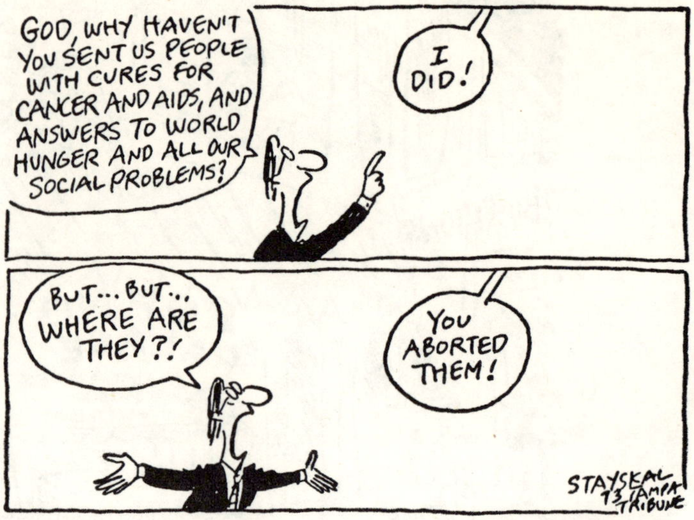

GOD, WHY HAVEN'T YOU SENT US PEOPLE WITH CURES FOR CANCER AND AIDS, AND ANSWERS TO WORLD HUNGER AND ALL OUR SOCIAL PROBLEMS?
I DID!
BUT... BUT... WHERE ARE THEY?!
YOU ABORTED THEM!
STAYSKAL

WAYNE STAYSKAL
Courtesy Tampa Tribune

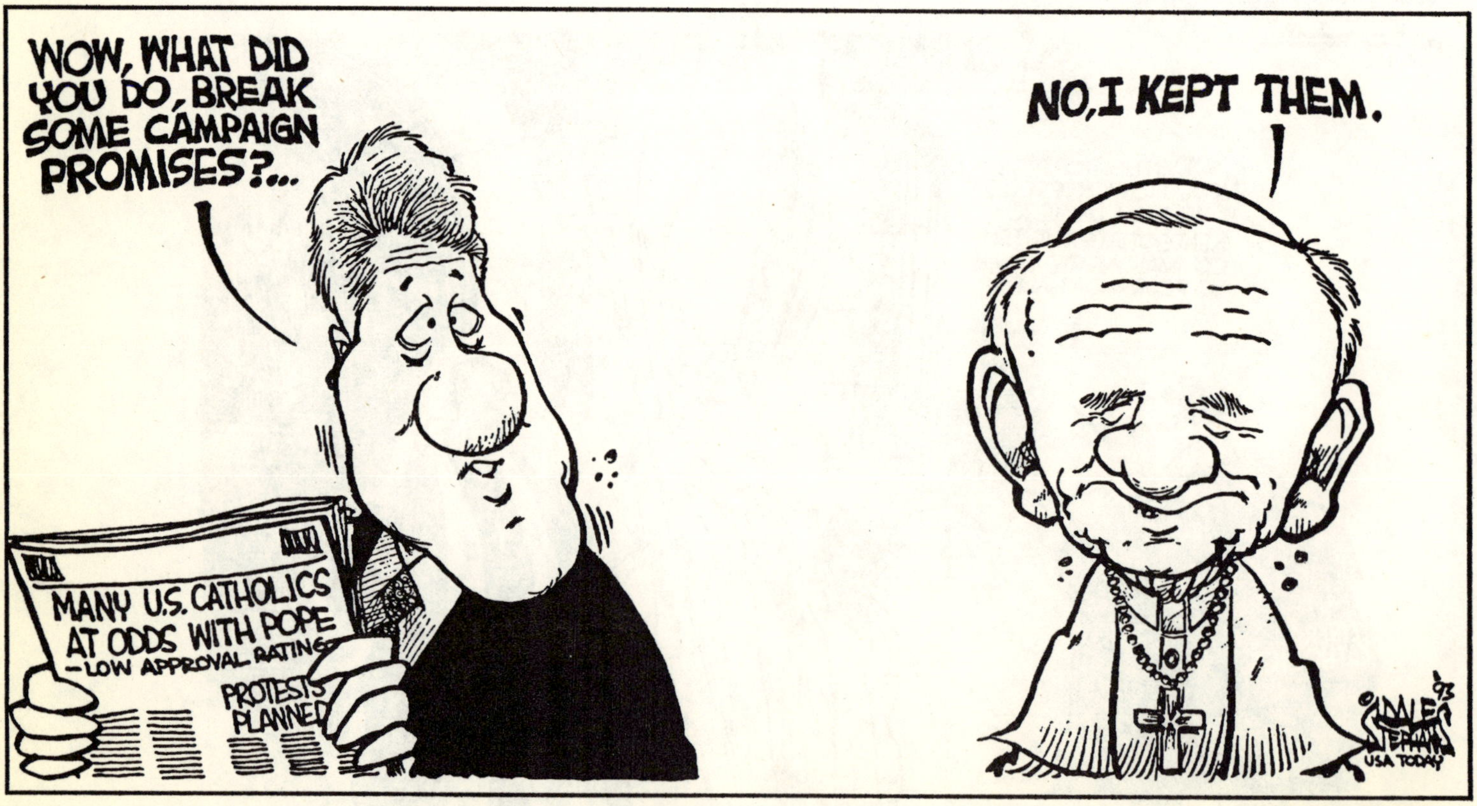

WOW, WHAT DID YOU DO, BREAK SOME CAMPAIGN PROMISES?...
NO, I KEPT THEM.
MANY U.S. CATHOLICS AT ODDS WITH POPE
—LOW APPROVAL RATING
PROTESTS PLANNED
USA TODAY

DALE STEPHANOS
Courtesy USA Today

JOHN BRANCH
Courtesy San Antonio Express-News

CHRIS OBRION
Courtesy Free Lance-Star (Va.)

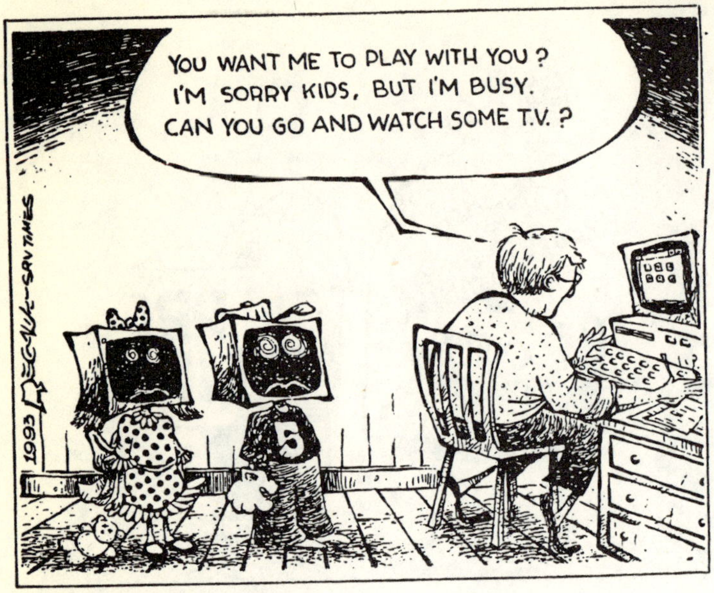
YOU WANT ME TO PLAY WITH YOU ? I'M SORRY KIDS, BUT I'M BUSY. CAN YOU GO AND WATCH SOME T.V. ?

DOUGLAS REGALIA
Courtesy San Ramon Valley Times
(Calif.)

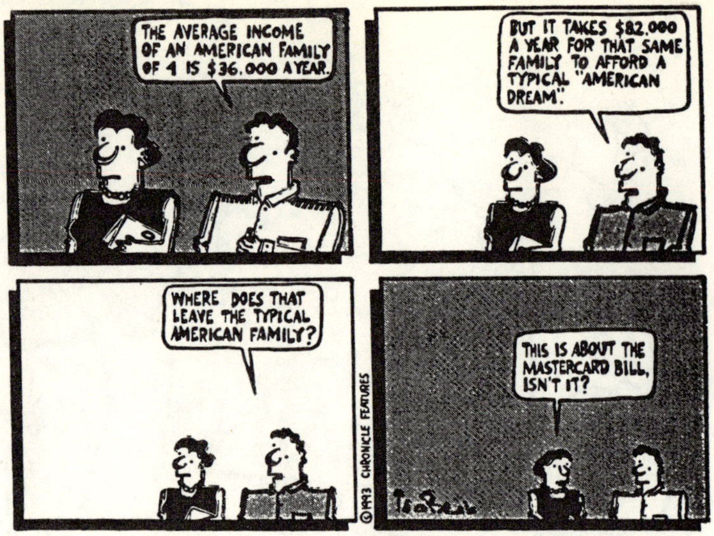
THE AVERAGE INCOME OF AN AMERICAN FAMILY OF 4 IS $36.000 A YEAR.
BUT IT TAKES $82,000 A YEAR FOR THAT SAME FAMILY TO AFFORD A TYPICAL "AMERICAN DREAM".
WHERE DOES THAT LEAVE THE TYPICAL AMERICAN FAMILY?
THIS IS ABOUT THE MASTERCARD BILL, ISN'T IT?
©1993 CHRONICLE FEATURES

TED RALL
Courtesy Chronicle Features

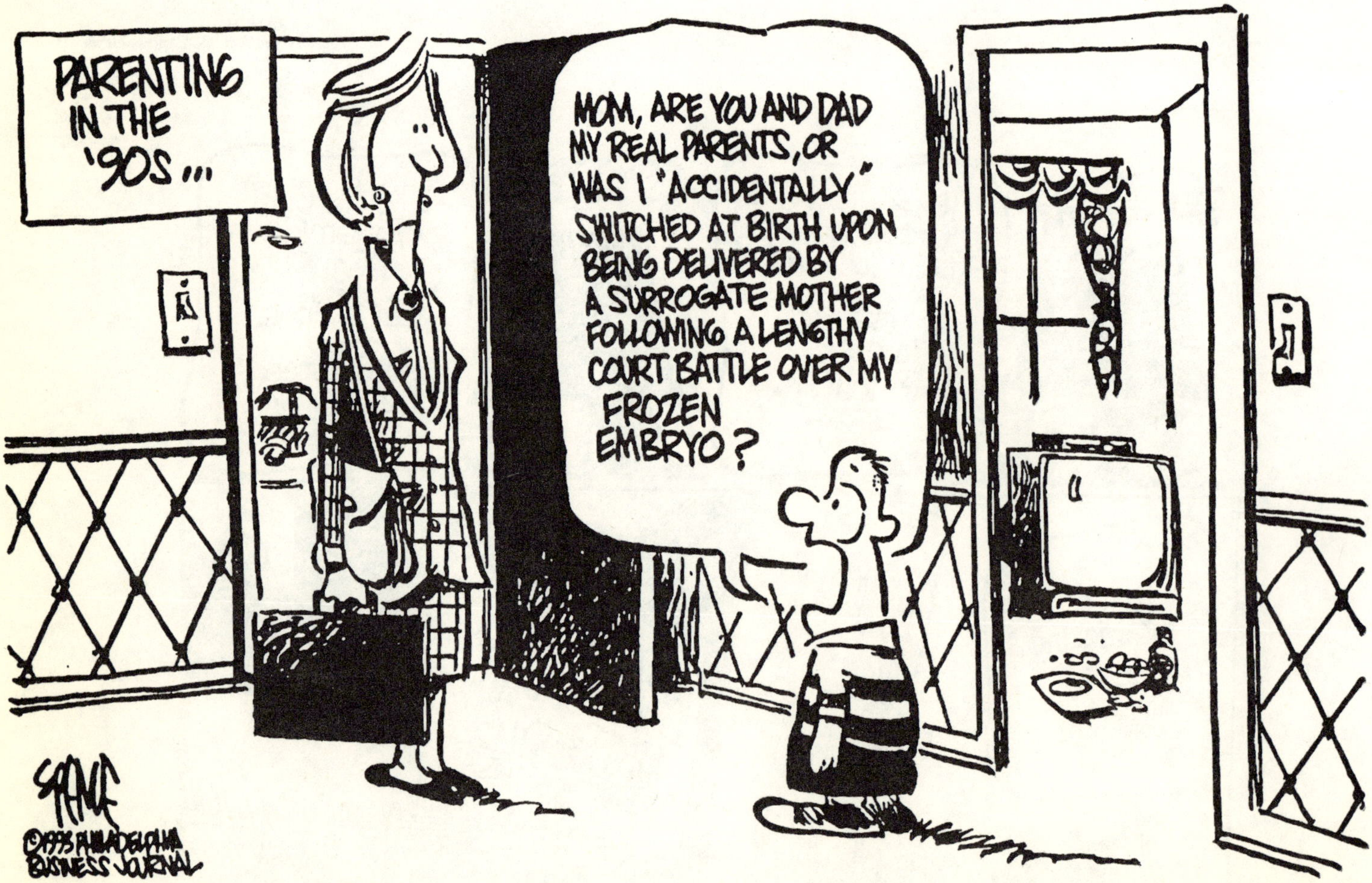
PARENTING IN THE '90S ...
MOM, ARE YOU AND DAD MY REAL PARENTS, OR WAS I "ACCIDENTALLY" SWITCHED AT BIRTH UPON BEING DELIVERED BY A SURROGATE MOTHER FOLLOWING A LENGTHY COURT BATTLE OVER MY FROZEN EMBRYO ?
SPENCE
©1993 PHILADELPHIA BUSINESS JOURNAL

JOHN SPENCER
Courtesy Philadelphia Business Journal

STEVE GREENBERG
Courtesy Seattle Post-Intelligencer

ROB ROGERS
Courtesy Pittsburgh Press

81

RICHARD CROWSON
Courtesy Wichita Eagle

JIM MORIN
Courtesy Miami Herald

The Economy

U.S. Commerce Department figures for the second quarter indicated that instead of the presumed 1.4 percent increase in the Gross Domestic Product, it actually was double that—2.8 percent. Experts concluded that recovery from the recession had begun in the spring of 1992 and had maintained a modest climb into 1993.

The job squeeze continued as manufacturers slashed payrolls across the country. IBM cut 85,000 workers, Sears laid off 50,000, and Boeing pared 28,000 as the defense industry retrenched. In most regions of the country shoppers continued to hold back on spending, but seemed to loosen the purse strings as the Christmas season approached. Late in the year, the overall employment picture brightened as the recovery appeared to be gaining momentum.

Part of the economic boost could be attributed to the fact that Detroit was making a strong comeback against Japanese automakers. The value of the yen against the dollar soared, forcing the Japanese to hike car prices substantially. All in all, consumer confidence seemed to be returning after the prolonged recession.

Mergers reached $265 billion during the year as companies sought ways to remain competitive in a changing global economy. Some observers feared many small businesses would go under as a result of President Clinton's large tax increase and costly health care package.

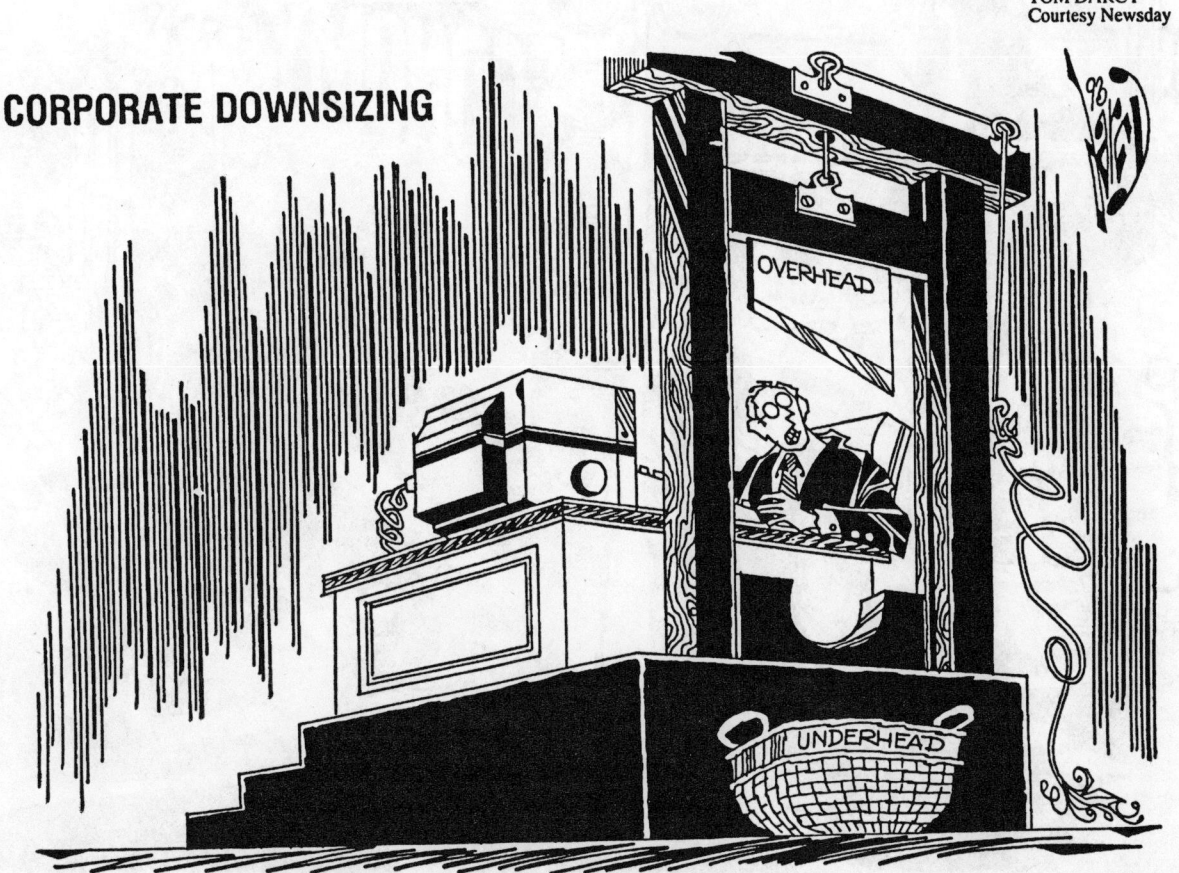

TOM DARCY
Courtesy Newsday

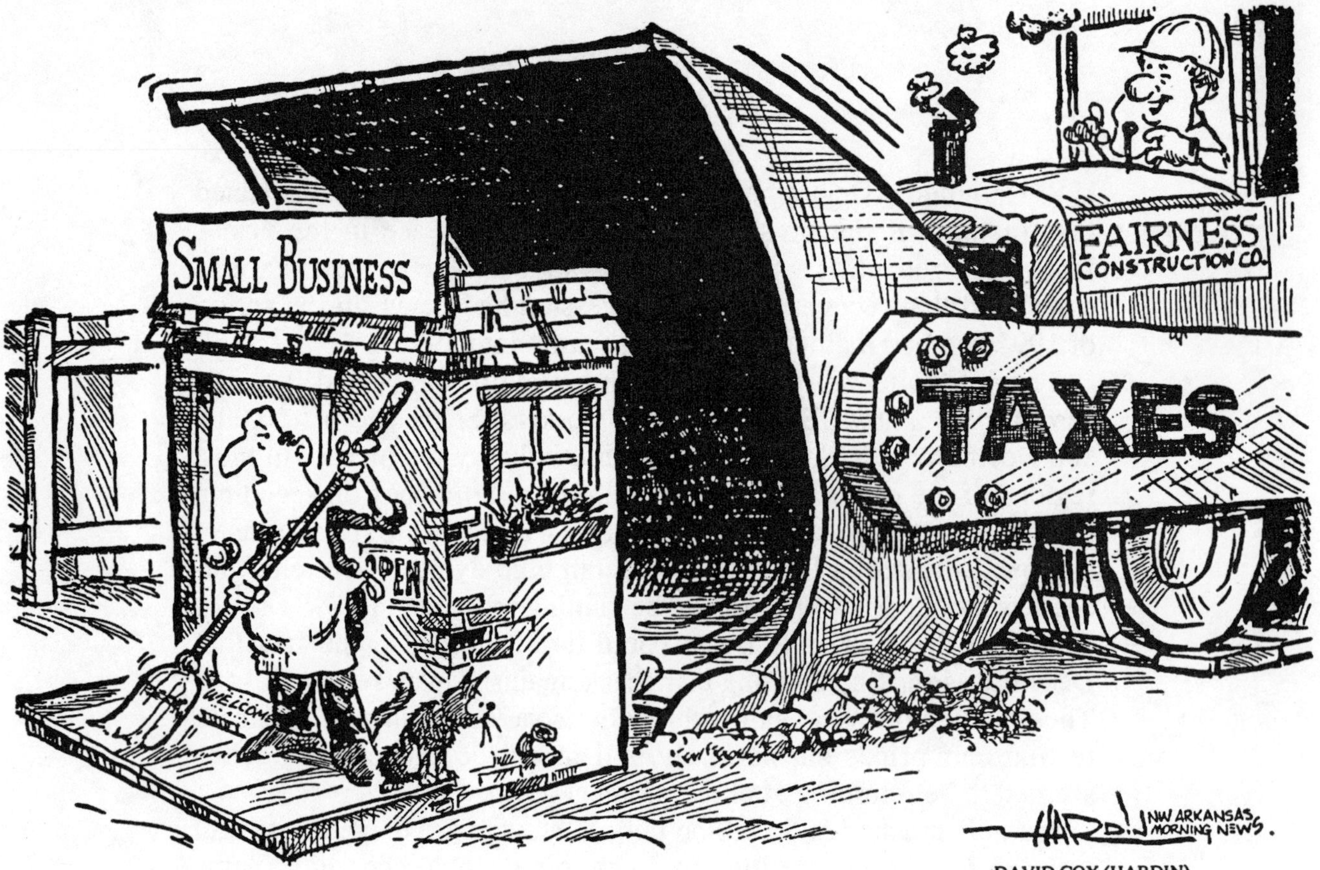
SMALL BUSINESS
OPEN
FAIRNESS CONSTRUCTION CO.
TAXES
HARDIN NW ARKANSAS MORNING NEWS

DAVID COX (HARDIN)
Courtesy N.W. Ark. Morning News

DICK LOCHER
Courtesy Chicago Tribune

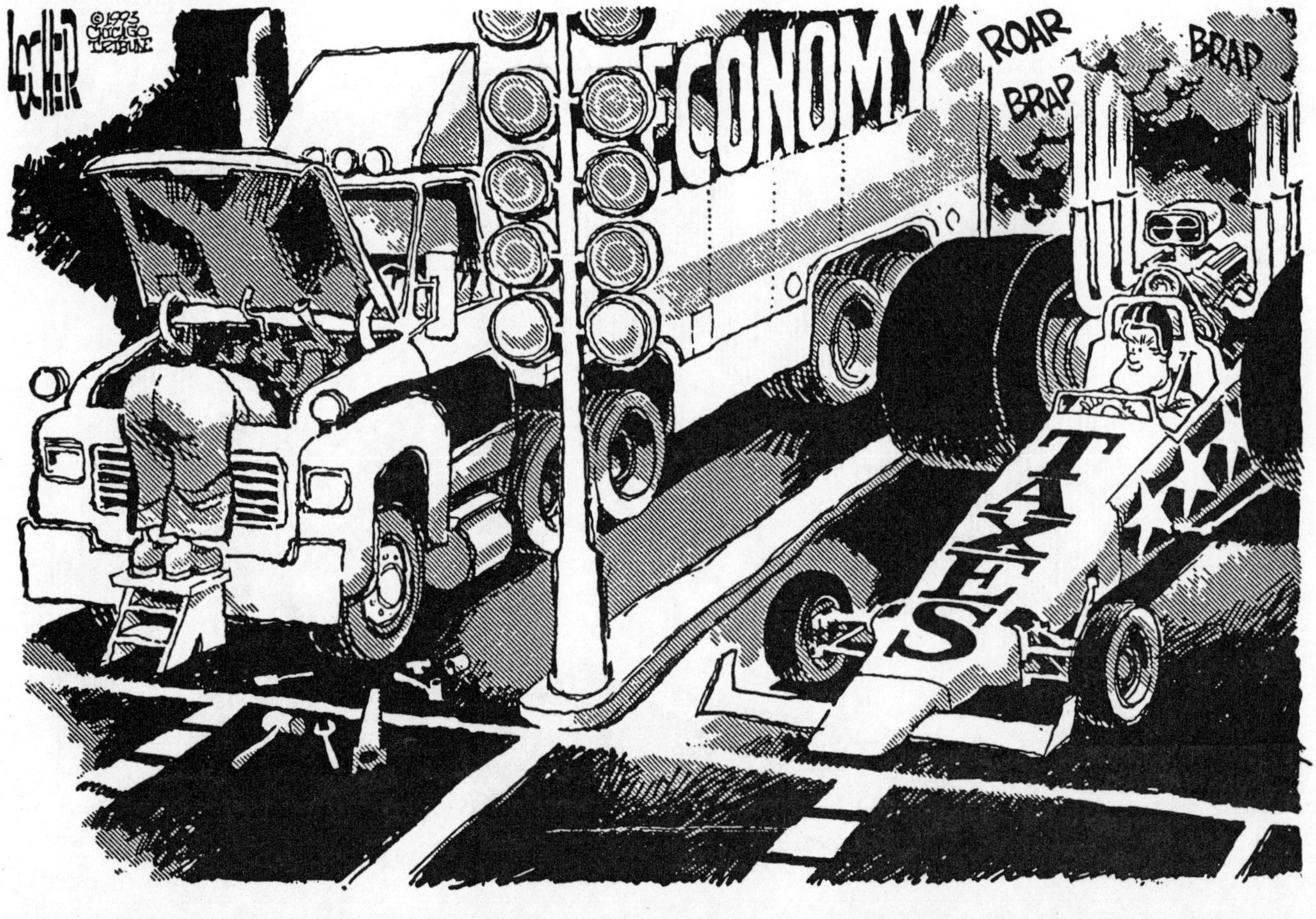
LOCHER ©1995 CHICAGO TRIBUNE
ECONOMY
ROAR
BRAP
BRAP
TAXES

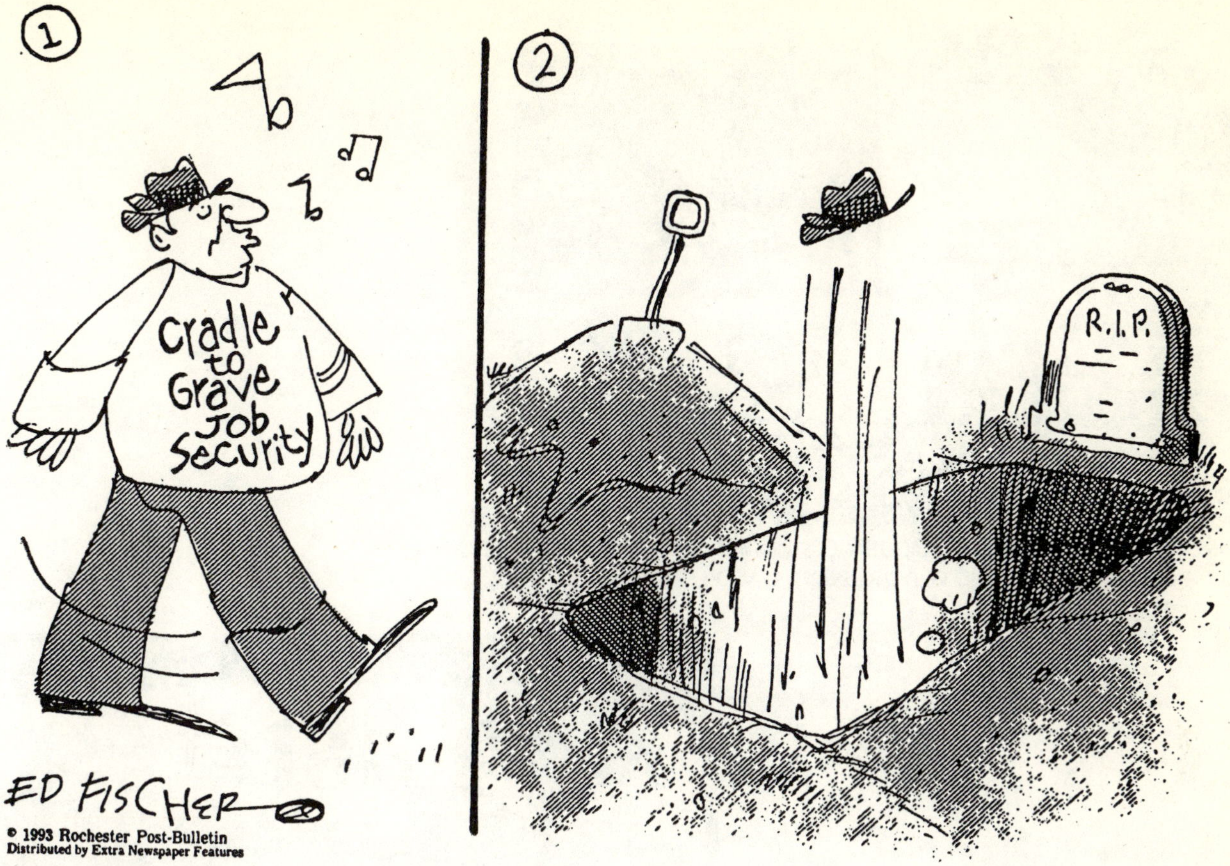
1
Cradle to Grave Job Security
2
R.I.P.
ED FISCHER

ED FISCHER
Courtesy Rochester Post-Bulletin

DENNY PRITCHARD
Courtesy Ottawa Citizen

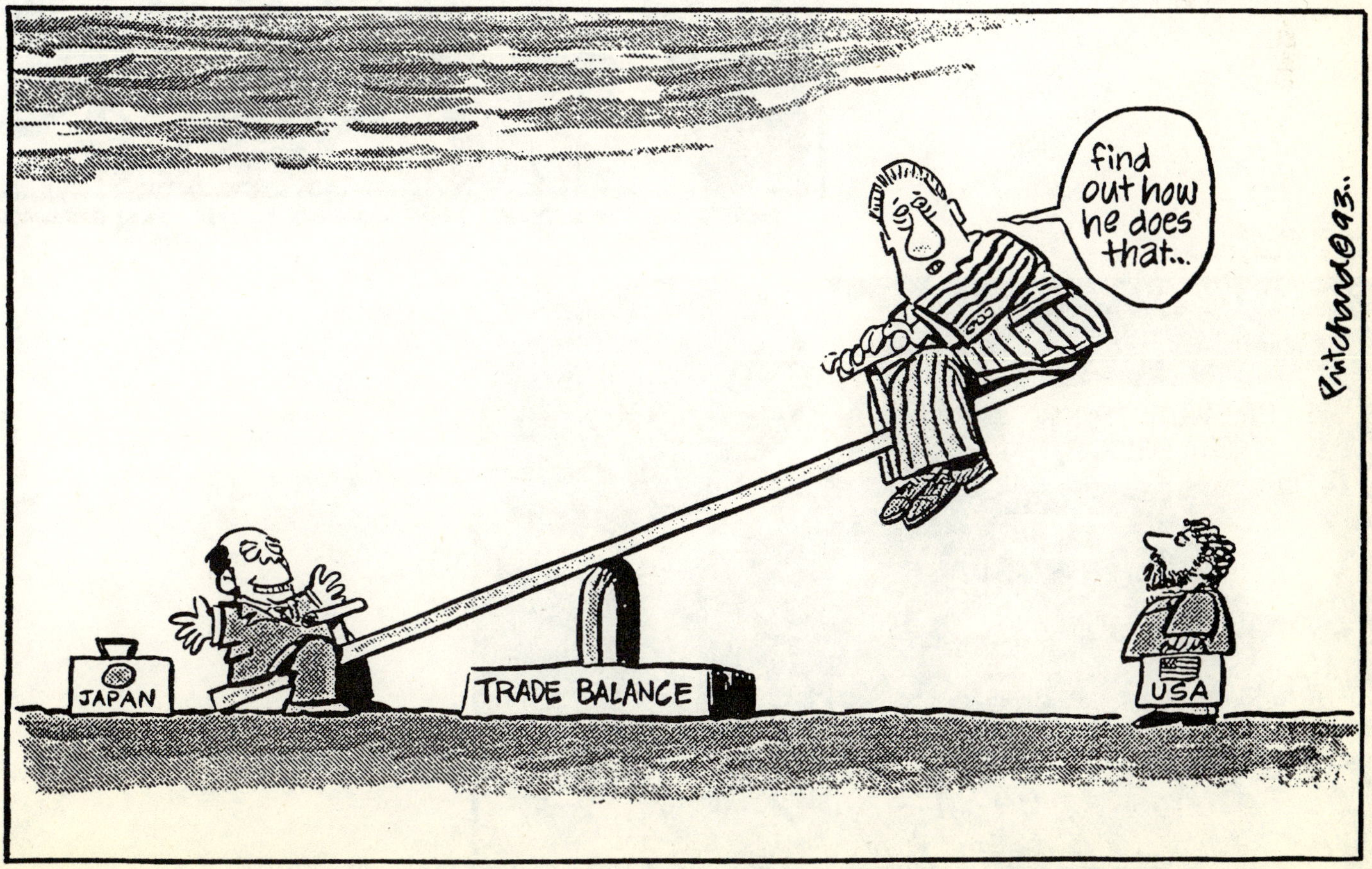
find out how he does that..
Pritchard©93..
JAPAN
TRADE BALANCE
USA

CHARLES BISSELL
Courtesy The Tennessean

"... AND THEN CHILDREN, THE BIGGER CORPORATION BOUGHT UP THE SMALLER CORPORATION, LAID OFF THOUSANDS, AND LIVED HAPPILY EVER..."

TED RALL
Courtesy Chronicle Features

"THERE'S ONLY ONE THING: WHAT HAPPENED TO OUR @**! CUSTOMERS?"

VIKRAM MADAN
Courtesy The Daily (Wash.)

CHUCK AYERS
Courtesy Akron Beacon Journal

HANK McCLURE
Courtesy Lawton Constitution

CHESTER COMMODORE
Courtesy Chicago Defender

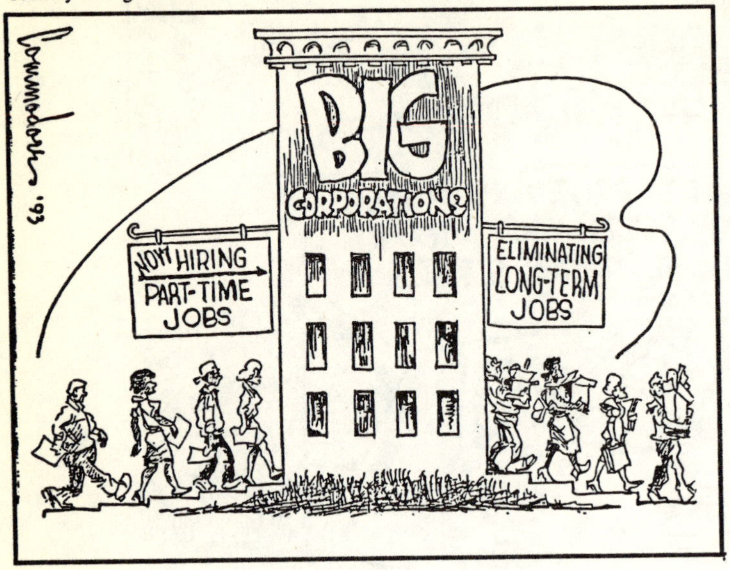
BIG
CORPORATIONS
NOW HIRING PART-TIME JOBS
ELIMINATING LONG-TERM JOBS
Commodore '93

STEPHEN TEMPLETON
Courtesy National Forum/Associated Features

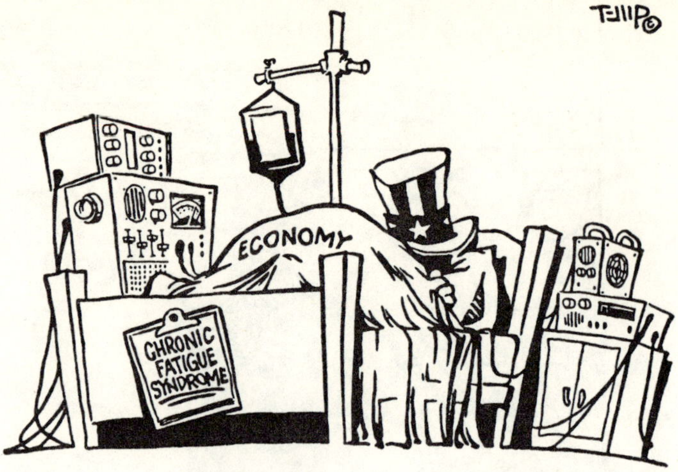
ECONOMY
CHRONIC FATIGUE SYNDROME

NICK ANDERSON
Courtesy Louisville Courier Journal

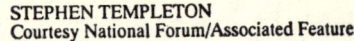

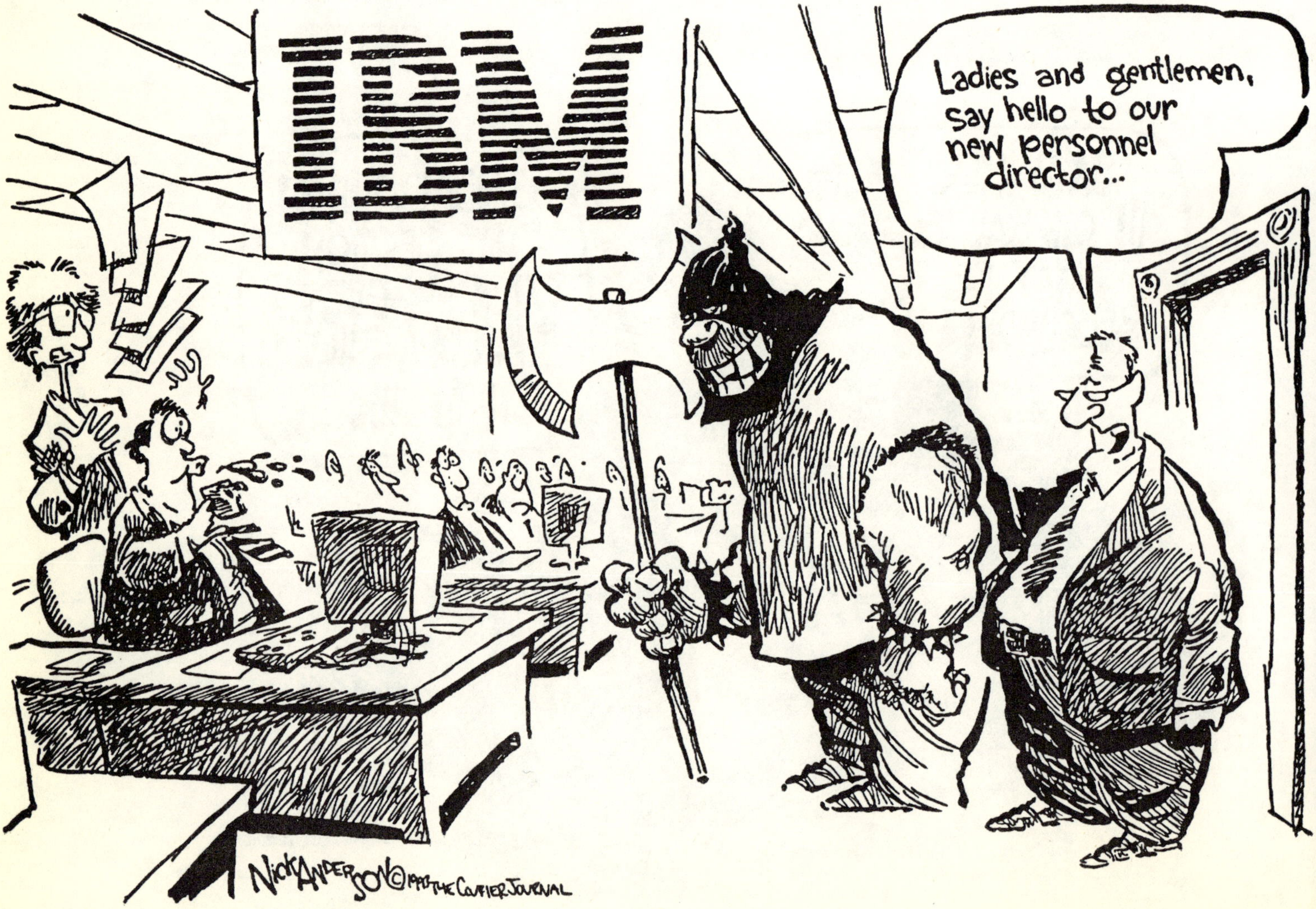
IBM
Ladies and gentlemen, say hello to our new personnel director...
NICK ANDERSON © THE COURIER JOURNAL

JIM BERRY
Courtesy NEA

BUBBA FLINT
Courtesy Ft. Worth Star-Telegram

DAVID HITCH
Courtesy Worcester Telegram & Gazette

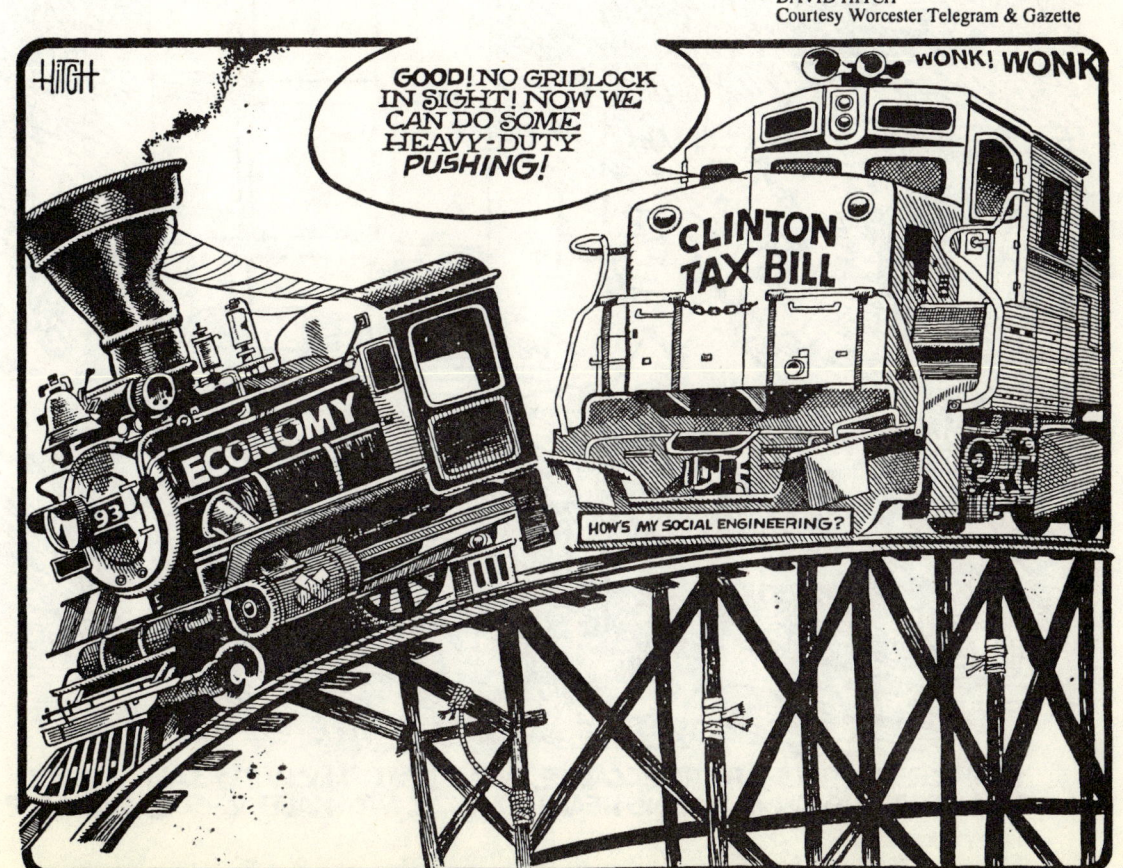

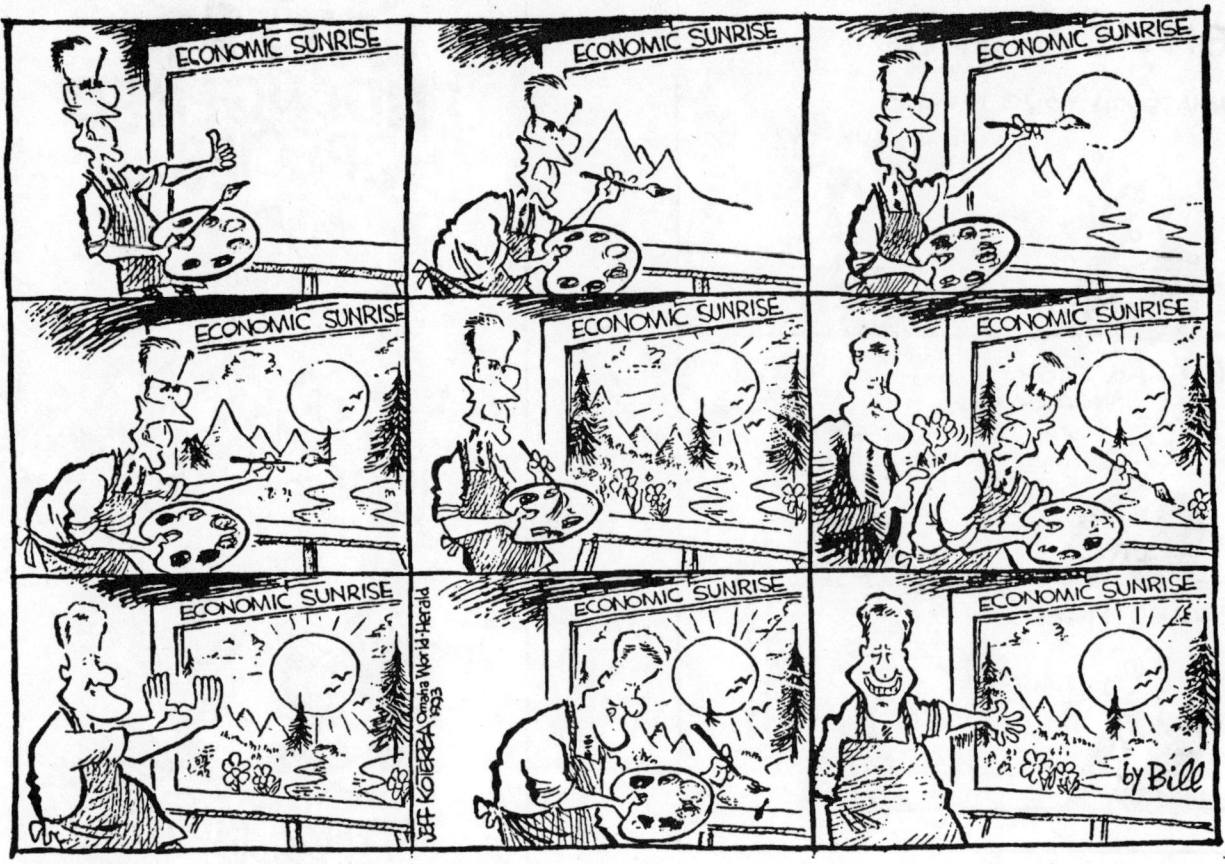

JEFF KOTERBA
Courtesy Omaha World-Herald

JERRY BUCKLEY
Courtesy Express Newspapers

Foreign Affairs

American troops were sent into Somalia in late 1992 by President George Bush to feed a starving population after famine and civil strife had created untold suffering. During 1993, more than thirty Americans and dozens of United Nations troops were killed in the action, including eighteen Army Rangers ambushed in a search for warlord Mohamed Farrah Aidid.

Europe's worst fighting since the end of World War II continued in beleaguered Bosnia. NATO attempted unsuccessfully to enforce a no-fly zone, and the U.S. air-dropped food and supplies as the killing continued.

After telling the people of Haiti that they would be welcome in the U.S. if he became president, Clinton reversed himself when he assumed office, and boatloads of Haitians were turned away. At year's end, the U.S. was still unsuccessful in its attempts to reinstall Haiti's ousted President Jean-Bertrand Aristide.

A major fire swept a wing of Windsor Castle in 1993, and Queen Elizabeth hit upon the idea of charging admission to Buckingham Palace to help pay for rebuilding. A pen stroke wrote the end to apartheid in South Africa, concluding two years of stormy negotiations between white and black leaders. More and more Cubans, including a relative of Fidel Castro, made their way to the U.S. to seek a better life.

TOM ENGELHARDT
Courtesy St. Louis Post-Dispatch

MARK STREETER
Courtesy Savannah Morning News

DAVID HORSEY
Courtesy Seattle Post-Intelligencer

ROBERT ARIAIL
Courtesy The State (S.C.)

DOUG MACGREGOR
Courtesy Ft. Meyers News-Press

BRIAN DUFFY
Courtesy Des Moines Register

RANAN LURIE
Courtesy Cartoonews International

LAZARO FRESQUET
Courtesy El Nuevo Herald (Miami)

MIKE RITTER
Courtesy Tribune Newspapers

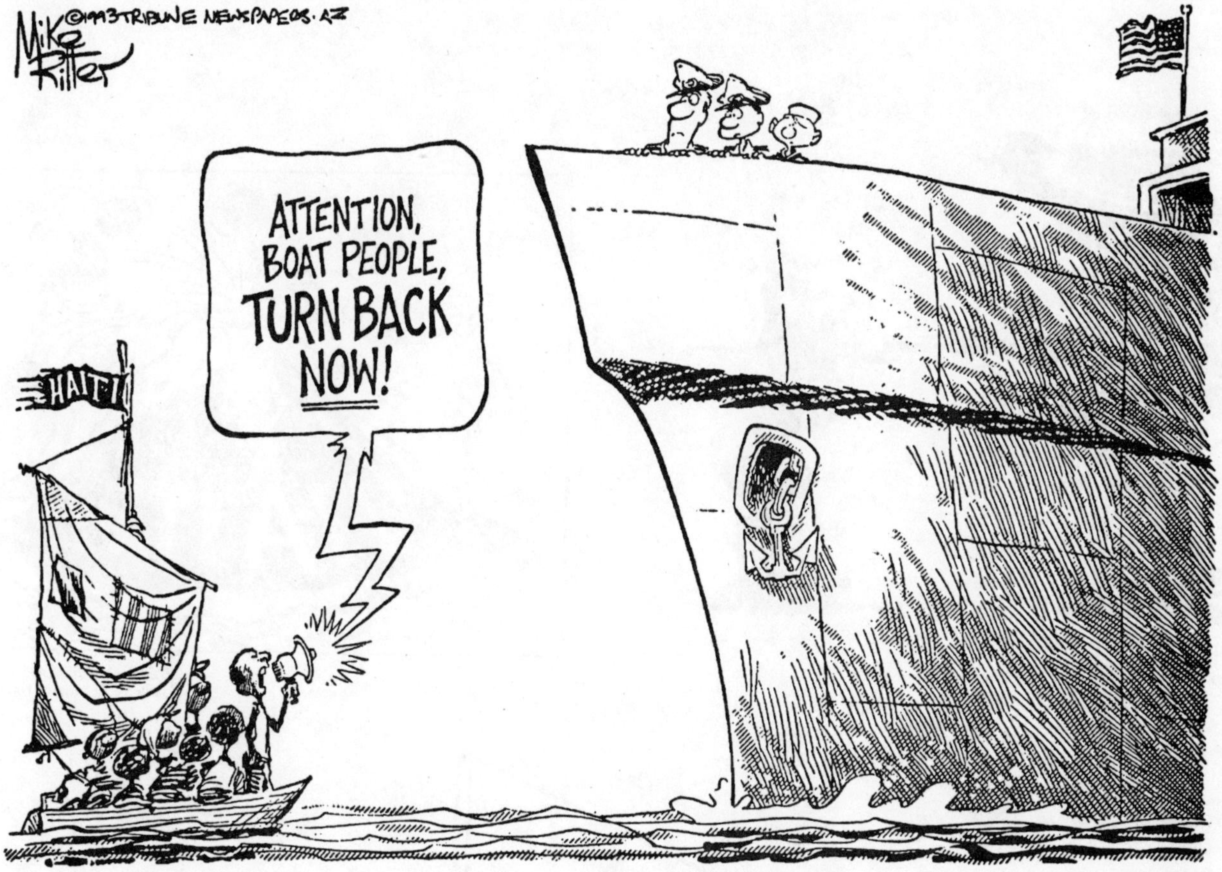

©1993 TRIBUNE NEWSPAPERS · AZ
Mike Ritter
ATTENTION, BOAT PEOPLE, TURN BACK NOW!
HAITI

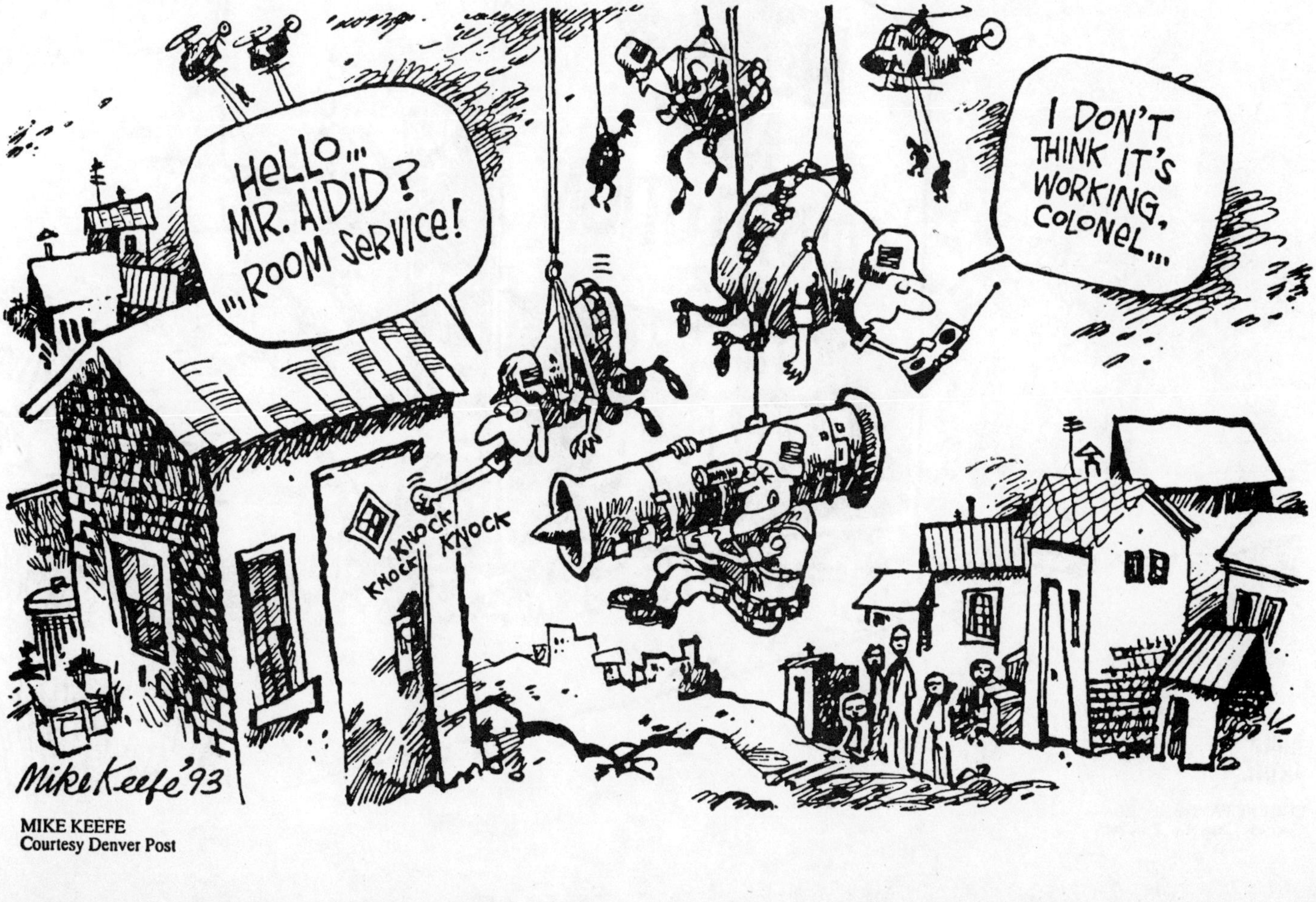

HELLO... MR. AIDID? ...ROOM SERVICE!
I DON'T THINK IT'S WORKING, COLONEL...
KNOCK KNOCK KNOCK
Mike Keefe '93

MIKE KEEFE
Courtesy Denver Post

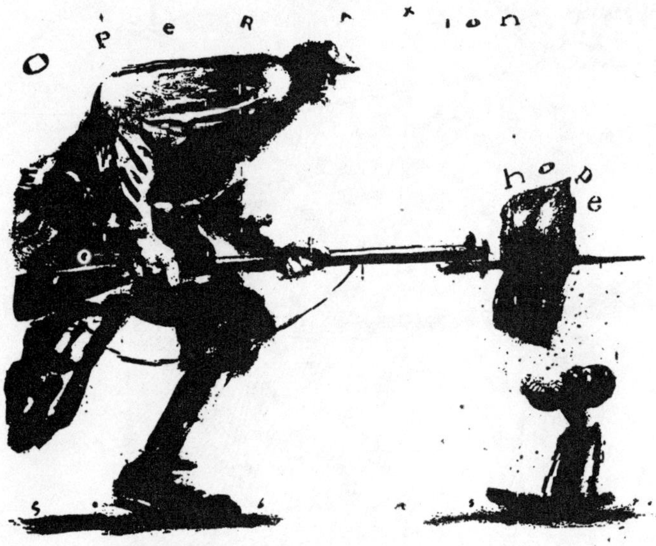
OpeRation
hope

FRED SEBASTIAN
Courtesy Ottawa Citizen

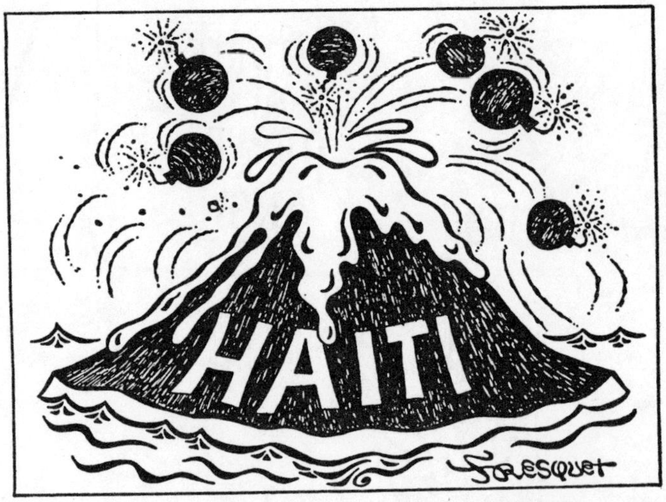
HAITI
FRESQUET

LAZARO FRESQUET
Courtesy El Nuevo Herald (Miami)

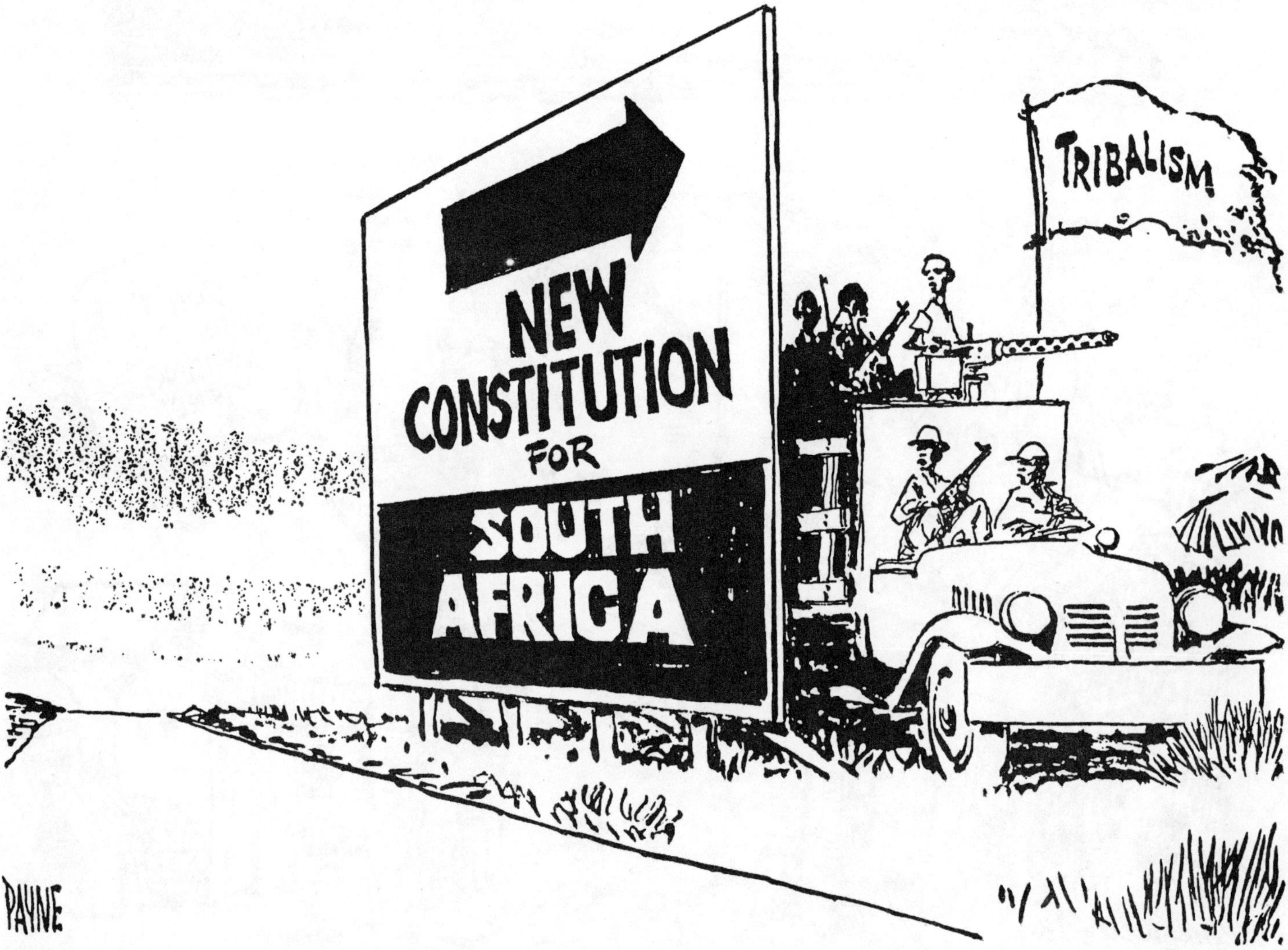
NEW CONSTITUTION FOR
SOUTH AFRICA
TRIBALISM
PAYNE

EUGENE PAYNE
Courtesy Charlotte Observer

BOB RICH
Courtesy Connecticut Post

DANA SUMMERS
Courtesy Orlando Sentinel

NEAL BLOOM
Courtesy Bloom Toons, INK

ETTA HULME
Courtesy Ft. Worth Star-Telegram

DENNY PRITCHARD
Courtesy Ottawa Citizen

STEVE GREENBERG
Courtesy Seattle Post-Intelligencer

MARK CULLUM
Courtesy Birmingham News

SITTING DUCK

ERIC SMITH
Courtesy Capital Gazette Newspapers

JAMES MERCADO
Courtesy Honolulu Star-Bulletin

PAUL CONRAD
Courtesy Los Angeles Times

JOHN STAMPONE
Courtesy The Wave (Del.)

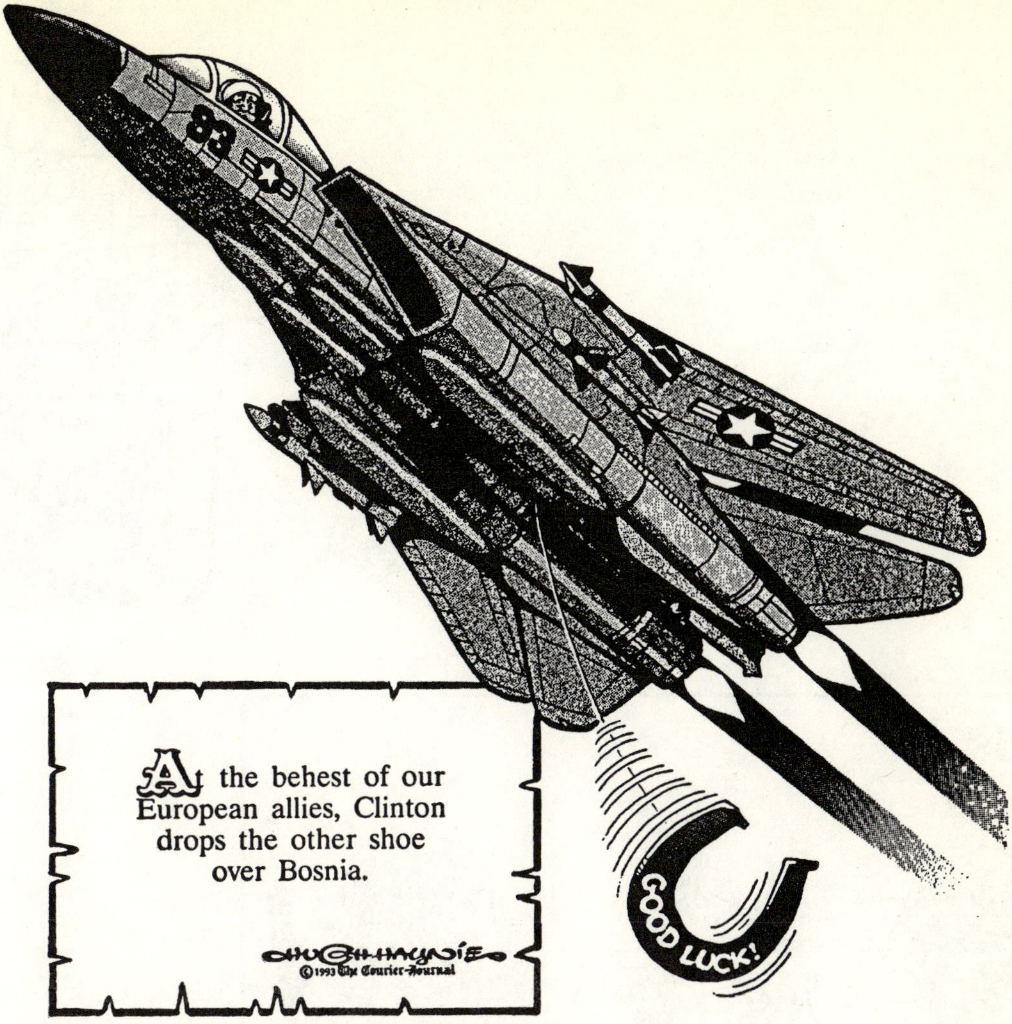
At the behest of our European allies, Clinton drops the other shoe over Bosnia.
83
GOOD LUCK!
©1993 The Courier-Journal

HUGH HAYNIE
Courtesy Louisville Courier Journal

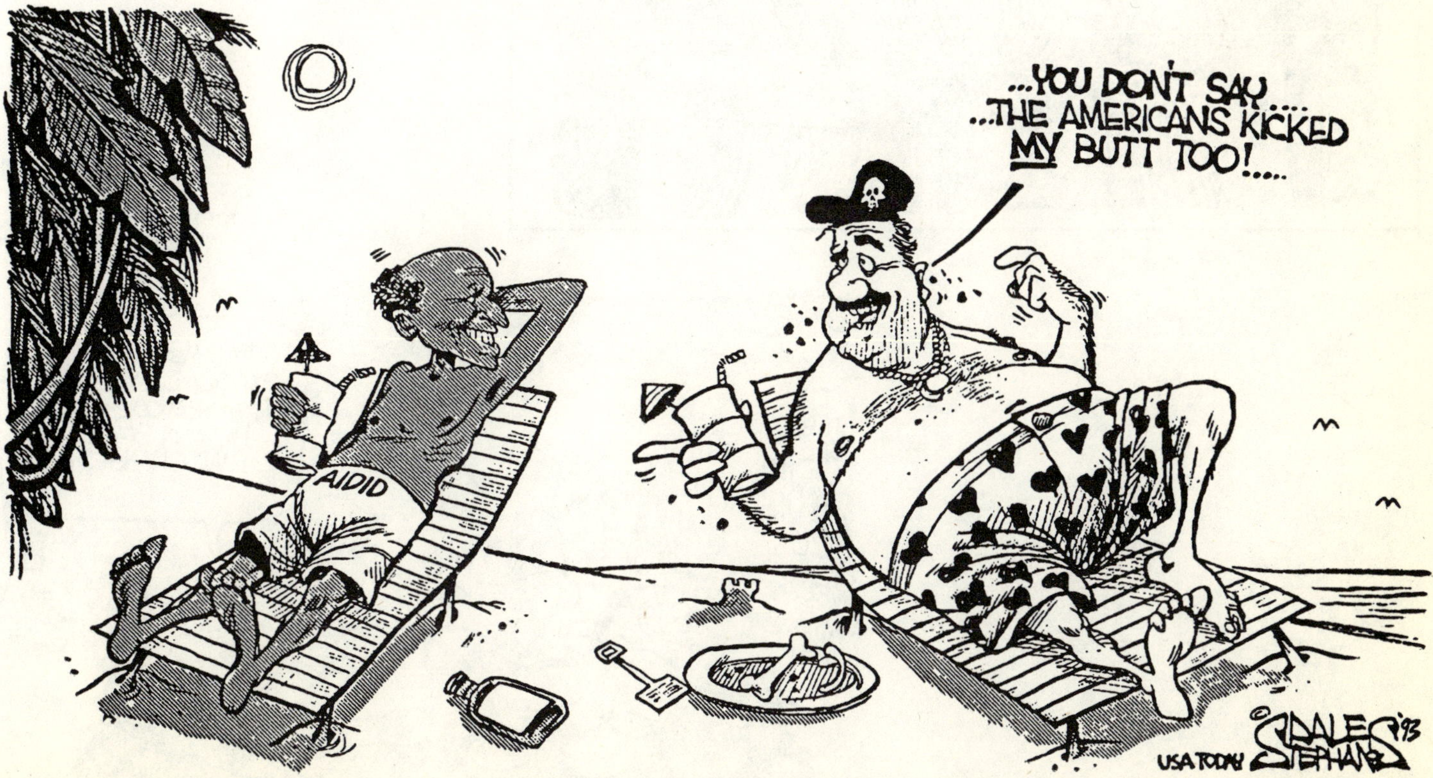
...YOU DON'T SAY.... ...THE AMERICANS KICKED MY BUTT TOO!....
AIDID
USA TODAY
DALE STEPHANOS '93

DALE STEPHANOS
Courtesy USA Today

DENNIS DRAUGHON
Courtesy Scranton Times

REX BABIN
Courtesy Times Union (N.Y.)

JOE HELLER
Courtesy Green Bay Press-Gazette

DAVID GRANLUND
Courtesy Middlesex News

CHARLES FAGAN
Courtesy Associated Features Syndicate

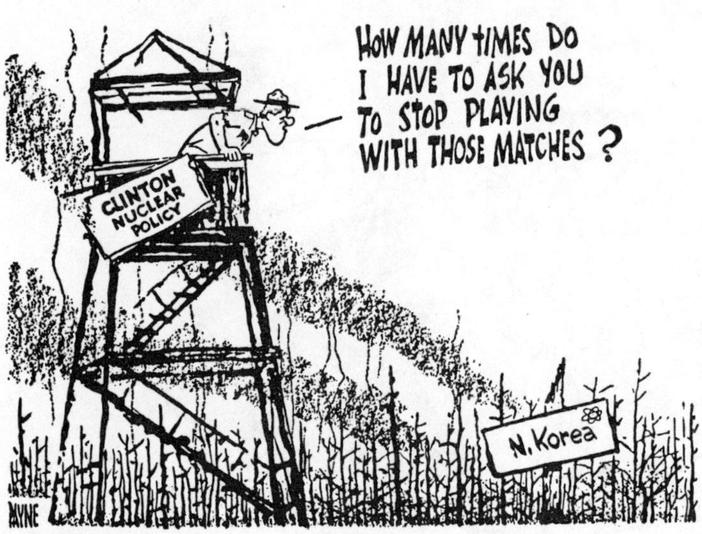
HOW MANY TIMES DO I HAVE TO ASK YOU TO STOP PLAYING WITH THOSE MATCHES ?
CLINTON NUCLEAR POLICY
N. Korea
PAYNE

EUGENE PAYNE
Courtesy Charlotte Observer

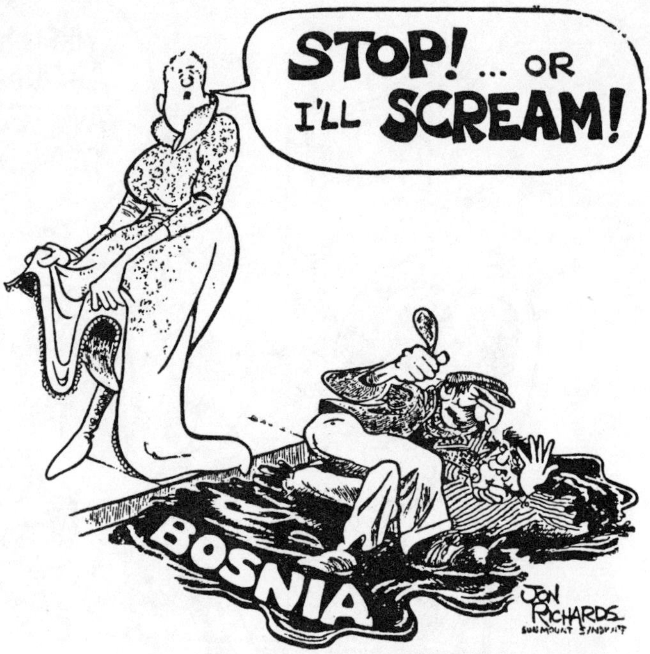
STOP! ... OR I'LL SCREAM!
BOSNIA
JON RICHARDS

JON RICHARDS
Courtesy Sun Mount Syndicate

PAUL SZEP
Courtesy Boston Globe

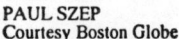

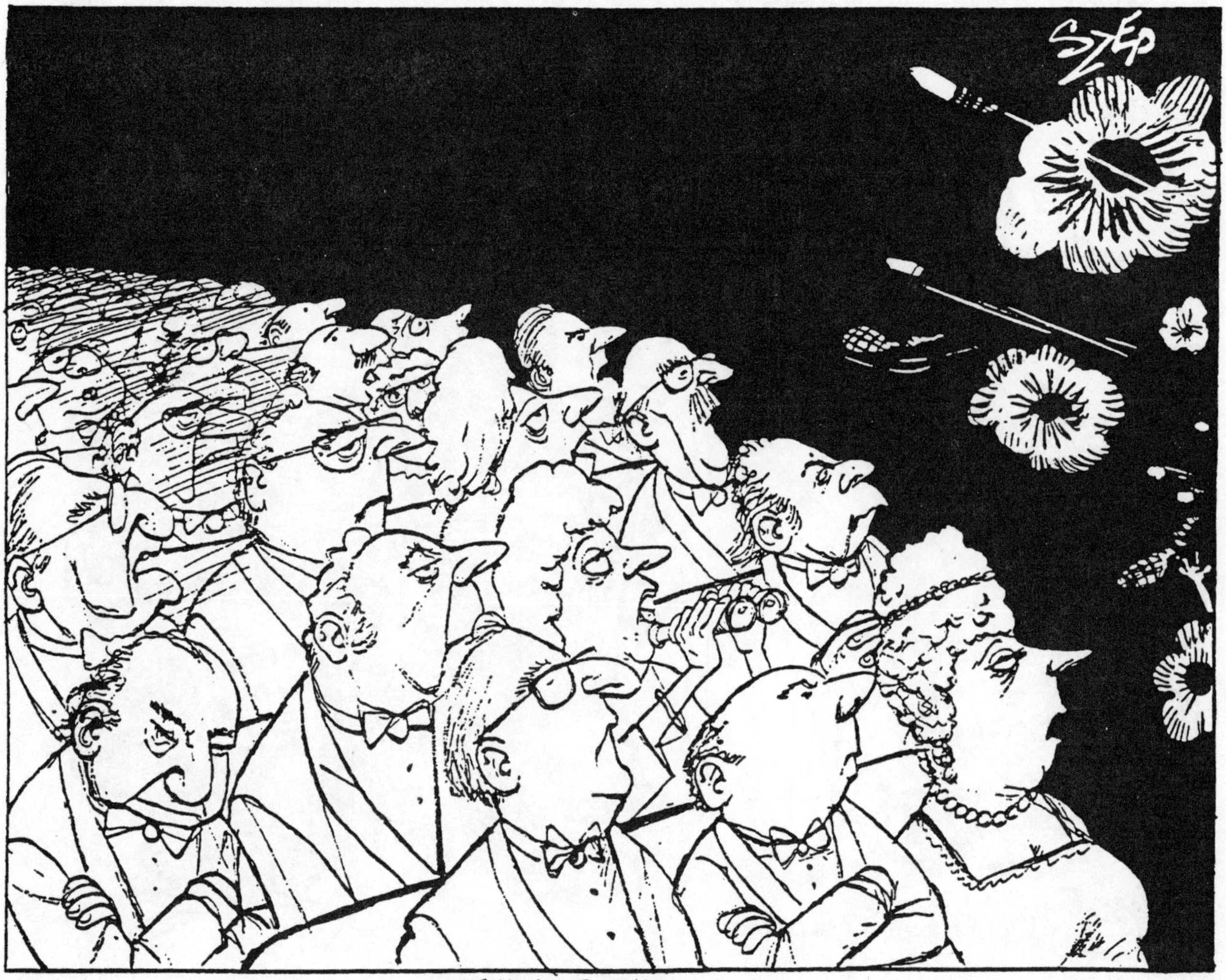
SZEP

WATCHING BOSNIA

DANA SUMMERS
Courtesy Orlando Sentinel

GLEN FODEN
Courtesy Patuxent Pub. Co.

RANAN LURIE
Courtesy Cartoonews International

CHUCK WERNER
Courtesy Indianapolis Star

LINDA BOILEAU
Courtesy Frankfort State Journal

Politics

Republican Sen. Robert Dole has been a thorn in President Clinton's side since he was elected to the White House. The Senate minority leader led the attack on Clinton's job stimulus bill that resulted in its defeat. Dole also opposed the president's deficit reduction bill, maintaining that while it was the largest tax increase in history, it was too short on spending cuts.

Dole, however, supported the administration on the North American Free Trade Agreement, as did two former GOP presidents—George Bush and Gerald Ford. On health care reform, Dole seems to be walking a tightrope. He feels that Republicans should not flatly oppose the plan, but rather should dilute it through substantial changes in the original proposal.

When Saddam Hussein invaded Kuwait, the majority of Democrats in Congress opposed going to war to stop him. They labeled the Gulf War a mistake and insisted it was none of America's business. But many of those same lawmakers in 1993 were calling for the U.S. to send troops to strife-torn Bosnia and Somalia.

President Clinton lost the votes of a sizeable number of Democrats on the NAFTA issue, while Republicans generally supported the bill. The November races were a debacle for Democrats as the Republicans won big in New Jersey, Virginia, and New York City. Some observers concluded that voters were tired of having their taxes increased without tangible results.

DICK LOCHER
Courtesy Chicago Tribune

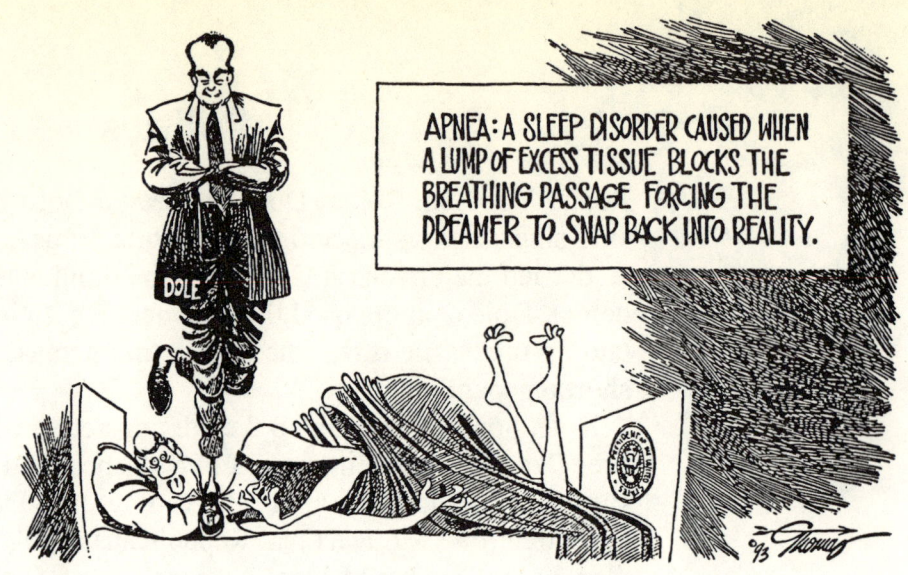

GARY THOMAS
Courtesy Des Moines Business Record

JOE MAJESKI
Courtesy The Times-Leader (Pa.)

MARK BREWER
Courtesy The Hour (Conn.)

JIM BERRY
Courtesy NEA

TOM BECK
Courtesy Freeport Journal-Standard (Ill.)

MICHAEL GILLETT
Courtesy Marion Star (Ohio)

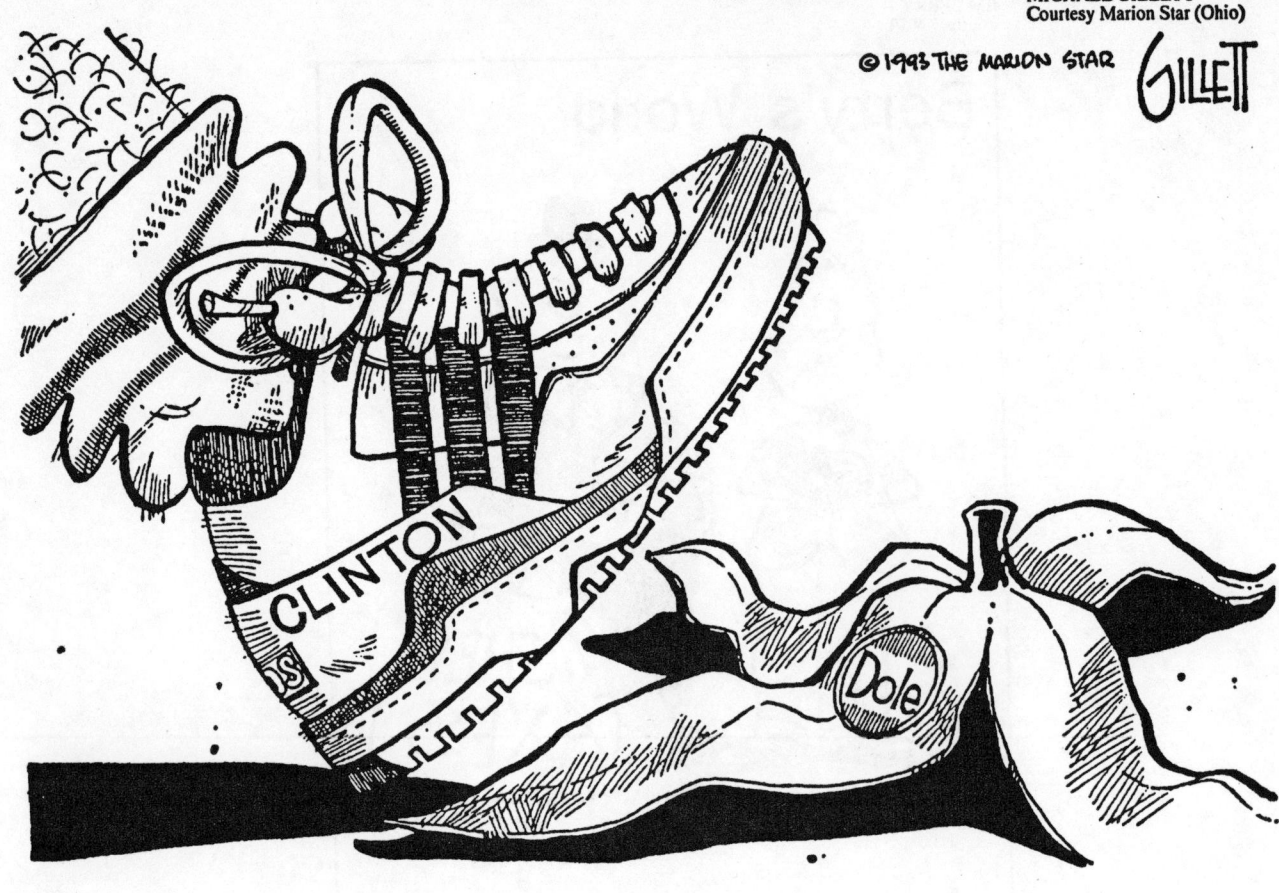

JIM MCCLOSKEY
Courtesy Staunton Daily News Leader

Congress

One of the most powerful men in Washington is chairman of the House Ways and Means Committee, because that body is where tax policy is actually made. Democrat Dan Rostenkowski of Illinois, who holds this position, found himself under an expanding cloud during 1993. The powerful lawmaker was being investigated for allegedly converting some $21,000 in taxpayer-funded office vouchers and campaign checks into cash by making fake stamp purchases at the House post office. He had not been formally charged at year's end, but he did hire a high-powered lawyer, Robert Bennett, to represent him. Clearly, the Rostenkowski flap added to the growing sentiment against Congress generally.

Democratic Speaker of the House Tom Foley's personal finances also came under suspicion when it was reported that he received more than $100,000 in profits by buying and then quickly selling initial public stock offerings on the advice of a banker friend.

Many colleagues called for the resignation of Sen. Robert Packwood when it was alleged that he had made unwanted sexual advances to more than two dozen women over the past twenty years. An ethics committee investigation was trying to force Packwood to release his private diary.

As usual, not a great deal was being done to control the national deficit. At the end of September the government owed about $340 billion more than a year before.

CLYDE WELLS
Courtesy Augusta Chronicle

JOHN TREVER
Courtesy Albuquerque Journal

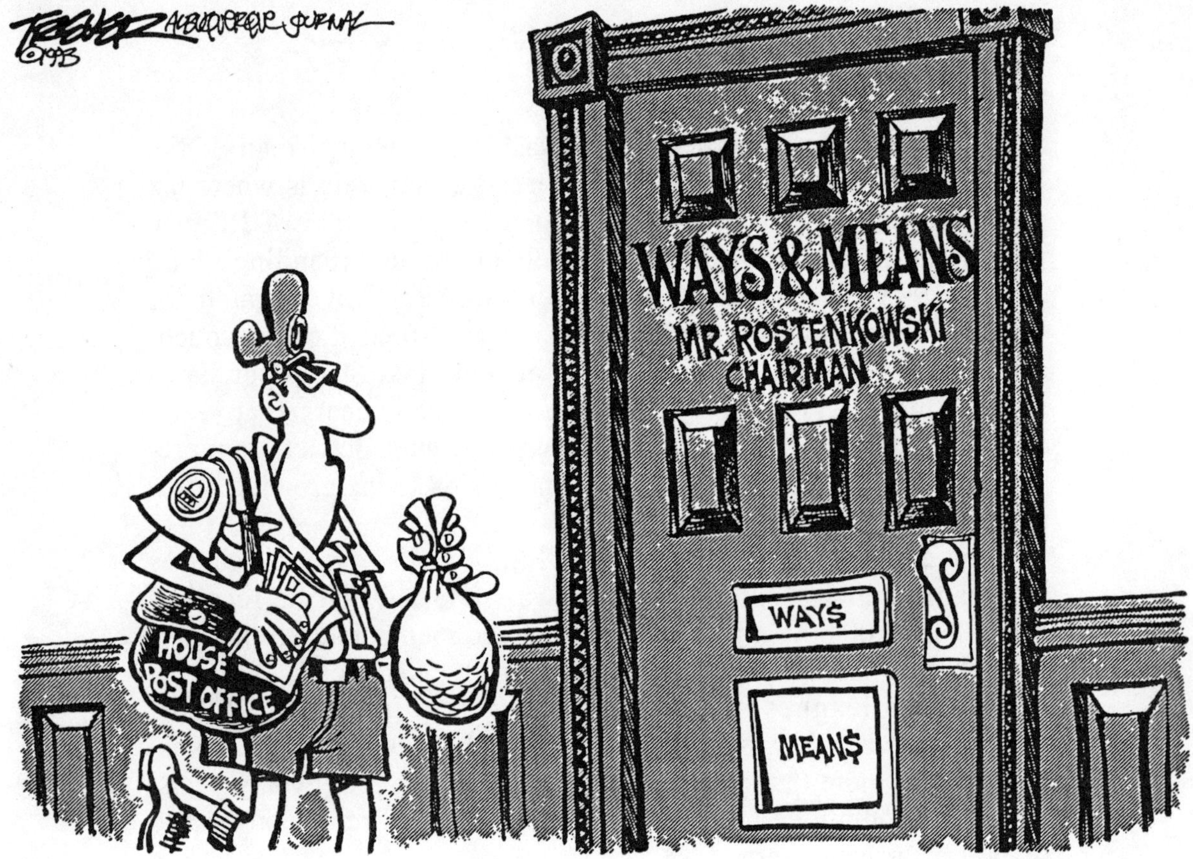
TREVER ALBUQUERQUE JOURNAL ©1993
WAYS & MEANS
MR. ROSTENKOWSKI
CHAIRMAN
WAY$
MEAN$
HOUSE
POST OFFICE

STEVE MCBRIDE
Courtesy Independence Daily Reporter (Kan.)

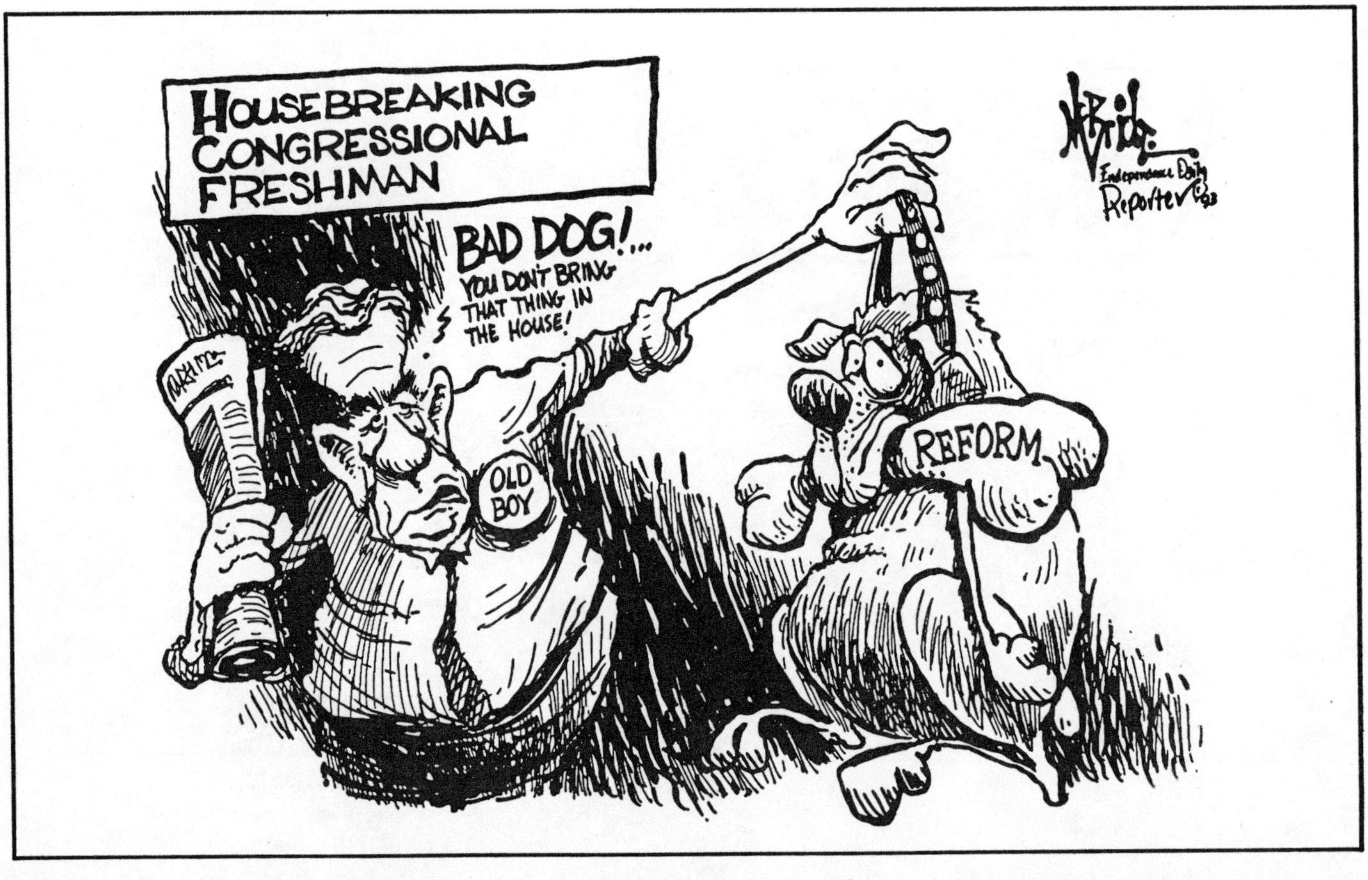
HOUSEBREAKING
CONGRESSIONAL
FRESHMAN
BAD DOG!...
YOU DON'T BRING THAT THING IN THE HOUSE!
OLD BOY
REFORM
McBride Independence Daily Reporter ©93

CLAY BENNETT
Courtesy St. Petersburg Times

MARK CULLUM
Courtesy Birmingham News

RANDY BISH
Courtesy Tribune-Review (Pa.)

NICK ANDERSON
Courtesy Louisville Courier Journal

SCOTT BATEMAN
Courtesy Baker City Herald (Oreg.)

STEVE MCBRIDE
Courtesy Independence Daily Reporter (Kan.)

PAUL DUGINSKI
Courtesy McClatchy News Service

DALE STEPHANOS
Courtesy Haverhill Gazette (Mass.)

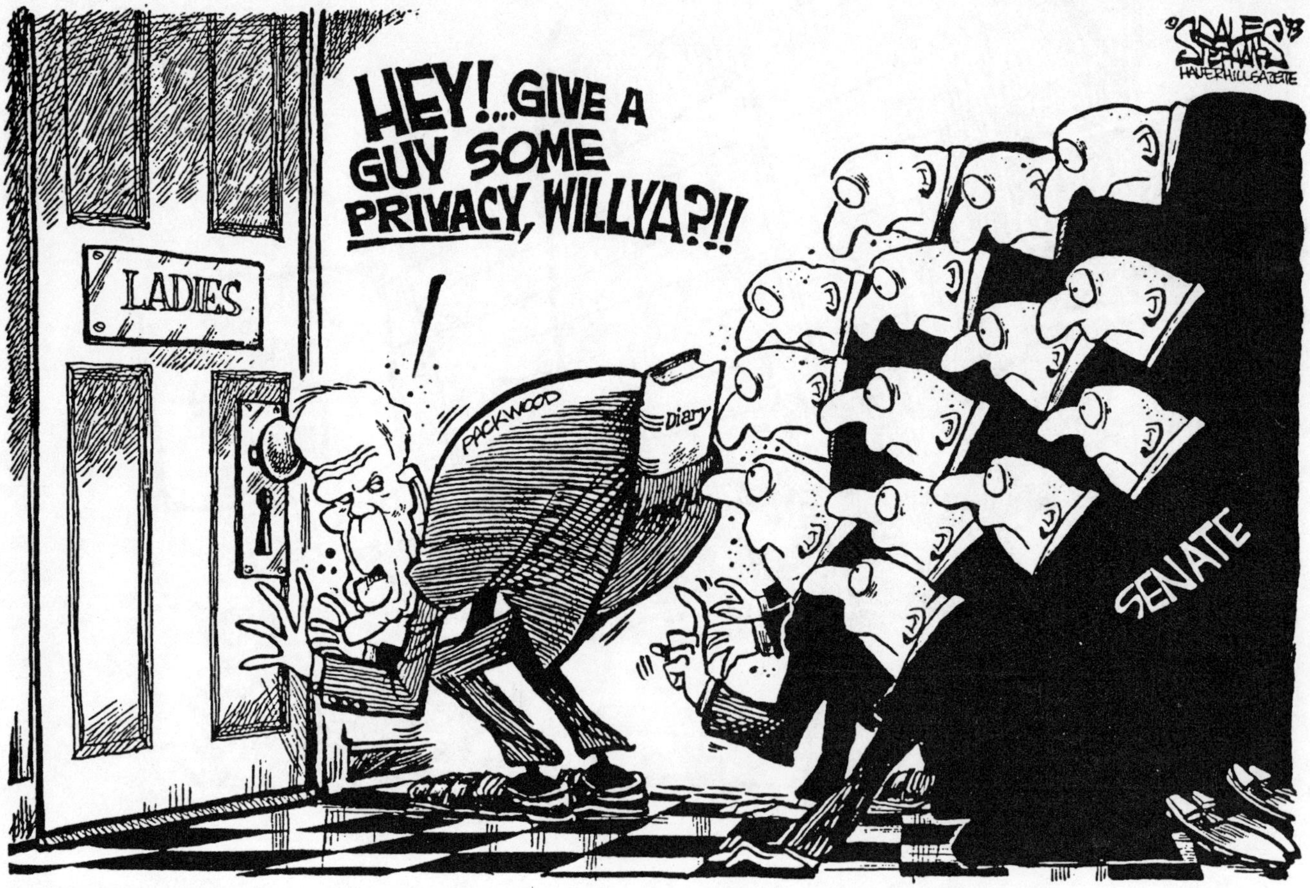
HAVERHILL GAZETTE
HEY!...GIVE A GUY SOME PRIVACY, WILLYA?!!
LADIES
PACKWOOD
Diary
SENATE

KIRK WALTERS
Courtesy Toledo Blade

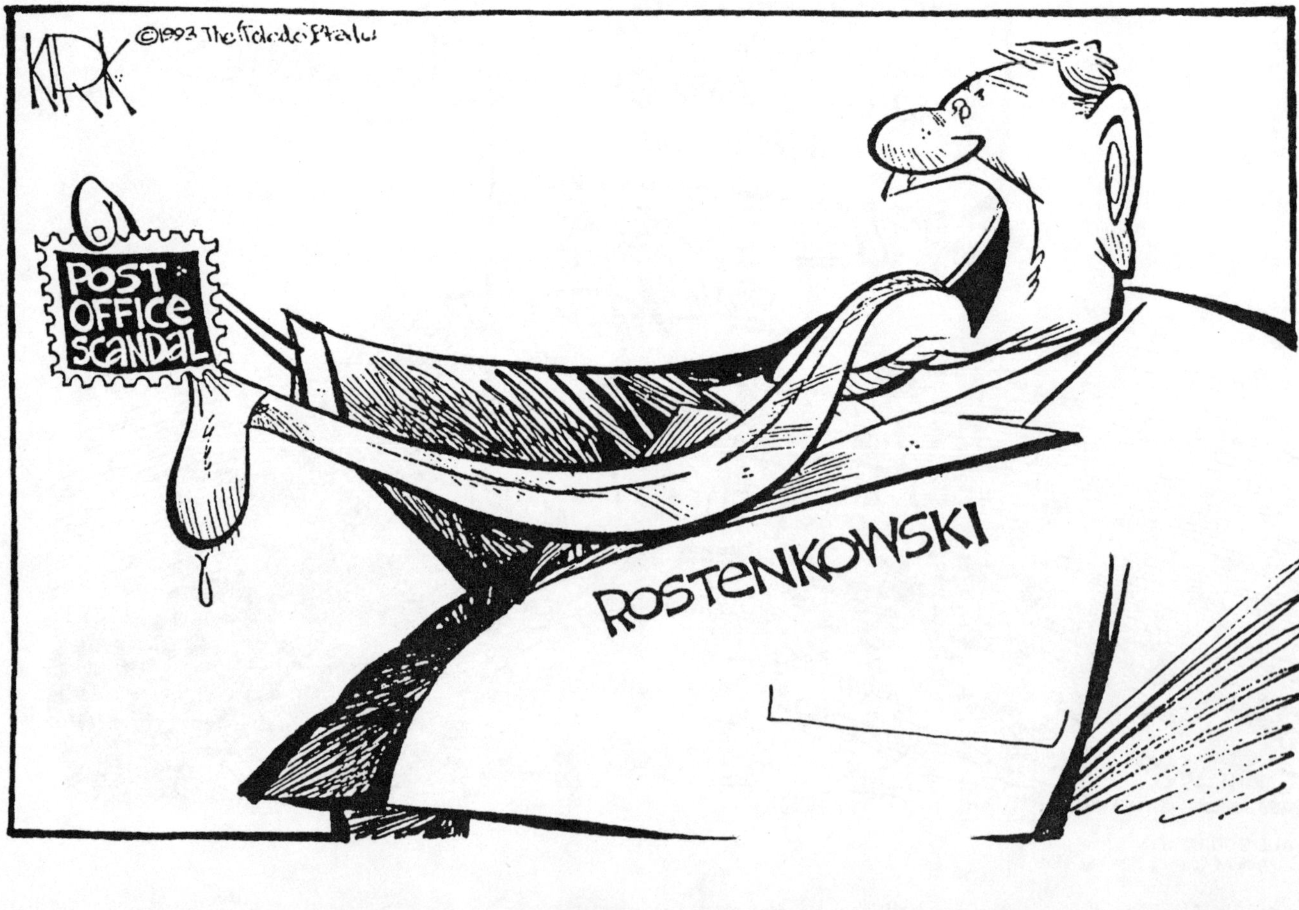
KIRK
POST OFFICE SCANDAL
ROSTENKOWSKI

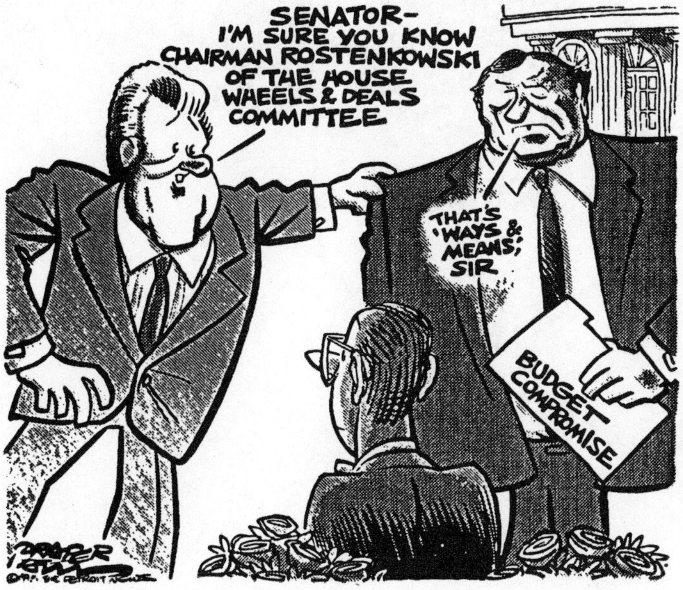
SENATOR- I'M SURE YOU KNOW CHAIRMAN ROSTENKOWSKI OF THE HOUSE WHEELS & DEALS COMMITTEE
THAT'S 'WAYS & MEANS,' SIR
BUDGET COMPROMISE

DRAPER HILL
Courtesy Detroit News

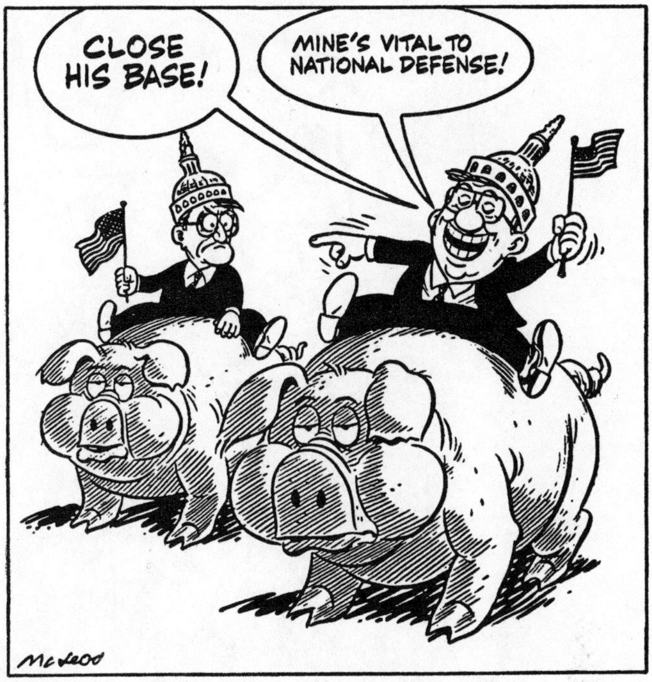
CLOSE HIS BASE!
MINE'S VITAL TO NATIONAL DEFENSE!

JACK MCLEOD
Courtesy Federal Times

CHUCK WERNER
Courtesy Indianapolis Star

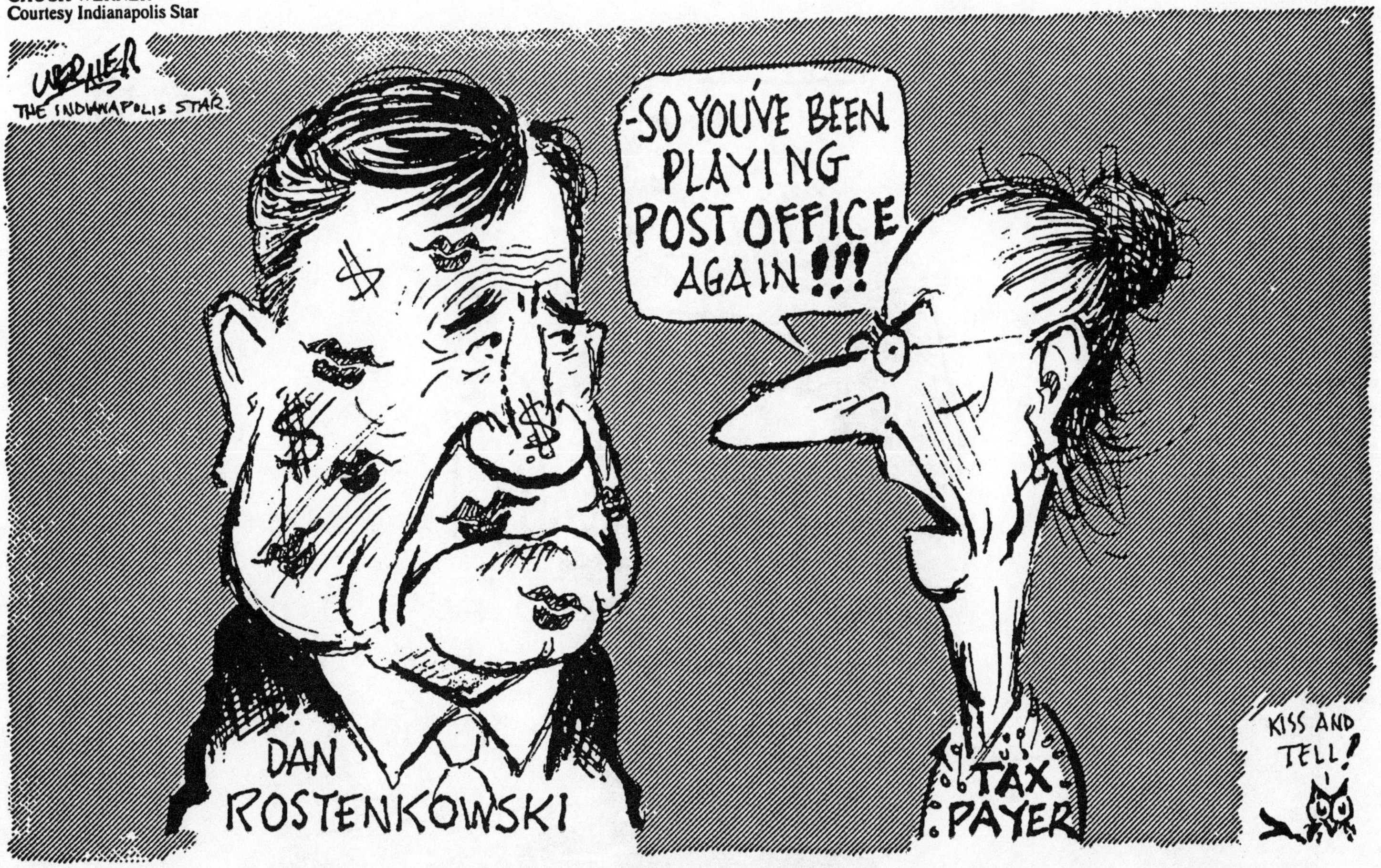
THE INDIANAPOLIS STAR
-SO YOU'VE BEEN PLAYING POST OFFICE AGAIN!!!
DAN ROSTENKOWSKI
TAX PAYER
KISS AND TELL!

KEN CATALINO
Courtesy Anchorage Times

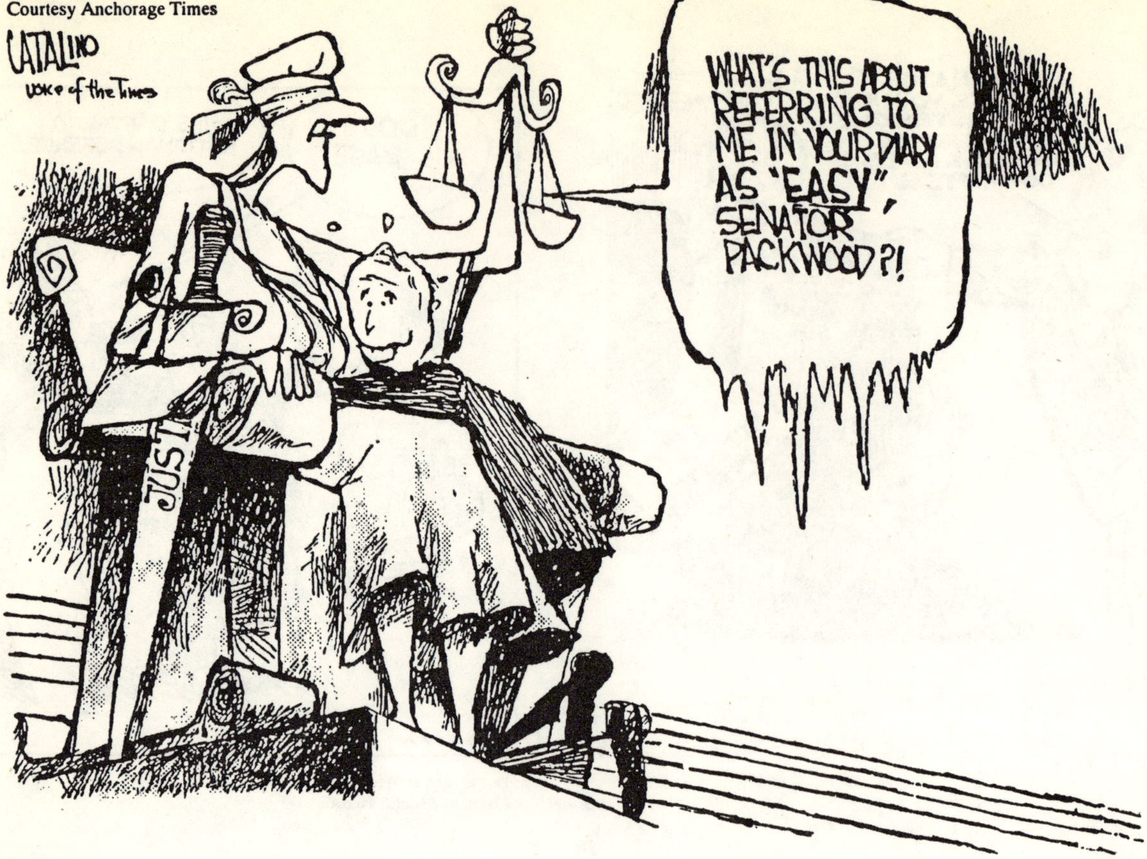
CATALINO
Voice of the Times
WHAT'S THIS ABOUT REFERRING TO ME IN YOUR DIARY AS "EASY", SENATOR PACKWOOD?!
JUST

VIC HARVILLE
Courtesy Arkansas
Democrat-Gazette

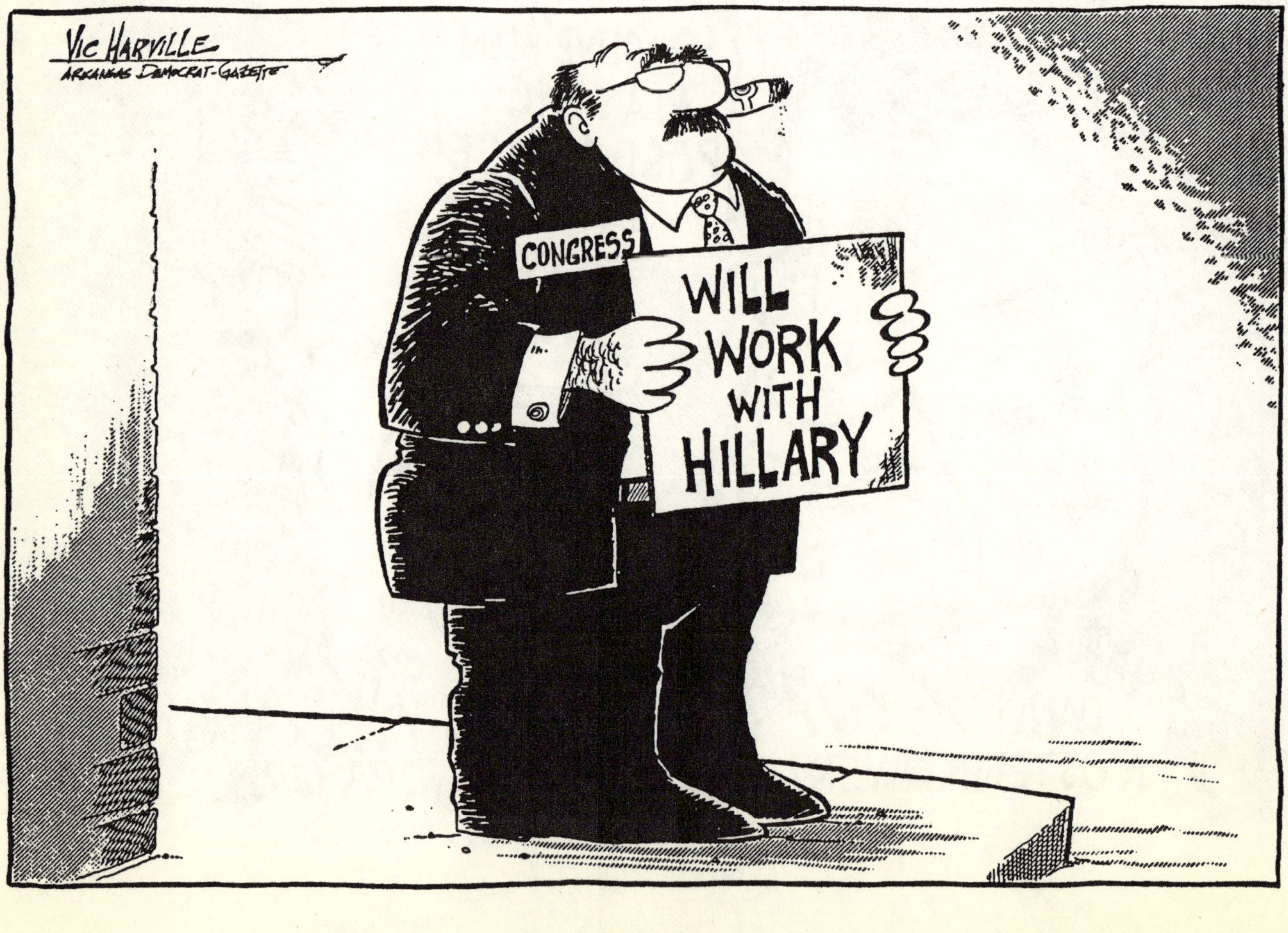
VIC HARVILLE
ARKANSAS DEMOCRAT-GAZETTE
CONGRESS
WILL WORK WITH HILLARY

The Courts

For months before the trial of two men charged with attempted murder in the videotaped beating of truck driver Reginald Denny, Los Angeles community leaders claimed the pair could not possibly receive a fair court hearing. But when a jury acquitted the two of almost all felony charges, the same leaders were vocal in their praise of "real justice." Most Americans, however, were astounded and outraged.

The men were depicted on videotape hurling bricks into the head of a man who had done nothing to provoke the attack. The unusual defense had contended that poverty, unjust treatment of minorities, and the jury verdict that acquitted four policemen in the beating of Rodney King had caused the two defendants to lose control. The decision was difficult for many Americans to believe, particularly in light of the videotape showing the assault—and a taped confession from one of the men on the day of his arrest.

The U.S. Supreme Court let stand the policy of the Boy Scouts of America that excluded self-declared agnostics and atheists. A youngster and his father had sued the organization because the Scouts' induction oath contains a promise to "love God." The court action left God in the Boy Scouts.

MIKE SMITH
Courtesy Las Vegas Sun

GARY MCCOY
Courtesy Suburban Journals

MIKE PETERS
Courtesy Dayton Daily News

MIKE PETERS
Courtesy Dayton Daily News

JOE HELLER
Courtesy Green Bay Press-Gazette

JIM BERRY
Courtesy NEA

ED GAMBLE
Courtesy Florida Times-Union

JOHN SHERFFIUS
Courtesy Ventura Star-Free Press

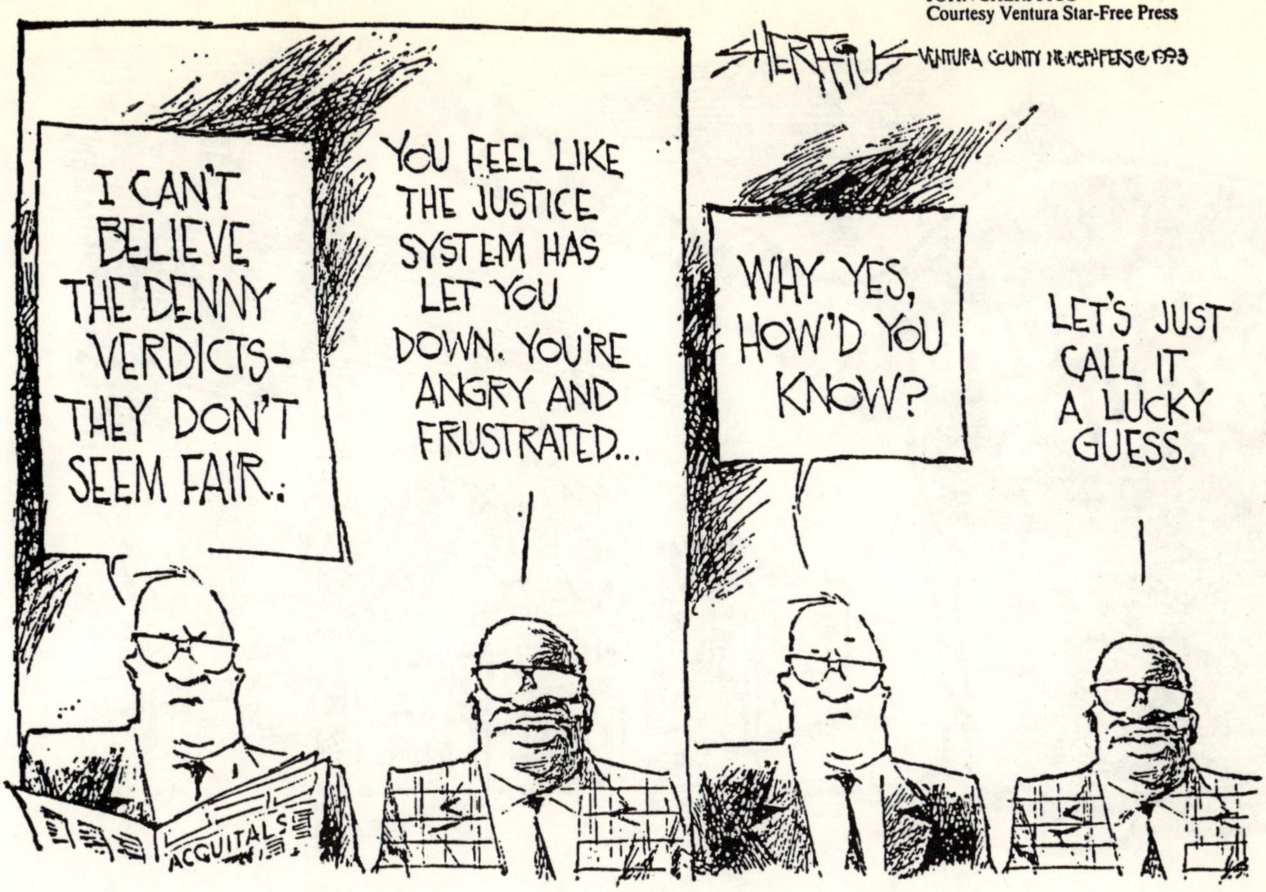
SHERFFIUS VENTURA COUNTY NEWSPAPERS © 1993
I CAN'T BELIEVE THE DENNY VERDICTS- THEY DON'T SEEM FAIR.
YOU FEEL LIKE THE JUSTICE SYSTEM HAS LET YOU DOWN. YOU'RE ANGRY AND FRUSTRATED...
WHY YES, HOW'D YOU KNOW?
LET'S JUST CALL IT A LUCKY GUESS.
ACQUITALS

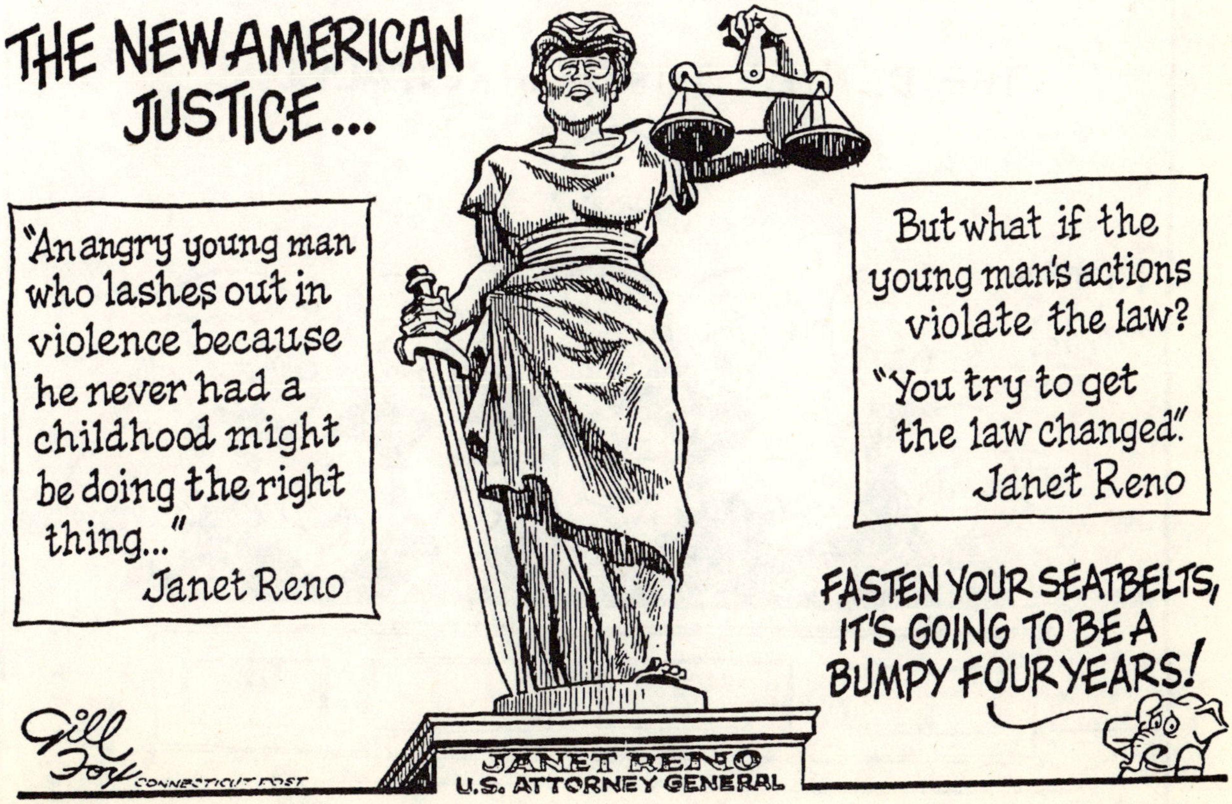
THE NEW AMERICAN JUSTICE...
"An angry young man who lashes out in violence because he never had a childhood might be doing the right thing..."
Janet Reno
But what if the young man's actions violate the law?
"You try to get the law changed."
Janet Reno
FASTEN YOUR SEATBELTS, IT'S GOING TO BE A BUMPY FOUR YEARS!
JANET RENO
U.S. ATTORNEY GENERAL
Gill Fox CONNECTICUT POST

GILL FOX
Courtesy Connecticut Post

ROD WARREN
Courtesy Bakersfield Californian

SCOTT NICKEL
Courtesy Antelope Valley Press (Calif.)

Crime

Terrorists set off a bomb in March that ripped a 180-foot crater through three floors of the world's tallest building, the 110-story twin towers of the World Trade Center in New York City. Seven people were killed and hundreds were injured. Several suspects were arrested.

A wave of murders of foreign tourists hit Florida during the year, causing a substantial decline in tourist bookings. The television networks were considering ways to better alert the viewing public to programs with high levels of violence, and Congress appeared ready to act on the matter. It is estimated that by age eighteen, youngsters have seen some 200,000 acts of violence on television, including 40,000 murders.

In November, the Senate passed an anti-crime bill calling for the hiring of 100,000 new policemen, construction of more prison cells, and a ban on the sale of combat weapons.

The Brady Bill, passed in late September after a seven-year campaign, requires a five-day waiting period for handgun purchasers and a police check of their backgrounds. Dr. Jack Kevorkian, also known as Dr. Death, was free on bail pending trial for assisting in still another suicide. Several individuals were arrested for falsely claiming they had found hypodermic needles in soda cans. Lorena Bobbitt made international headlines when she sliced off the penis of her allegedly abusive husband while he was sleeping. She was later acquitted.

MIKE LUCKOVICH
Courtesy Atlanta Constitution

JERRY FEARING
Courtesy St. Paul Pioneer Press-Dispatch

DAVID COX (HARDIN)
Courtesy N.W. Ark. Morning News

WAYNE STAYSKAL
Courtesy Tampa Tribune

JACK OHMAN
Courtesy Portland Oregonian

KEN CATALINO
Courtesy Anchorage Times

GLENN MCCOY
Courtesy Belleville News-Democrat (Ill.)

DAVID HORSEY
Courtesy Seattle Post-Intelligencer

JOE HELLER
Courtesy Green Bay Press-Gazette

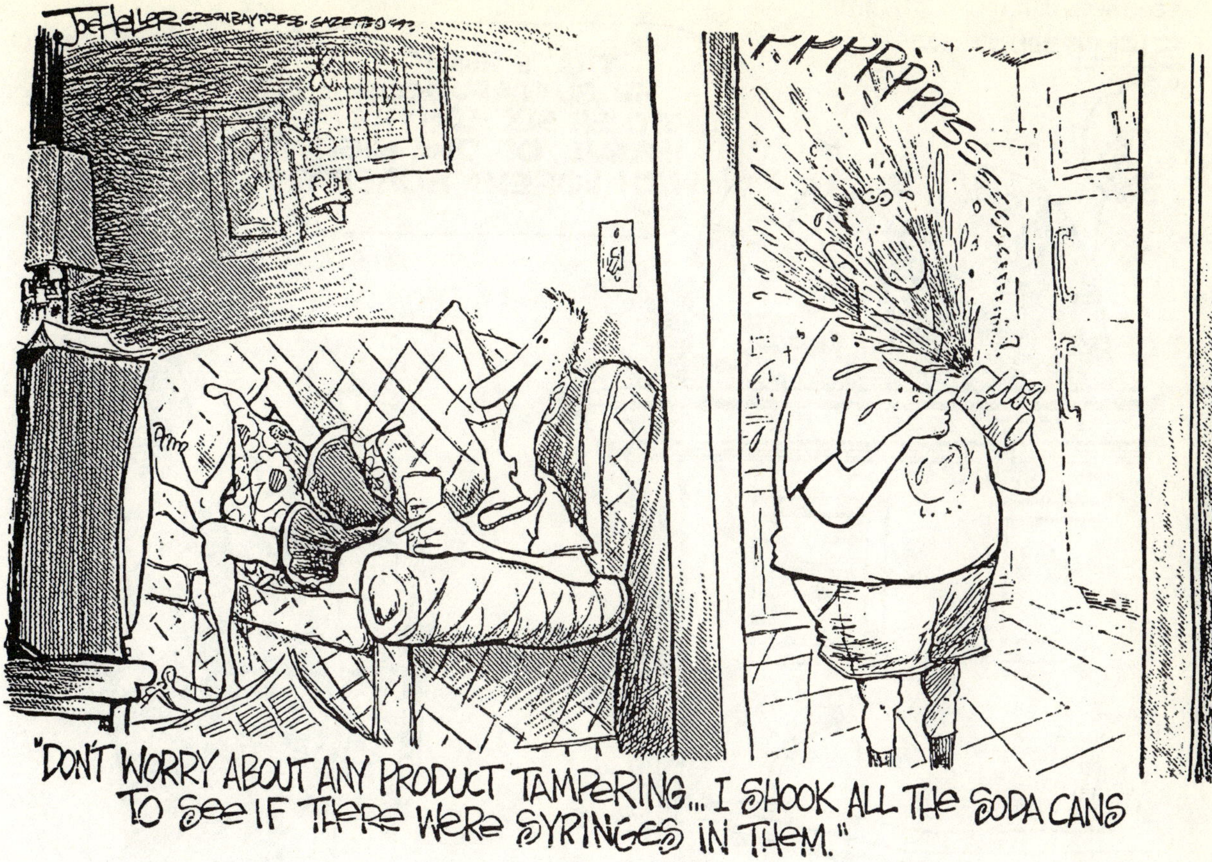
PPPPRRPPPSS
"DON'T WORRY ABOUT ANY PRODUCT TAMPERING... I SHOOK ALL THE SODA CANS TO SEE IF THERE WERE SYRINGES IN THEM."

DANI AGUILA
Courtesy Filipino Reporte-

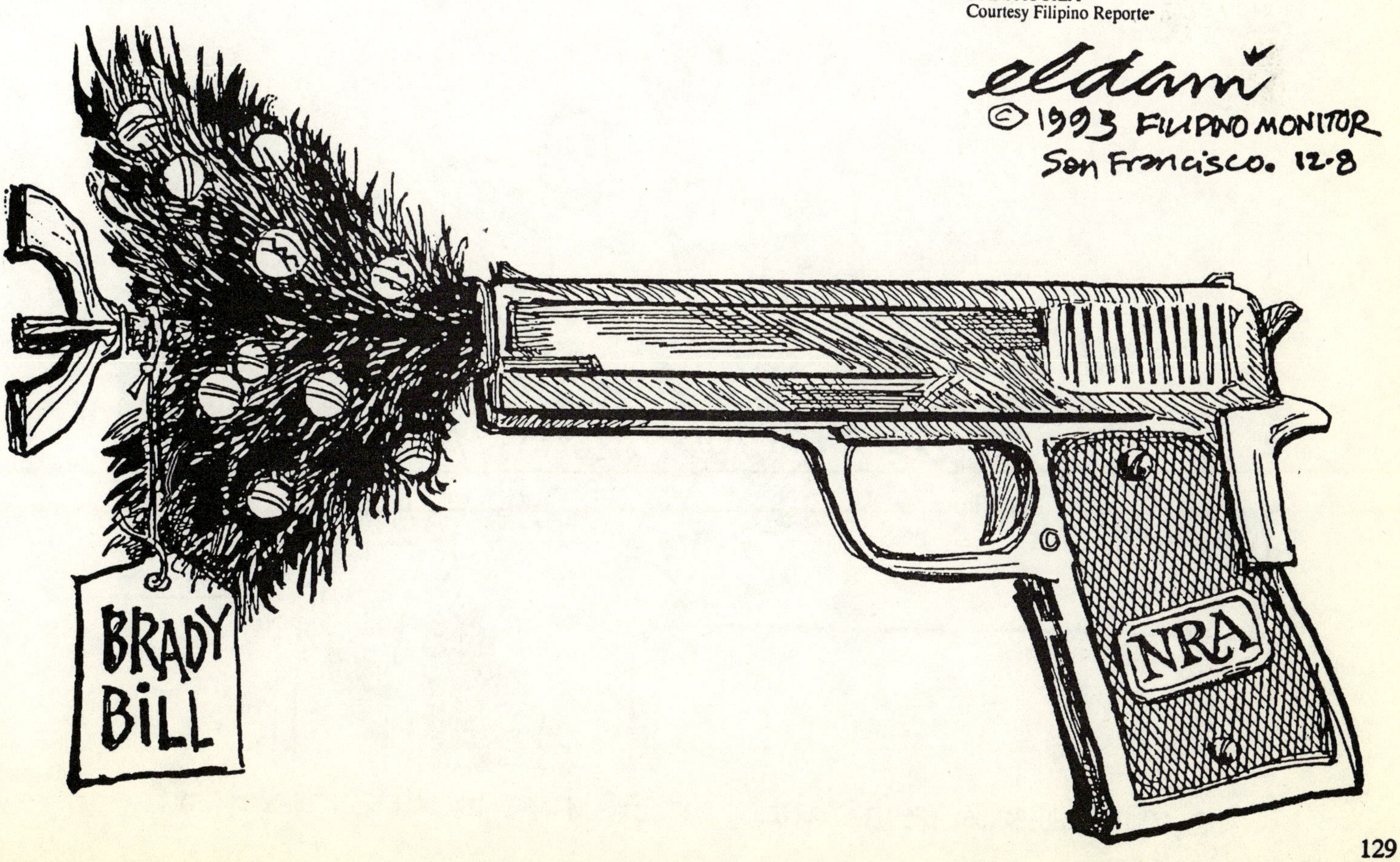
eldani
©1993 FILIPINO MONITOR
San Francisco. 12-8
BRADY BILL
NRA

STEVE KELLEY
Courtesy San Diego Union

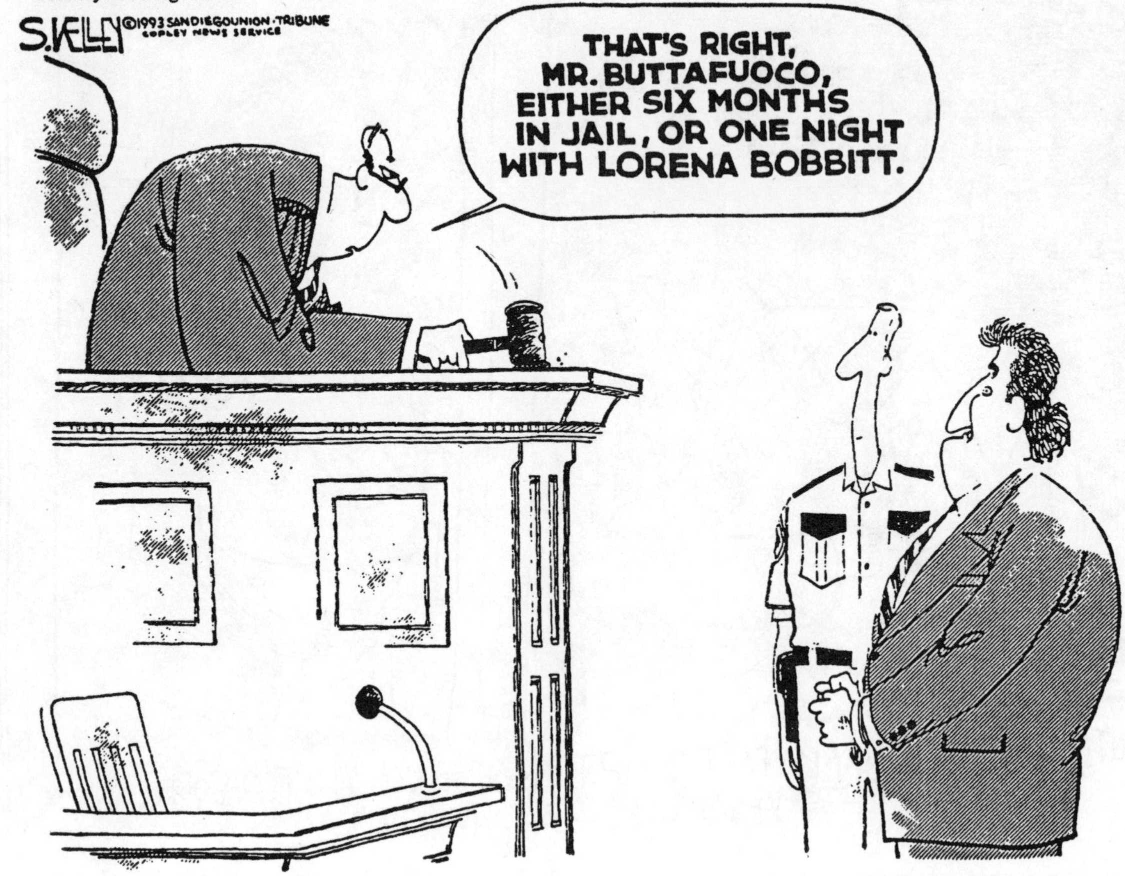
S.KELLEY ©1993 SANDIEGOUNION-TRIBUNE COPLEY NEWS SERVICE
THAT'S RIGHT, MR. BUTTAFUOCO, EITHER SIX MONTHS IN JAIL, OR ONE NIGHT WITH LORENA BOBBITT.

TOM GIBB
Courtesy Rothco

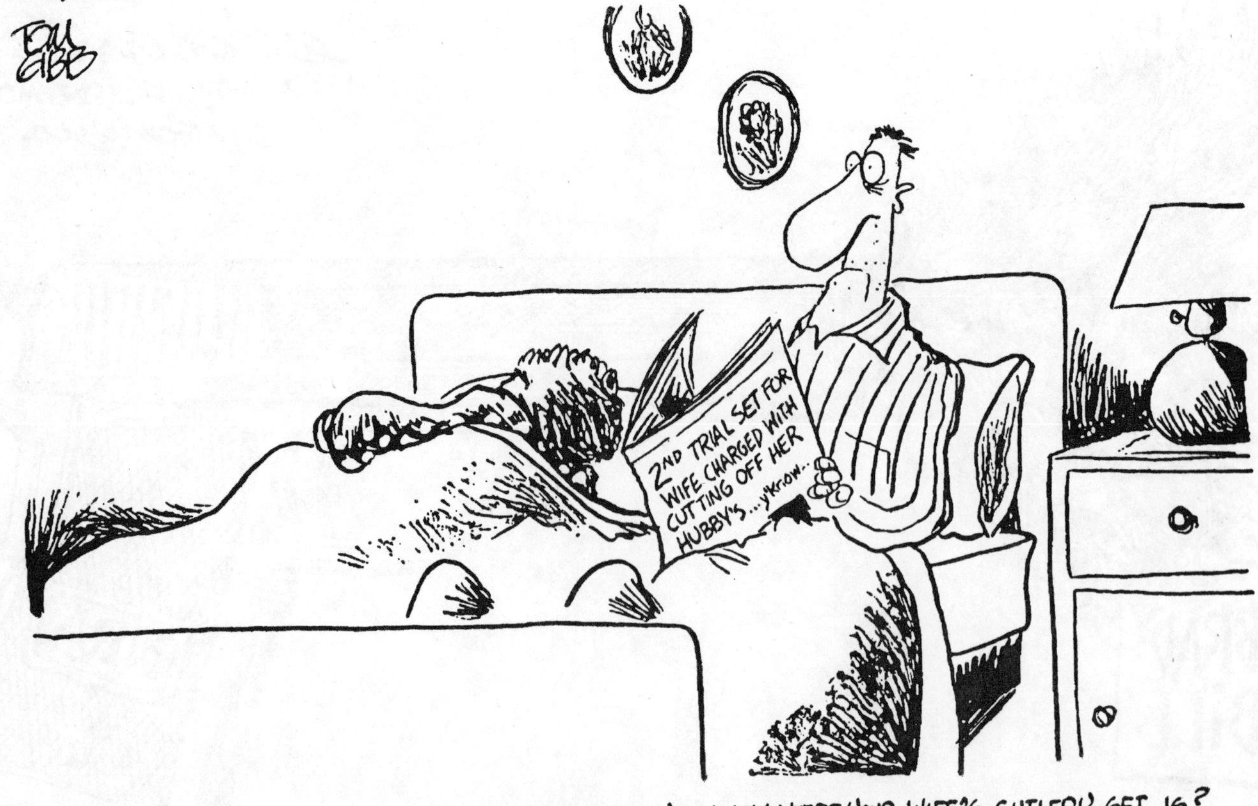
TOM GIBB
2ND TRIAL SET FOR WIFE CHARGED WITH CUTTING OFF HER HUBBY'S... y'know

CRUDE, LOUTISH HUSBANDS: IT'S 11 O'CLOCK. DO YOU KNOW WHERE YOUR WIFE'S CUTLERY SET IS?

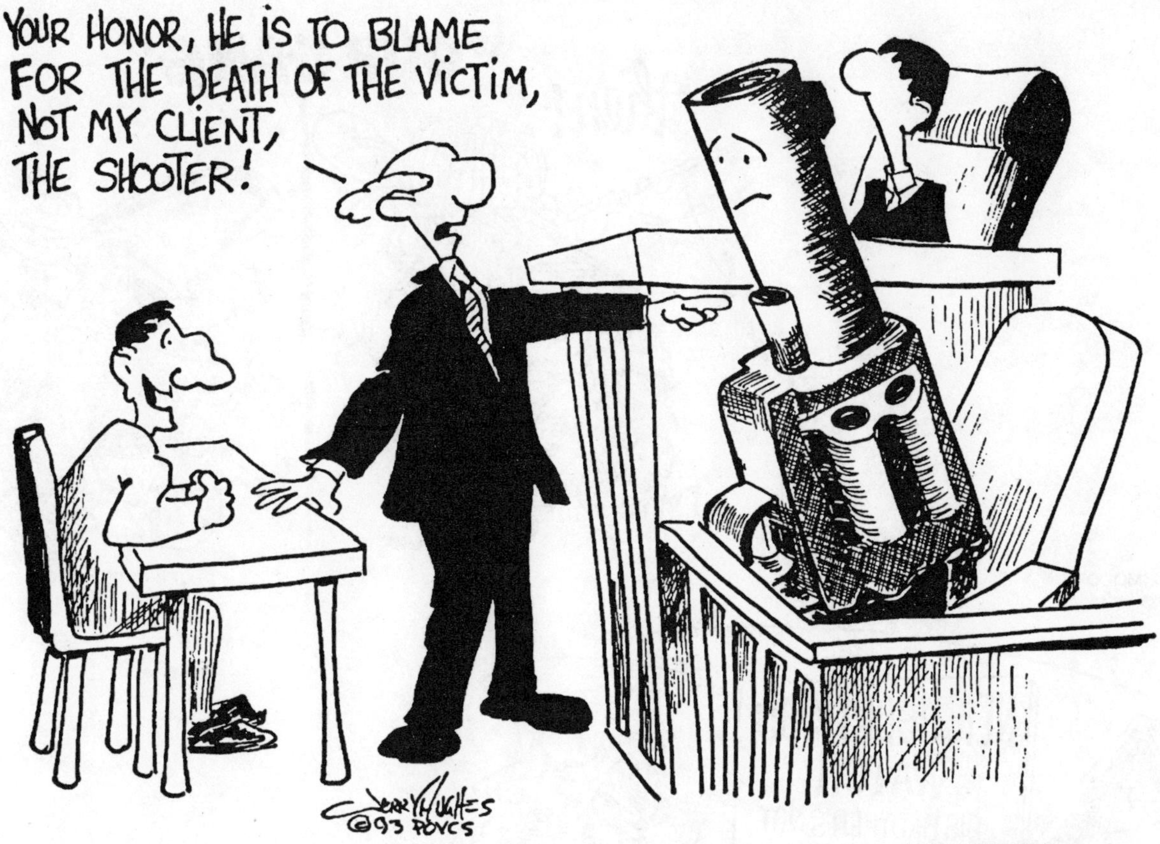
YOUR HONOR, HE IS TO BLAME FOR THE DEATH OF THE VICTIM, NOT MY CLIENT, THE SHOOTER!
JERRY HUGHES
©93 POVCS

JERRY HUGHES
Courtesy The Messenger (Ala.)

BOB GORRELL
Courtesy Richmond Times-Dispatch

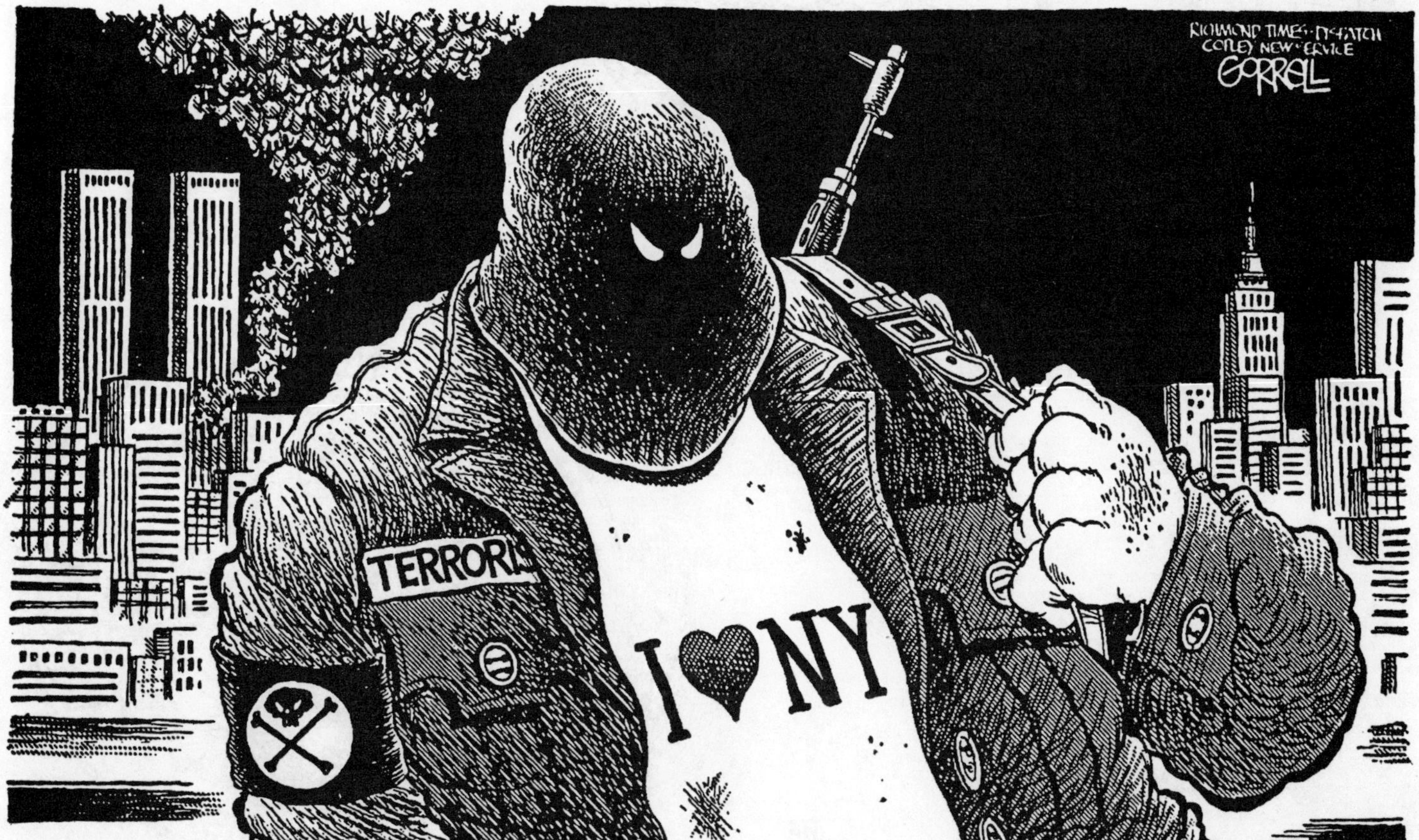
RICHMOND TIMES-DISPATCH
COPLEY NEWS SERVICE
GORRELL
TERRORI
I ♥ NY

CHESTER COMMODORE
Courtesy Chicago Defender

JERRY FEARING
Courtesy St. Paul Pioneer Press-Dispatch

JEFF PARKER
Courtesy Florida Today

ROB ROGERS
Courtesy Pittsburgh Press

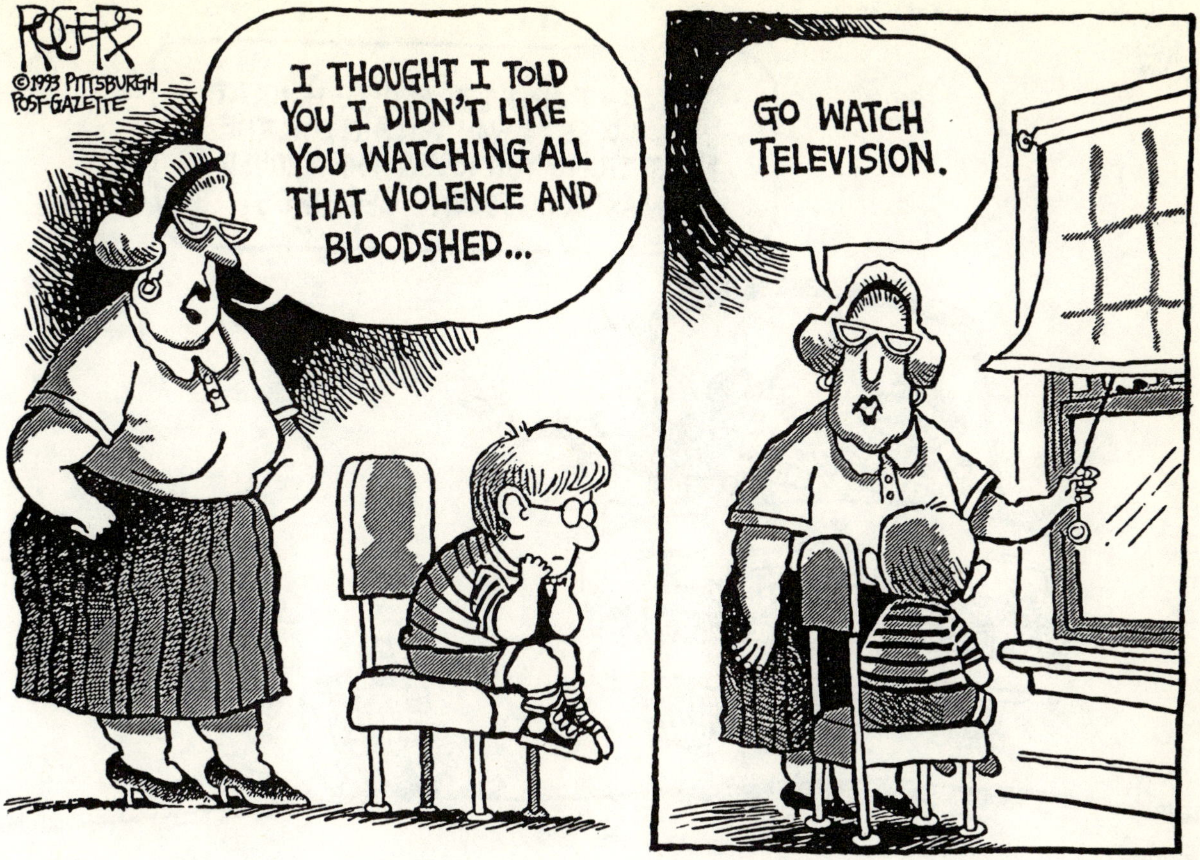
ROGERS
©1993 PITTSBURGH POST-GAZETTE
I THOUGHT I TOLD YOU I DIDN'T LIKE YOU WATCHING ALL THAT VIOLENCE AND BLOODSHED...
GO WATCH TELEVISION.

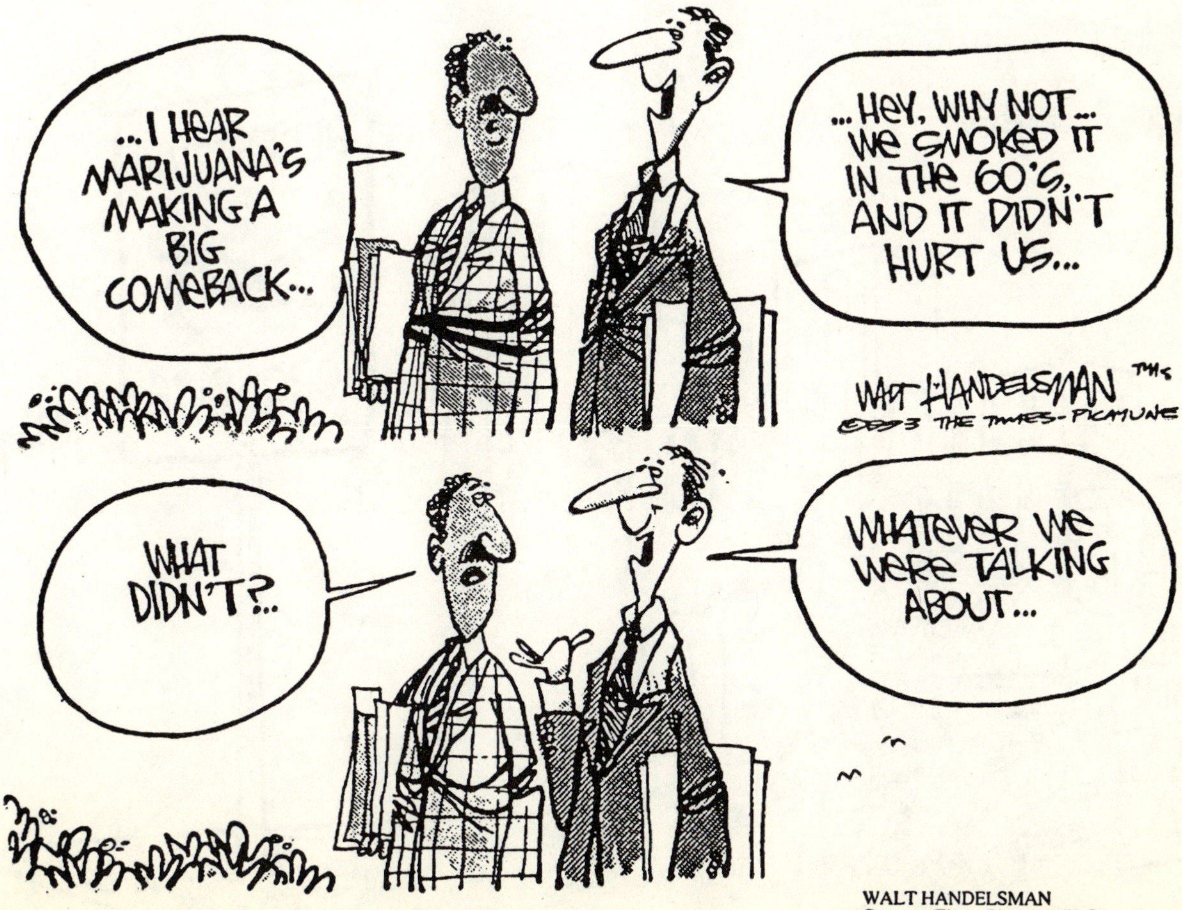
...I HEAR MARIJUANA'S MAKING A BIG COMEBACK...
...HEY, WHY NOT... WE SMOKED IT IN THE 60'S, AND IT DIDN'T HURT US...
WALT HANDELSMAN
WHAT DIDN'T?..
WHATEVER WE WERE TALKING ABOUT...

WALT HANDELSMAN
Courtesy Times-Picayune (N.O.)

ETTA HULME
Courtesy Ft. Worth Star-Telegram

JOHN BRANCH
Courtesy San Antonio Express-News

KEVIN SIERS
Courtesy Charlotte Observer

PATRICK RICE
Courtesy Jupiter Courier

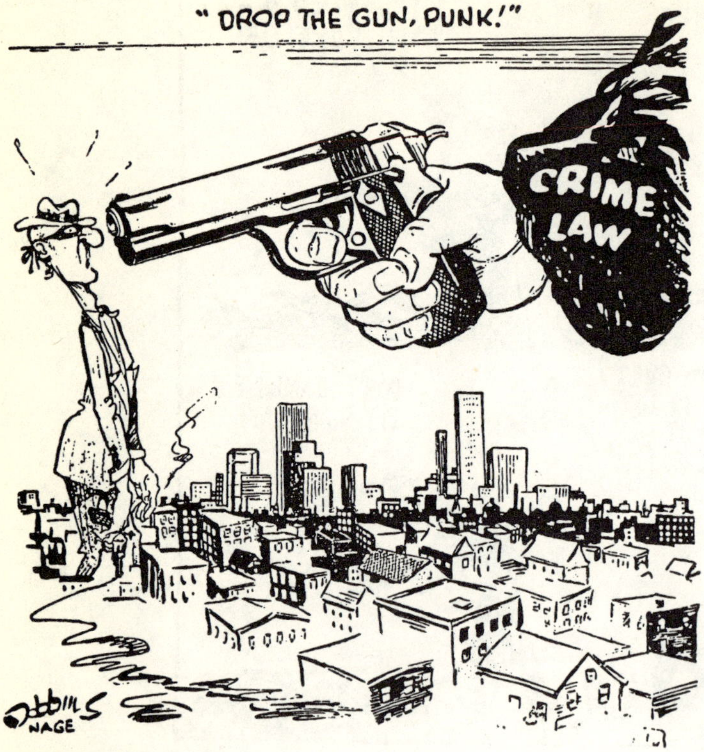
"DROP THE GUN, PUNK!"
CRIME LAW
Dobbins NAGE

JIM DOBBINS
Courtesy N.A.G.E. Reporter

EDGAR SOLLER
Courtesy California Examiner

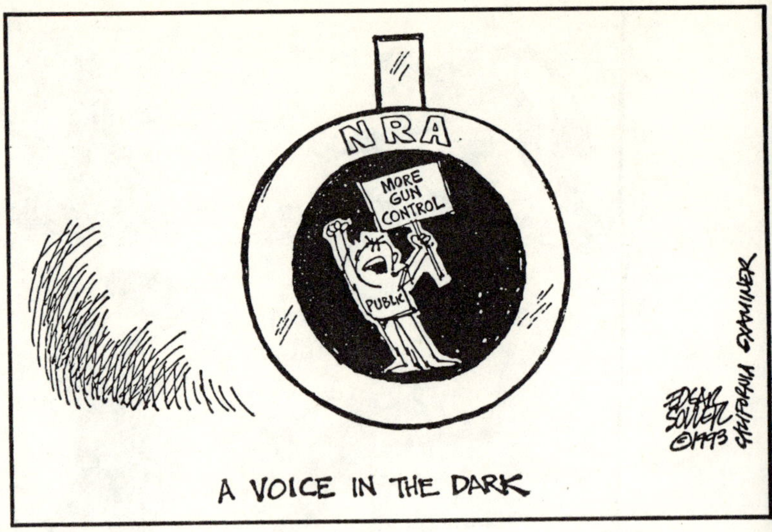
NRA
MORE GUN CONTROL
PUBLIC
A VOICE IN THE DARK

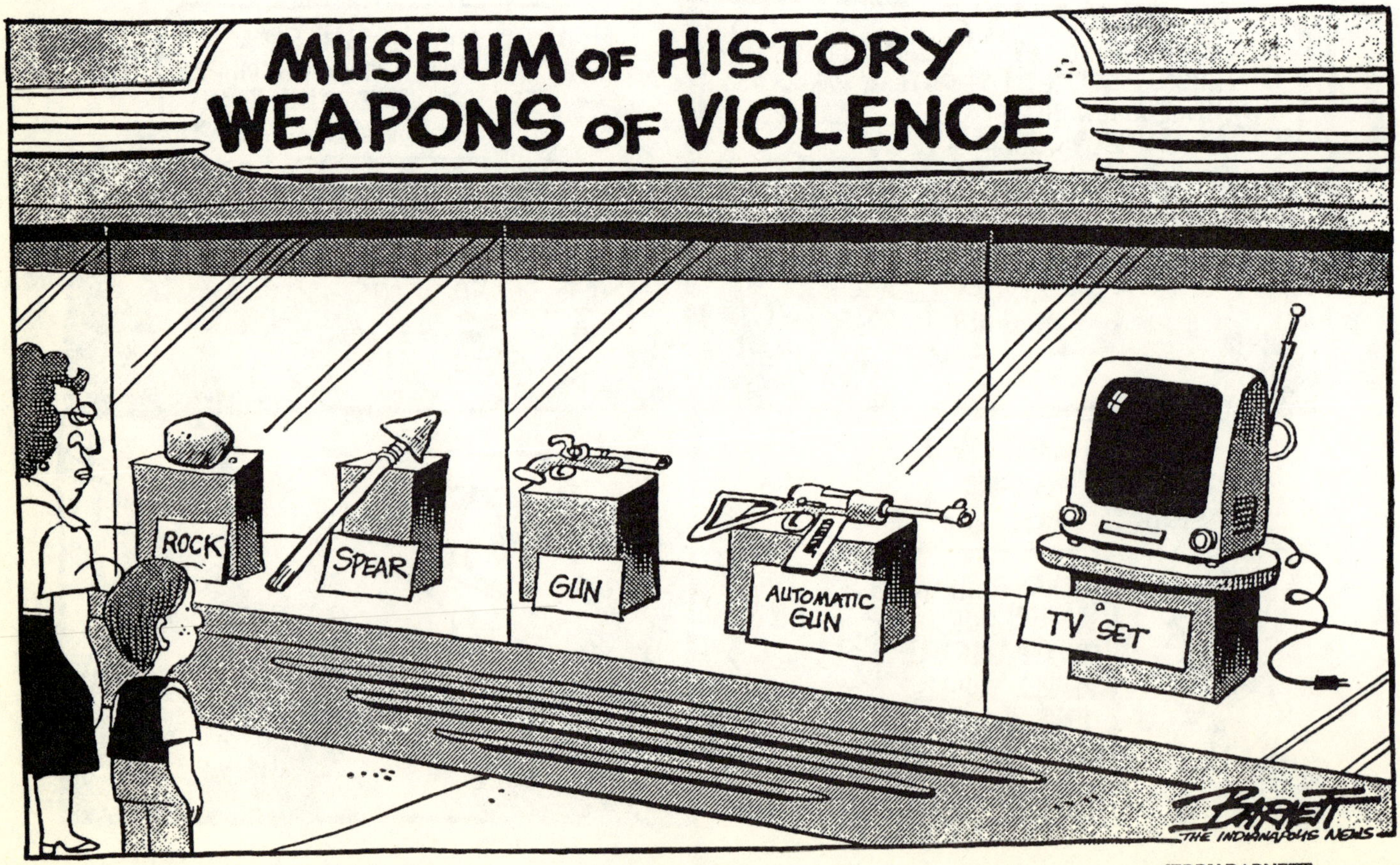
MUSEUM OF HISTORY
WEAPONS OF VIOLENCE
ROCK
SPEAR
GUN
AUTOMATIC GUN
TV SET
BARNETT
THE INDIANAPOLIS NEWS

JERRY BARNETT
Courtesy Indianapolis News

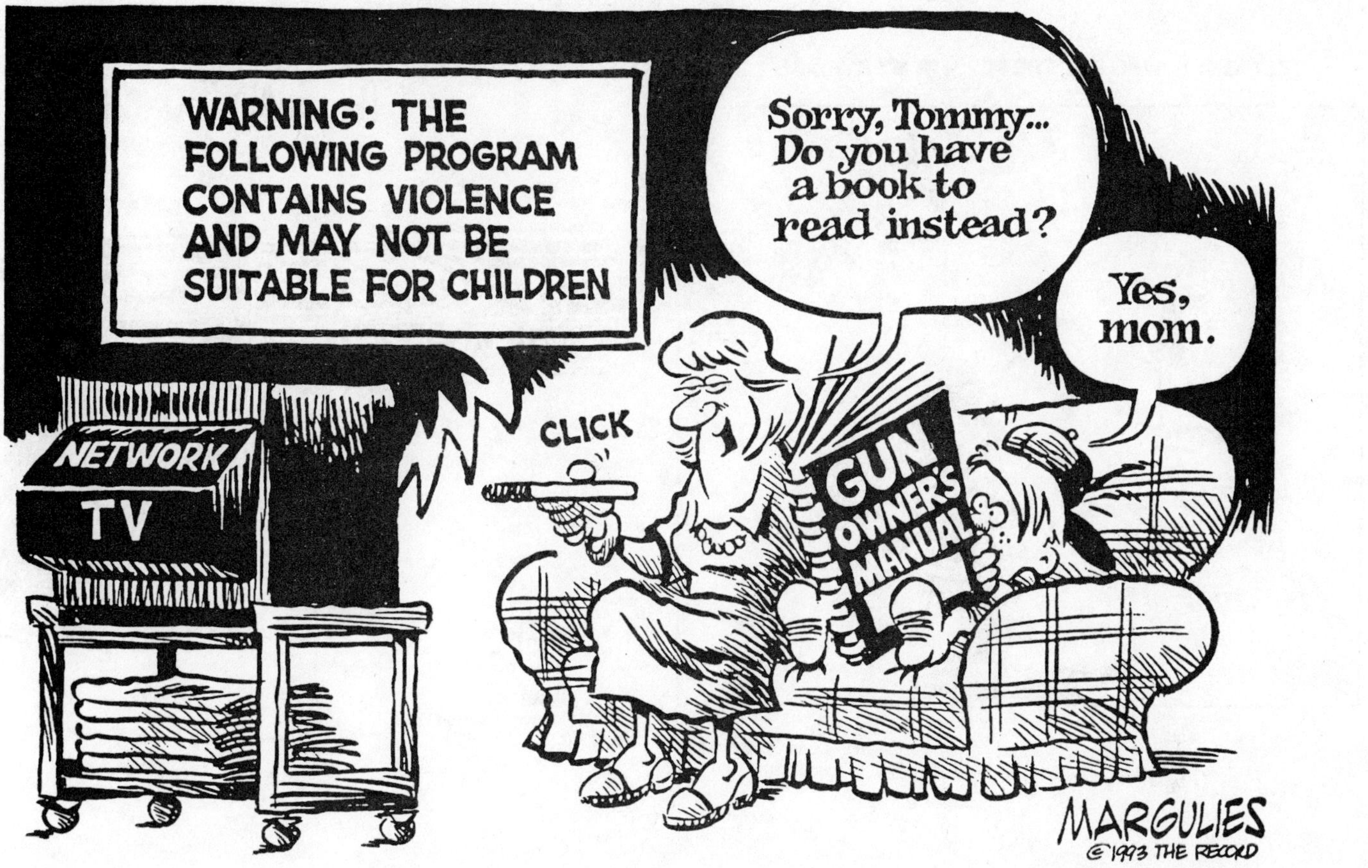
WARNING: THE FOLLOWING PROGRAM CONTAINS VIOLENCE AND MAY NOT BE SUITABLE FOR CHILDREN
Sorry, Tommy... Do you have a book to read instead?
Yes, mom.
NETWORK
TV
CLICK
GUN OWNER'S MANUAL
MARGULIES
©1993 THE RECORD

JIMMY MARGULIES
Courtesy The Record (N.J.)

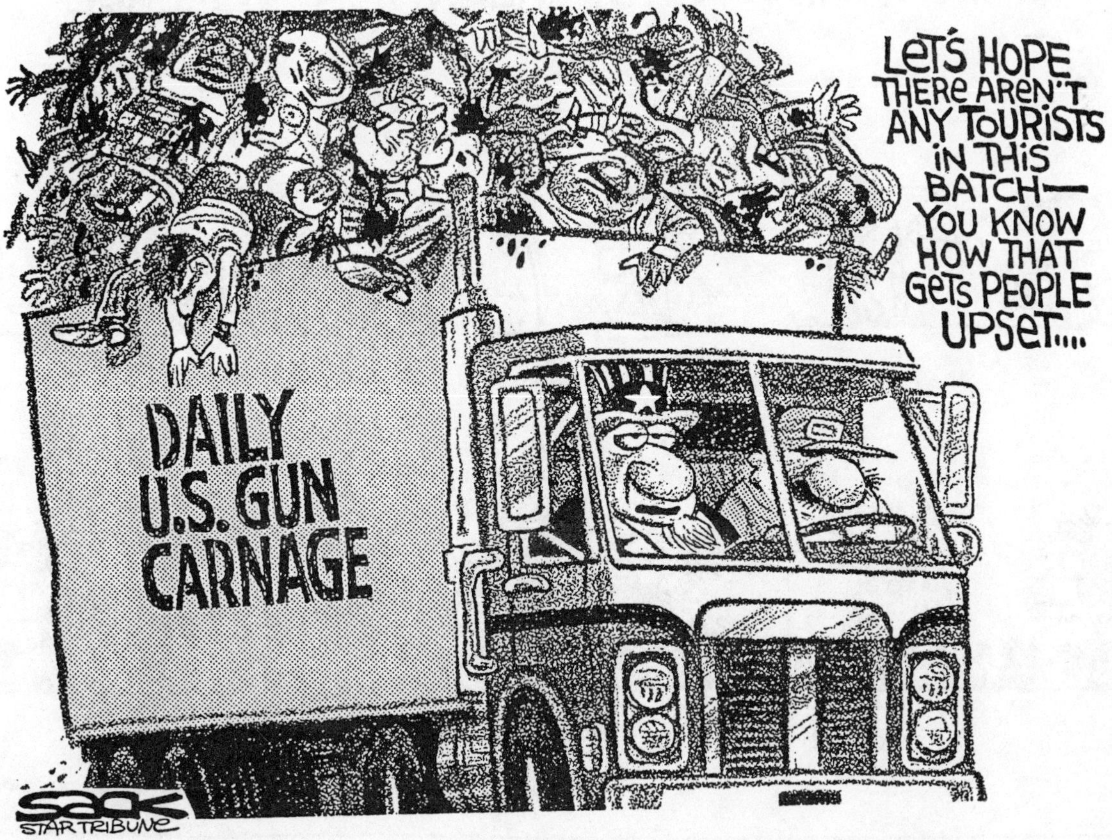
LET'S HOPE THERE AREN'T ANY TOURISTS IN THIS BATCH— YOU KNOW HOW THAT GETS PEOPLE UPSET....
DAILY U.S. GUN CARNAGE
SACK
STAR TRIBUNE

STEVE SACK
Courtesy Minneapolis Star-Tribune

"ALRIGHT!! WHO PUT THE PEPSI IN MY SYRINGE?"

JIM LANGE
Courtesy Daily Oklahoman

THE BRADY BUNCH

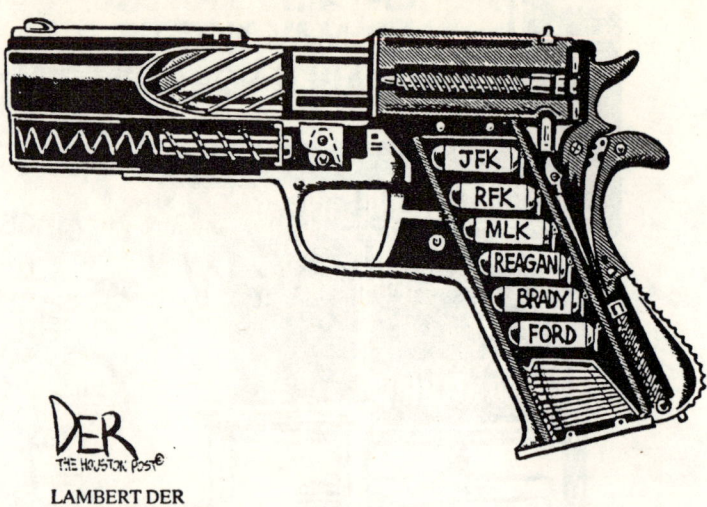

LAMBERT DER
Courtesy Houston Post

A SHORT HISTORY OF TELEVISION VIOLENCE

ETTA HULME
Courtesy Ft. Worth Star-Telegram

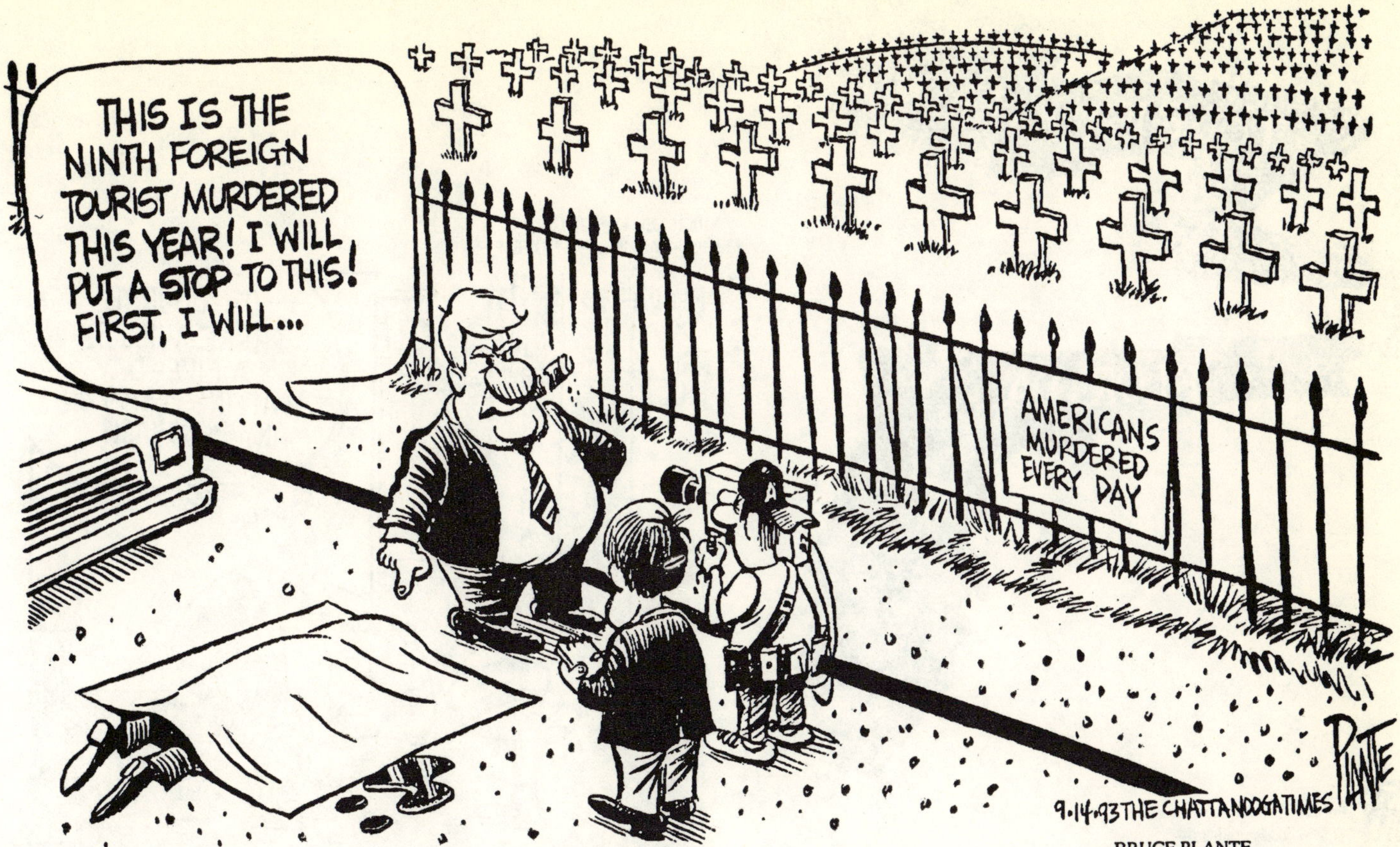
THIS IS THE NINTH FOREIGN TOURIST MURDERED THIS YEAR! I WILL PUT A STOP TO THIS! FIRST, I WILL...
AMERICANS MURDERED EVERY DAY
A
9·14·93 THE CHATTANOOGA TIMES
PLANTE

BRUCE PLANTE
Courtesy Chattanooga Times and
Extra Newspapers Features

CRAIG M. TERRY
Courtesy N.W. Florida Daily News

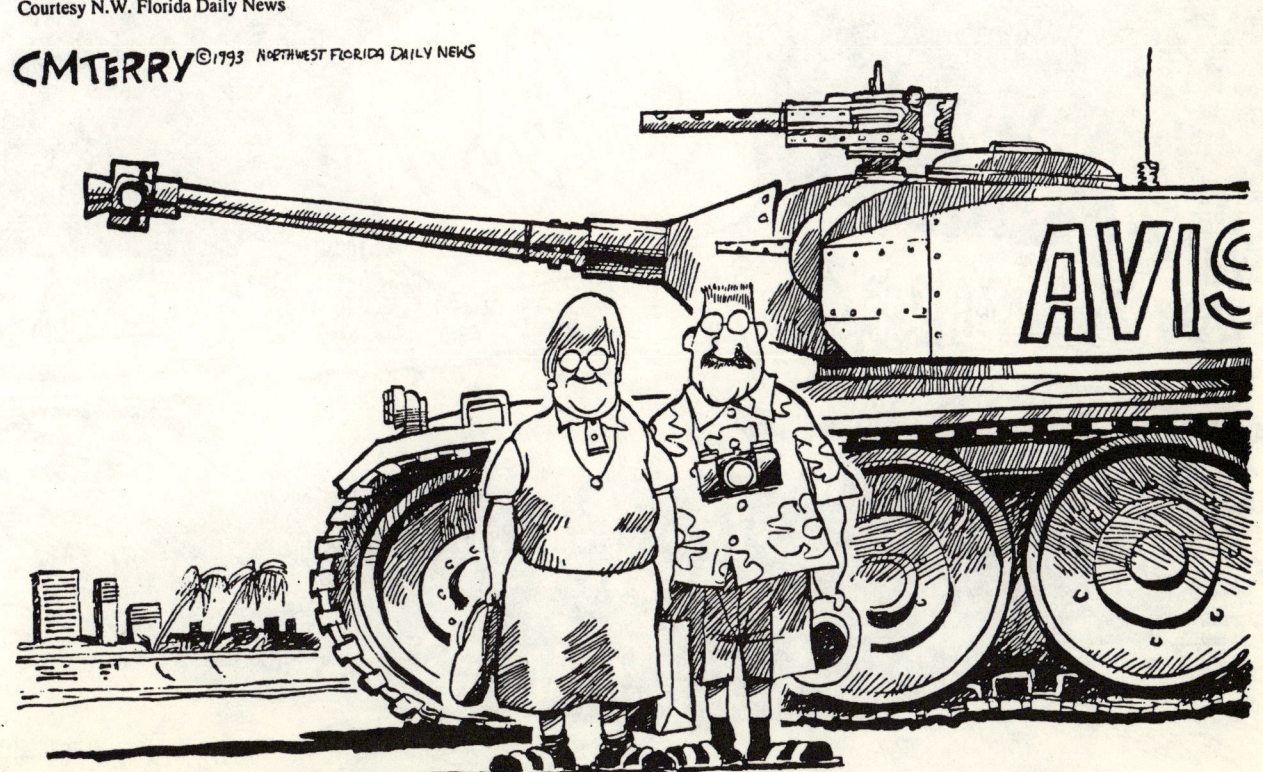

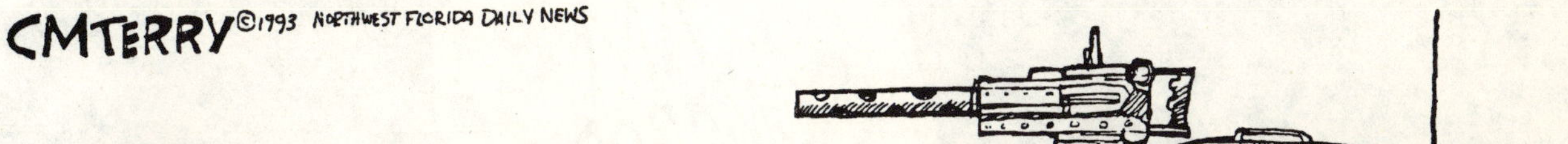
CMTERRY ©1993 NORTHWEST FLORIDA DAILY NEWS
AVIS
BRUNHILDA AND EDEL MUELLER, NEWLY ARRIVED GERMAN TOURISTS, POSE FOR A SNAPSHOT BEFORE EMBARKING ON A MOTOR TOUR OF GREATER MIAMI, FLORIDA.

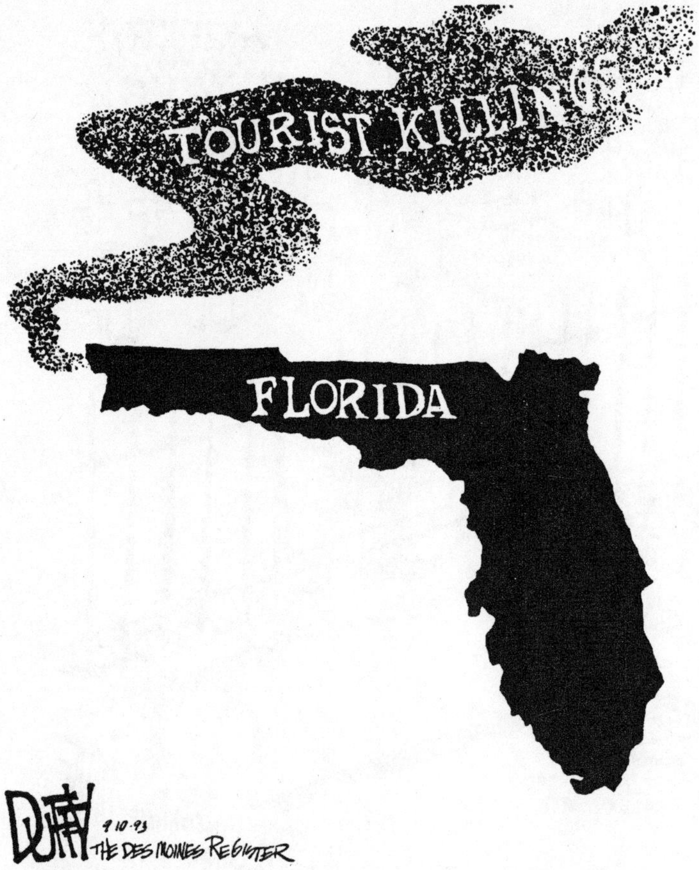
TOURIST KILLINGS
FLORIDA
DUFFY 9-10-93 THE DES MOINES REGISTER

BRIAN DUFFY
Courtesy Des Moines Register

MICHAEL D. RHODA
Courtesy Briargate/Cheyenne Editions

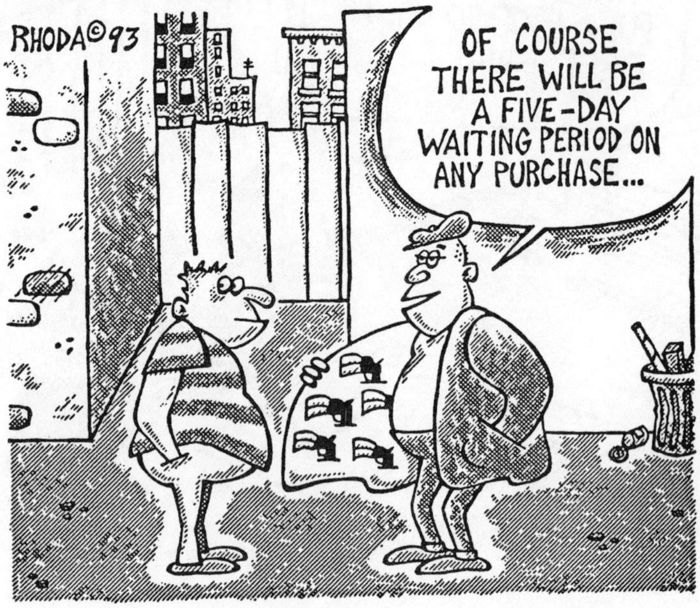
RHODA©93
OF COURSE THERE WILL BE A FIVE-DAY WAITING PERIOD ON ANY PURCHASE...

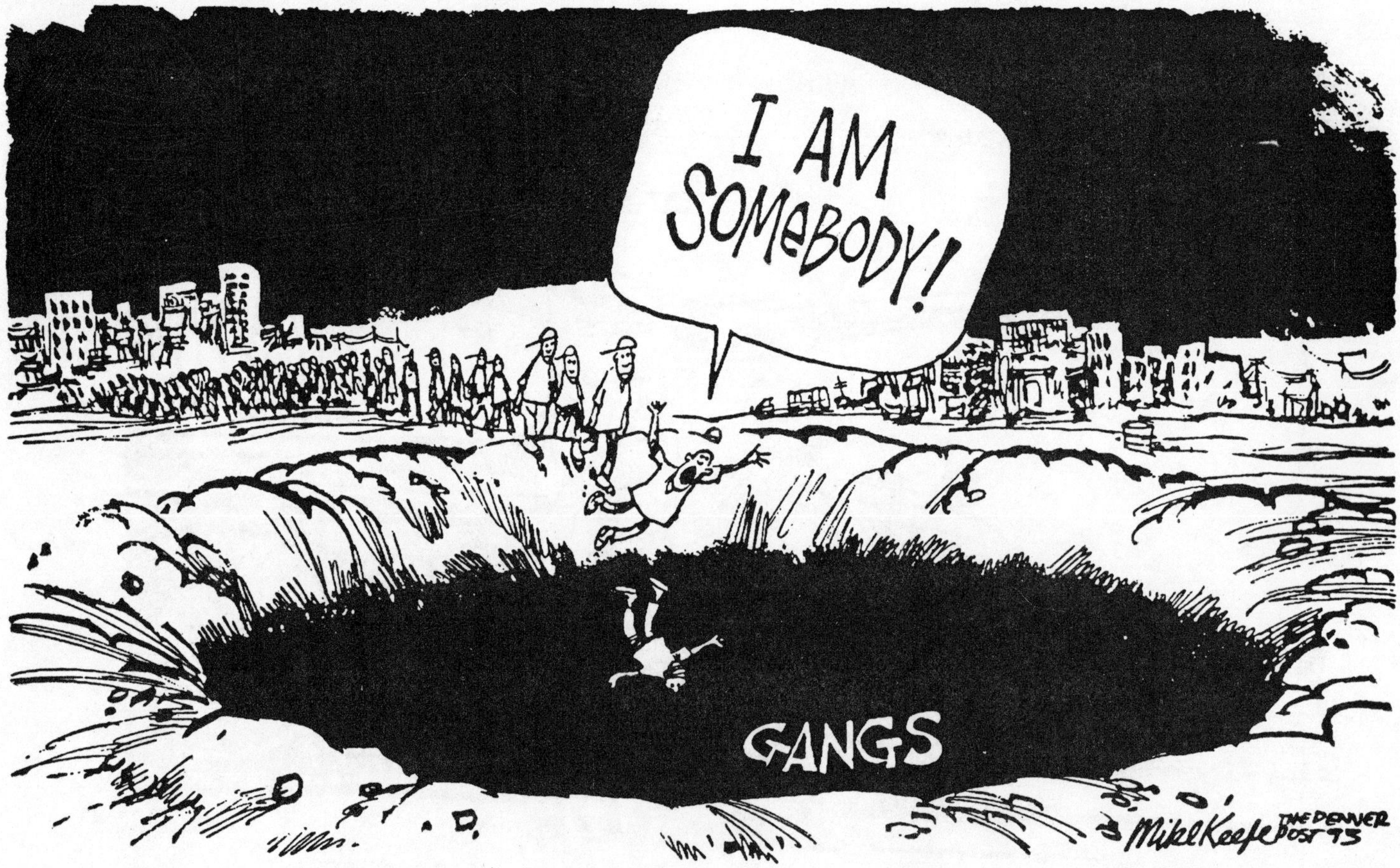
I AM SOMEBODY!
GANGS
Mike Keefe THE DENVER POST '93

MIKE KEEFE
Courtesy Denver Post

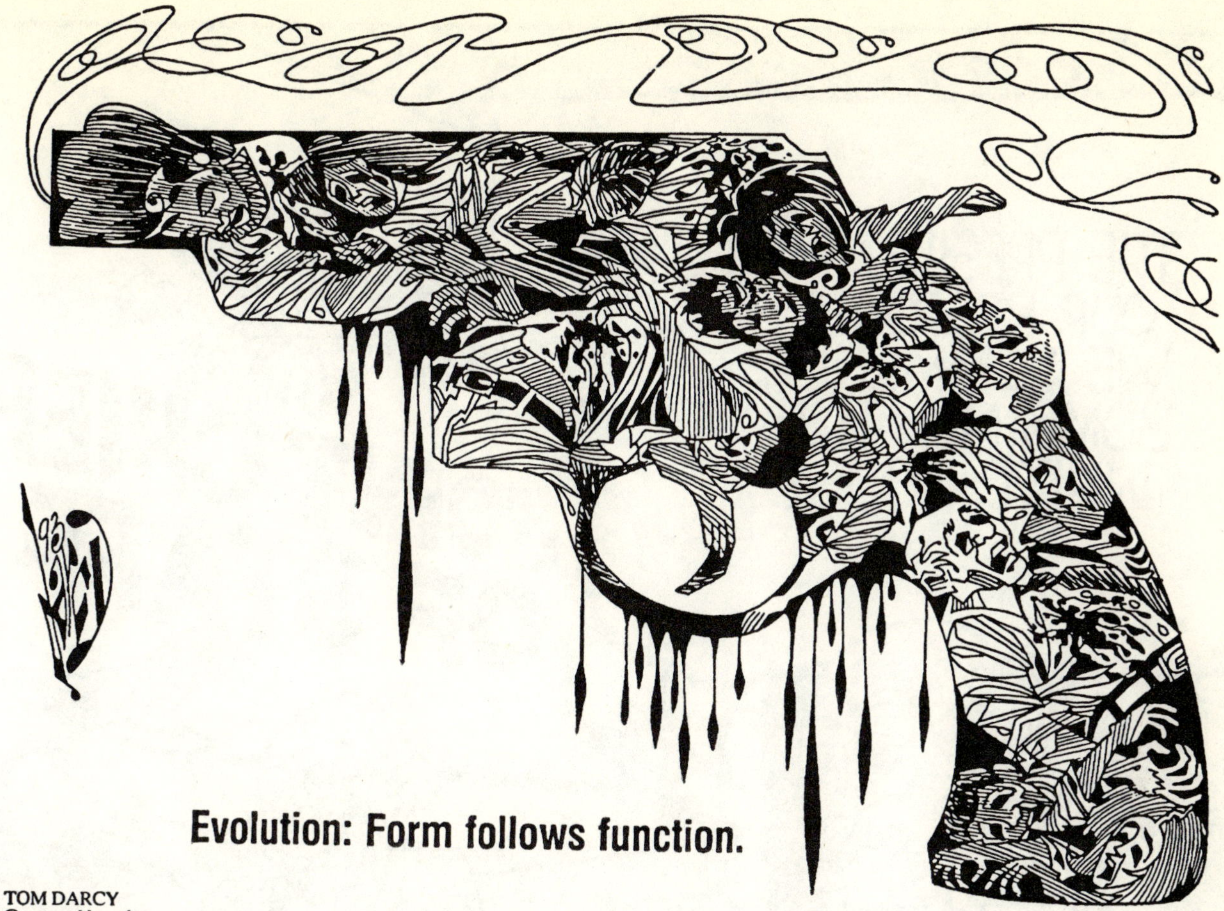
Evolution: Form follows function.

TOM DARCY
Courtesy Newsday

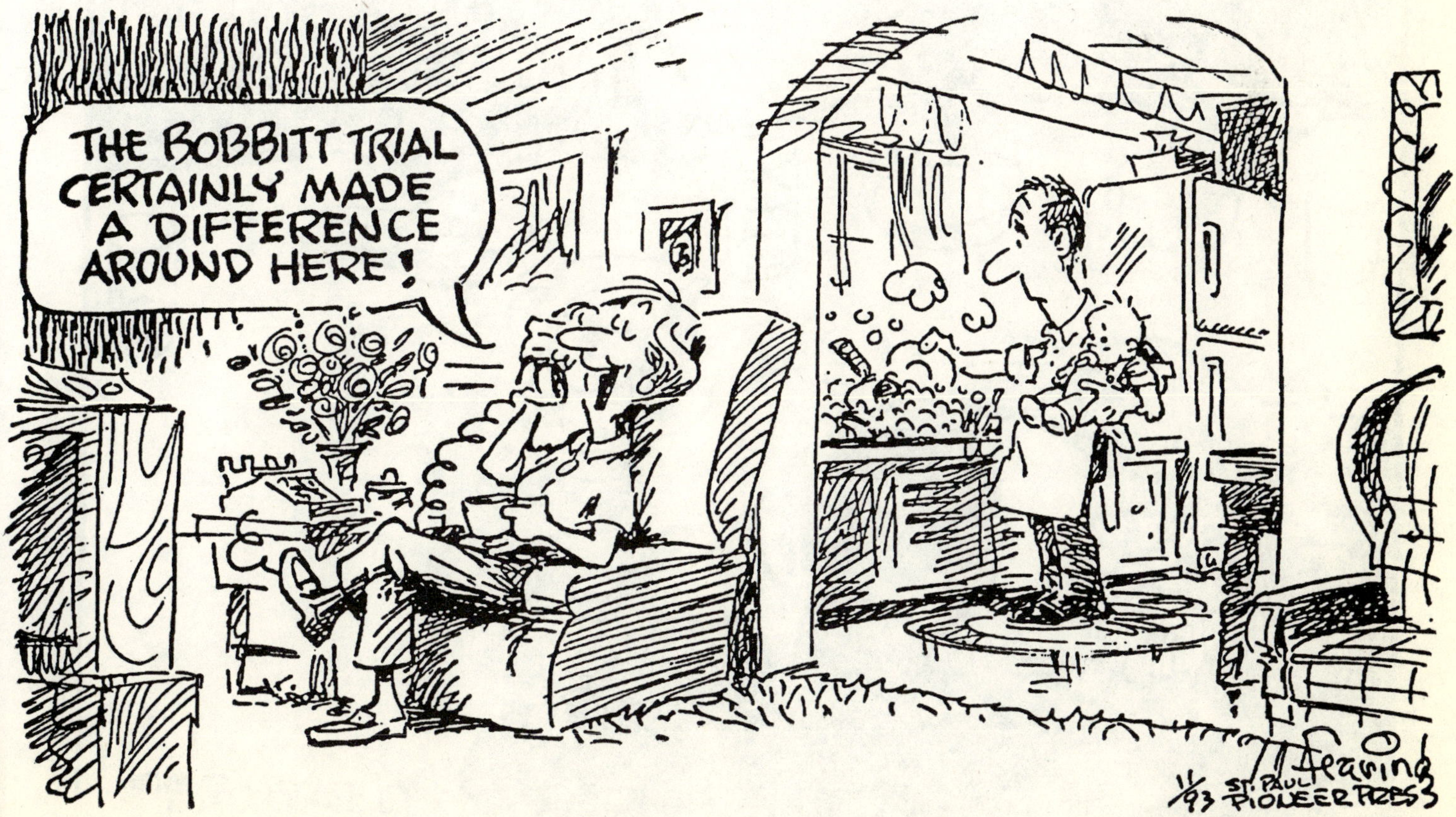
THE BOBBITT TRIAL CERTAINLY MADE A DIFFERENCE AROUND HERE!
Fearing
1/93 ST. PAUL PIONEER PRESS

JERRY FEARING
Courtesy St. Paul Pioneer Press-Dispatch

FRED CURATOLO
Courtesy Edmonton Sun

U.S. Military

President Clinton ran into a stone wall after his campaign promise to scrap the military's long-standing ban on gays. The wall was composed of Gen. Colin Powell, chairman of the Joint Chiefs of Staff, Sen. Sam Nunn, and top brass in the armed forces. Under the "Don't Ask, Don't Tell" compromise that finally was reached, new recruits are no longer asked if they are homosexual. But, once in uniform, they will be barred from openly identifying themselves as gay, except to a chaplain, a lawyer, or a doctor. Now there must be a specific act of disruptive misconduct before homosexuals can be forced out of service. The Defense Department considers the compromise to be in line with the past court rulings on such matters.

The Pentagon finally closed its two-year investigation of the Navy's Tailhook incident, in which women service members alleged systematic sexual harassment at an annual gathering. The secretary of the Navy was removed from office and four admirals were replaced or relieved of duty. Nearly half of the cases were dismissed for lack of evidence.

The prohibition against women serving in combat was lifted in 1993, largely because of the performance of women pilots during Desert Storm. Not all doors have opened to women, however, and the various services are pondering the removal of other barriers to jobs for women in the military.

JOHN TREVER
Courtesy Albuquerque Journal

DICK WRIGHT
Courtesy Providence Journal-Bulletin

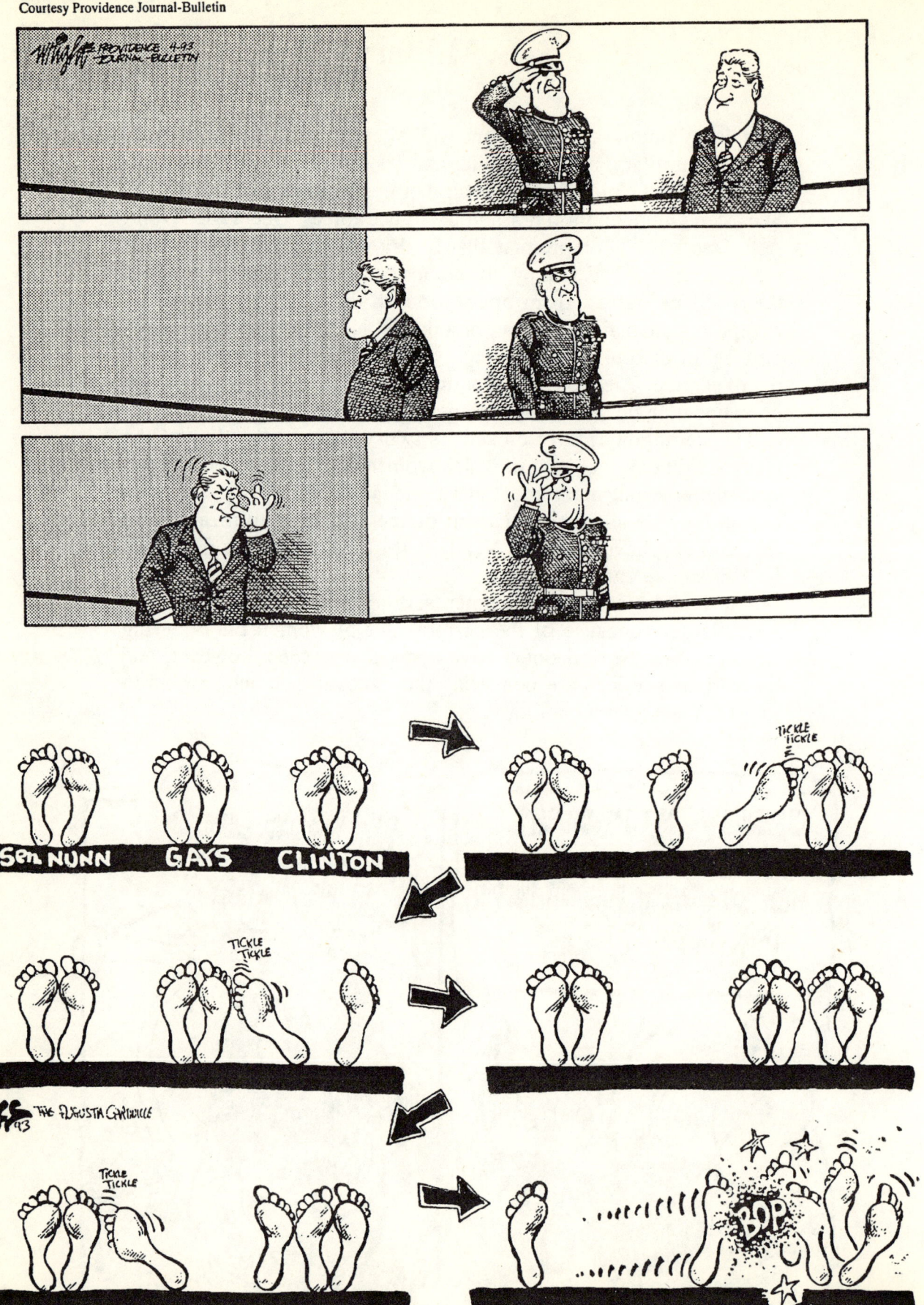

CLYDE WELLS
Courtesy Augusta Chronicle

JACK OHMAN
Courtesy Portland Oregonian

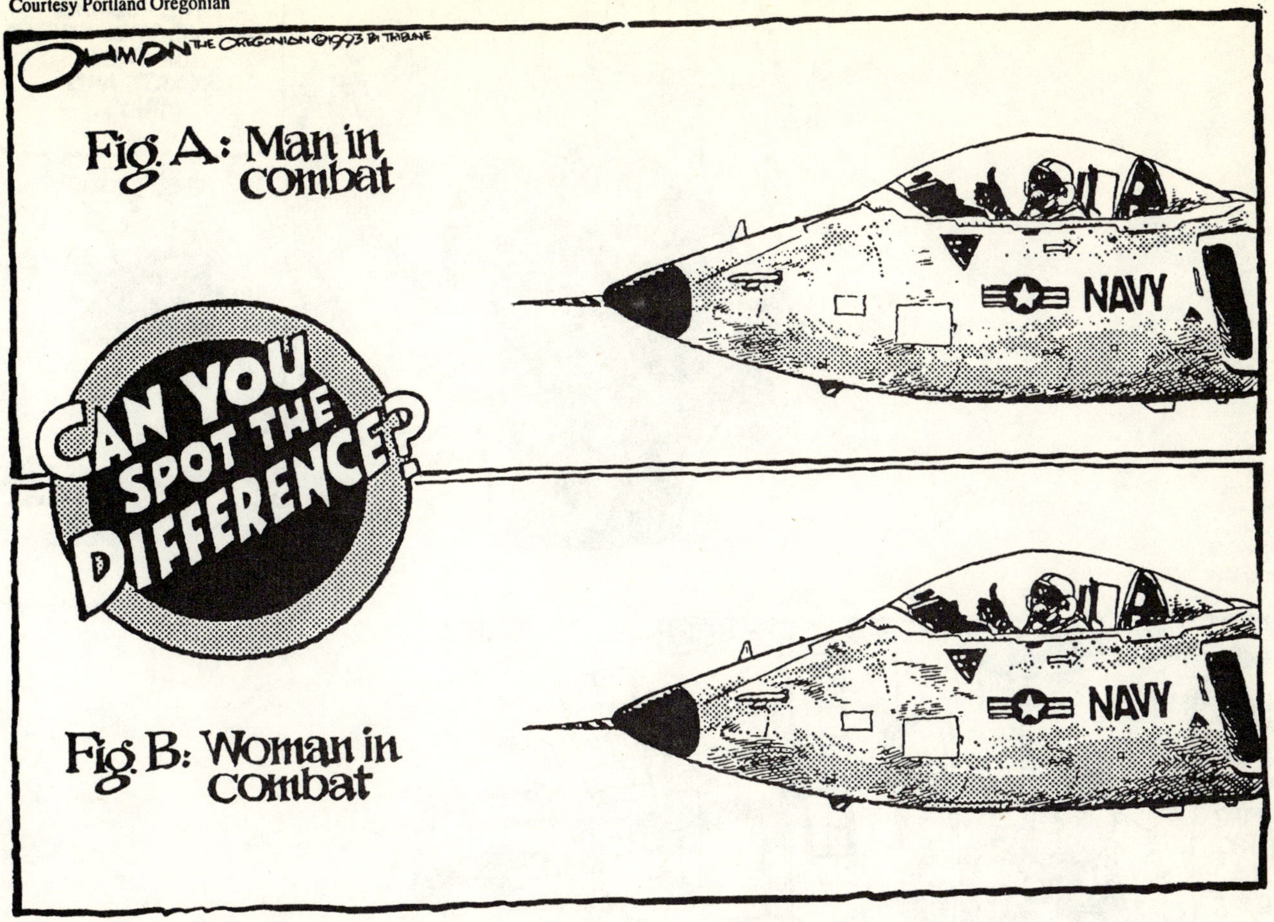
OHMAN THE OREGONIAN ©1993 BY TRIBUNE
Fig. A: Man in combat
NAVY
CAN YOU SPOT THE DIFFERENCE?
NAVY
Fig. B: Woman in combat

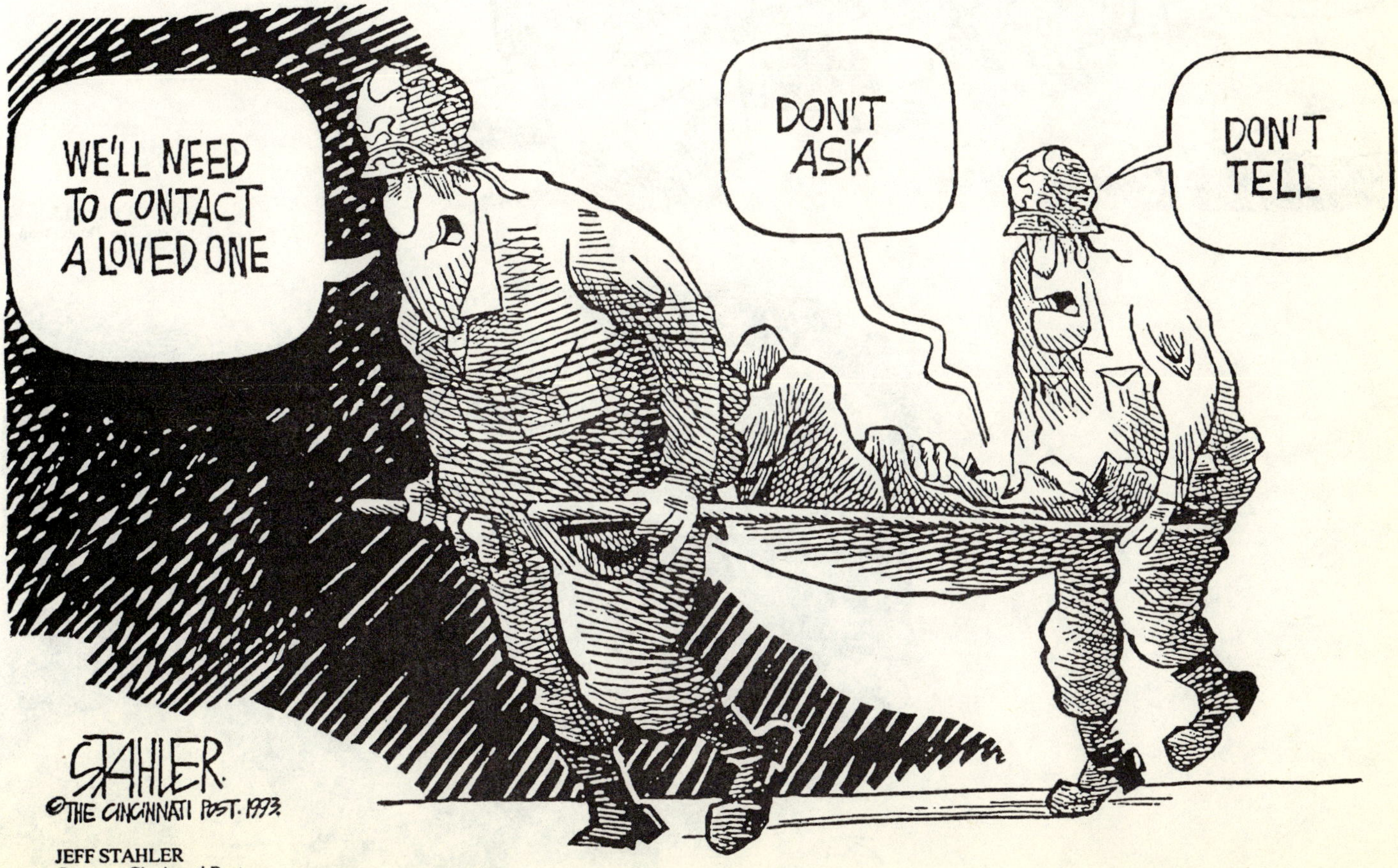
WE'LL NEED TO CONTACT A LOVED ONE
DON'T ASK
DON'T TELL
STAHLER ©THE CINCINNATI POST. 1993.

JEFF STAHLER
Courtesy Cincinnati Post

MIKE KEEFE
Courtesy Denver Post

CHAN LOWE
Courtesy The News/Sun-Sentinel (Fla.)

CHARLES BISSELL
Courtesy The Tennessean

"U.S. DEFENSE SEEMS TO BE THE BRAVEST, MOST FORMIDABLE FORCE ON EARTH. THEY FEAR ONLY ONE THING—GAYS IN THE SHOWER."

BRIAN GABLE
Courtesy Toronto Globe and Mail

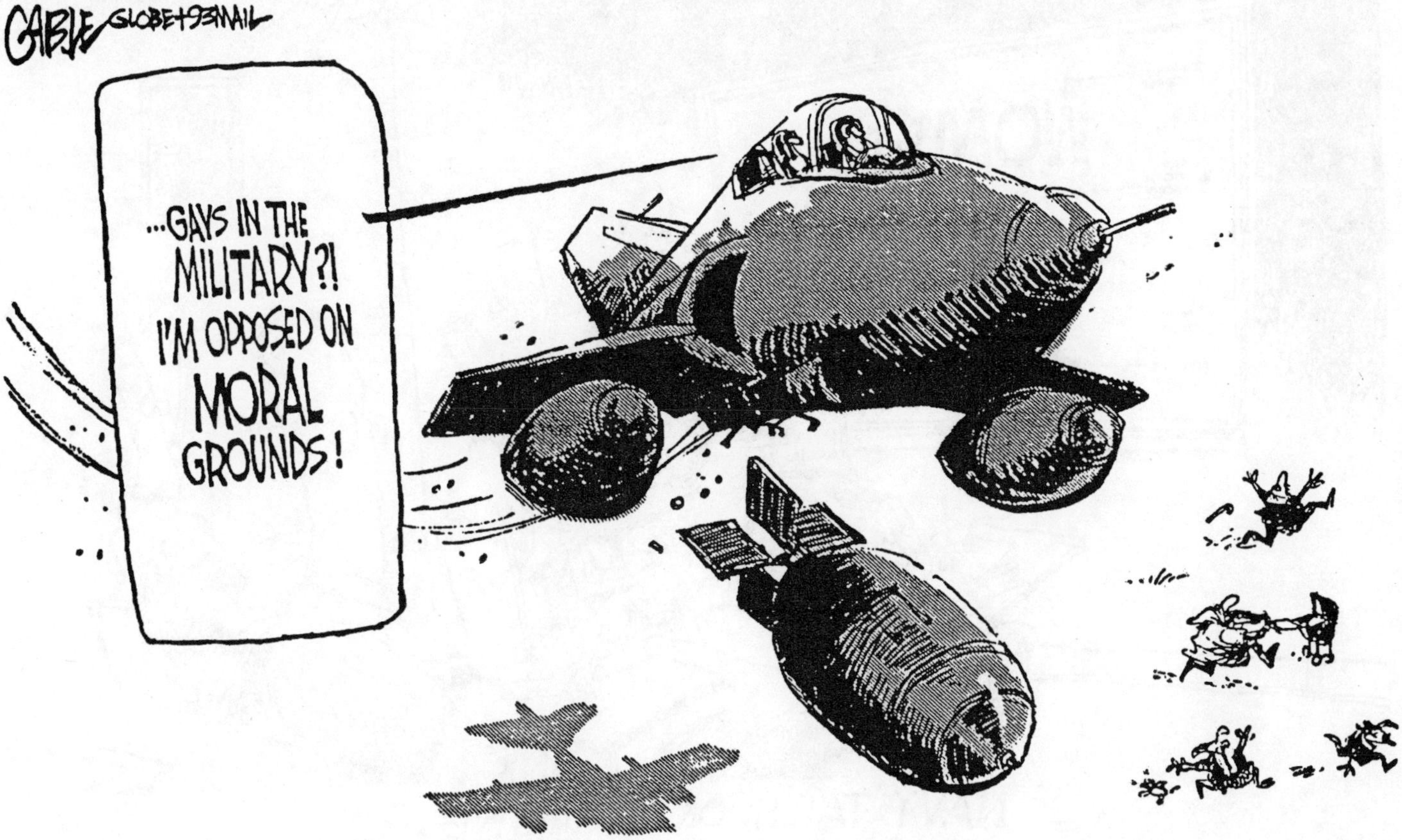
GABLE GLOBE+MAIL
...GAYS IN THE MILITARY?! I'M OPPOSED ON MORAL GROUNDS!

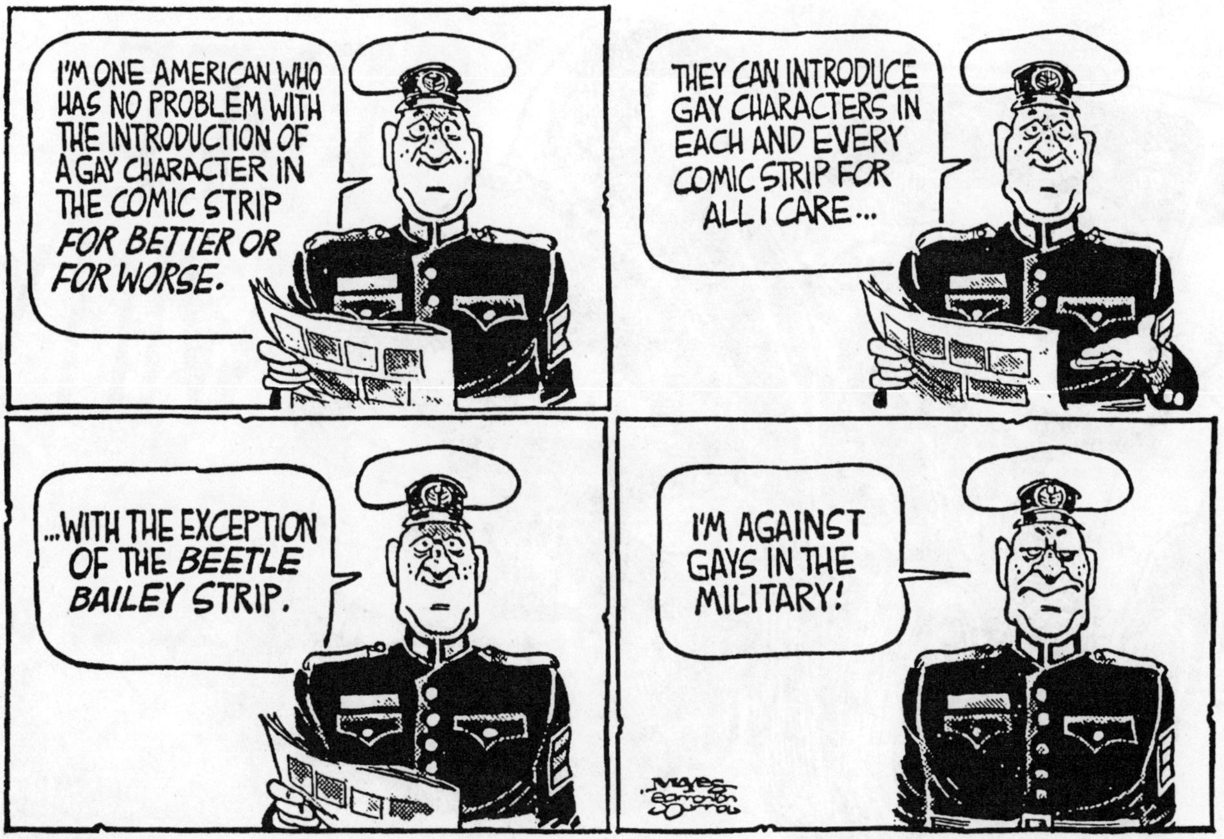
I'M ONE AMERICAN WHO HAS NO PROBLEM WITH THE INTRODUCTION OF A GAY CHARACTER IN THE COMIC STRIP *FOR BETTER OR FOR WORSE*.
THEY CAN INTRODUCE GAY CHARACTERS IN EACH AND EVERY COMIC STRIP FOR ALL I CARE...
...WITH THE EXCEPTION OF THE *BEETLE BAILEY* STRIP.
I'M AGAINST GAYS IN THE MILITARY!
MAYES Edmonton Journal

MALCOLM MAYES
Courtesy Edmonton Journal

DAVID SWANN
Courtesy Huntsville Times (Ala.)

WOMEN ARE HUMAN BEINGS

NAVY "TAILHOOK" TRAINING

FREE WILLY

DNT ASK DNT TELL

KEN CATALINO
Courtesy Anchorage Times

PAUL CONRAD
Courtesy Los Angeles Times

JACK HIGGINS
Courtesy Chicago Sun-Times

JACK MCLEOD
Courtesy Federal Times

LINDA BOILEAU
Courtesy Frankfort State Journal

LARRY WRIGHT
Courtesy Detroit News

PAUL CONRAD
Courtesy Los Angeles Times

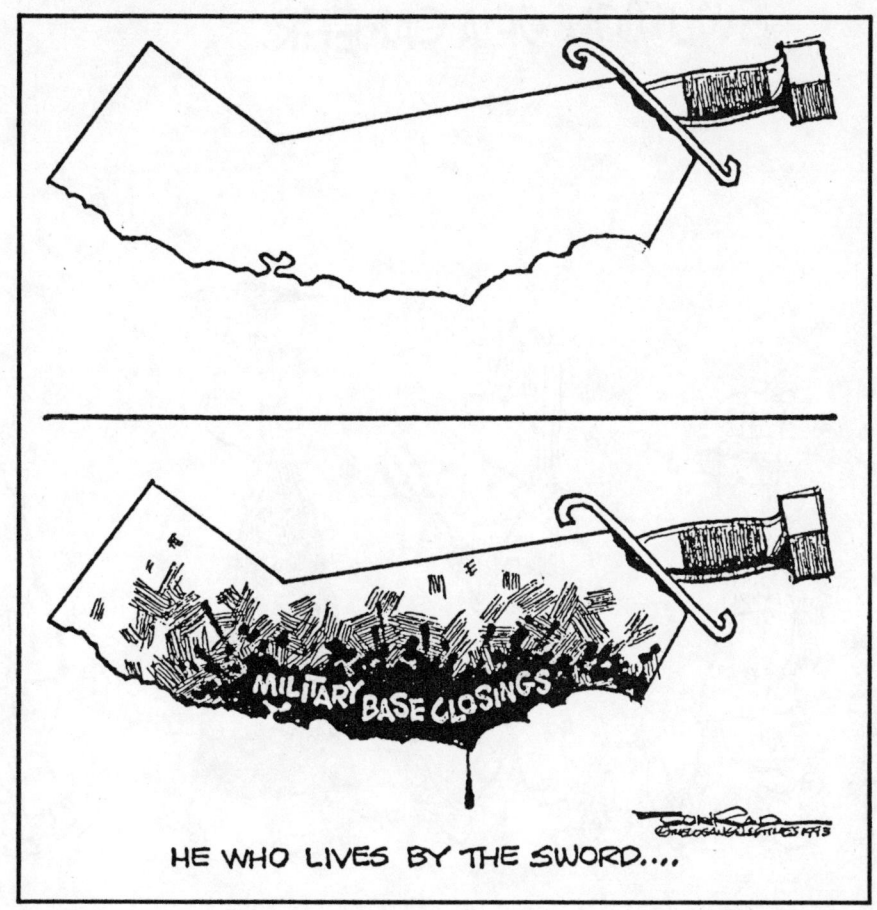

DAVE COVERLY
Courtesy Bloomington Herald-Times

JEFF STAHLER
Courtesy Cincinnati Post

EVOLUTION OF A CAREER...

CLAY BENNETT
Courtesy St. Petersburg Times

Education

During 1993, more than 3 million crimes were committed in or near the 85,000 public schools in the United States. In October, New York City authorities announced plans to station police officers in all 1,069 of the city's public schools, at a cost of $460 million to taxpayers.

School crimes were becoming increasingly violent, and studies showed that 9 percent of eighth-grade students carry a gun, knife, or club to school at least once a month. An estimated 270,000 guns are in schools every day. Many schools have fenced their campuses, initiated locker searches, and installed metal detectors.

School crimes are no longer confined to large cities, but have spread across America to towns of all sizes. School rape continued to grow during the year, with some teachers the targets. Some schools began dispensing condoms to students, drawing the ire of parents.

The U.S. Supreme Court has outlawed prayer in schools, including prayer to open football games. Some schools, however, have openly ignored the ban.

As businesses across the country continued to trim workers in order to become more competitive in a changing economy, college and high-school graduates were finding jobs scarce. The day when companies flooded colleges with representatives bearing lucrative job offers apparently is over.

DICK WALLMEYER
Courtesy Long Beach Press-Telegram

CAMPUS ROULETTE

NEIL GRAHAME
Courtesy Spencer Newspapers

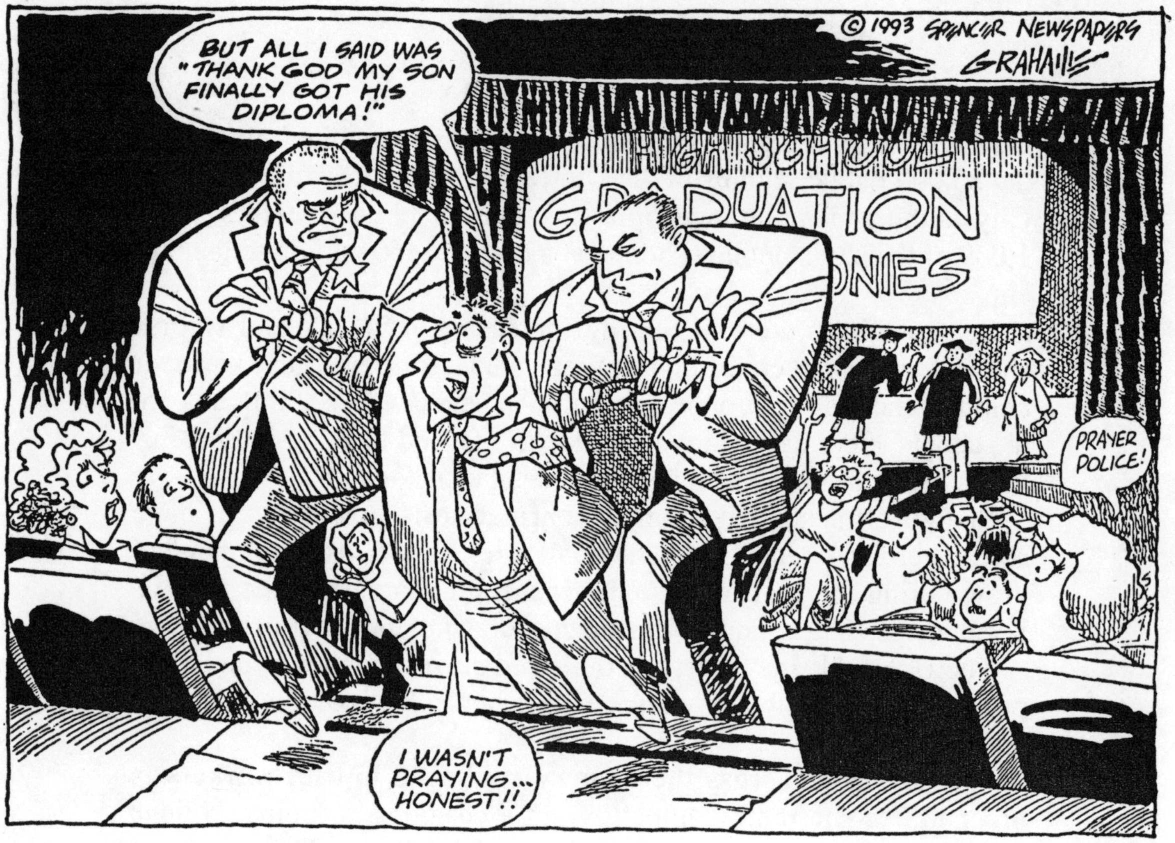
© 1993 SPENCER NEWSPAPERS
GRAHAME
BUT ALL I SAID WAS "THANK GOD MY SON FINALLY GOT HIS DIPLOMA!"
GRADUATION CEREMONIES
PRAYER POLICE!
I WASN'T PRAYING... HONEST!!

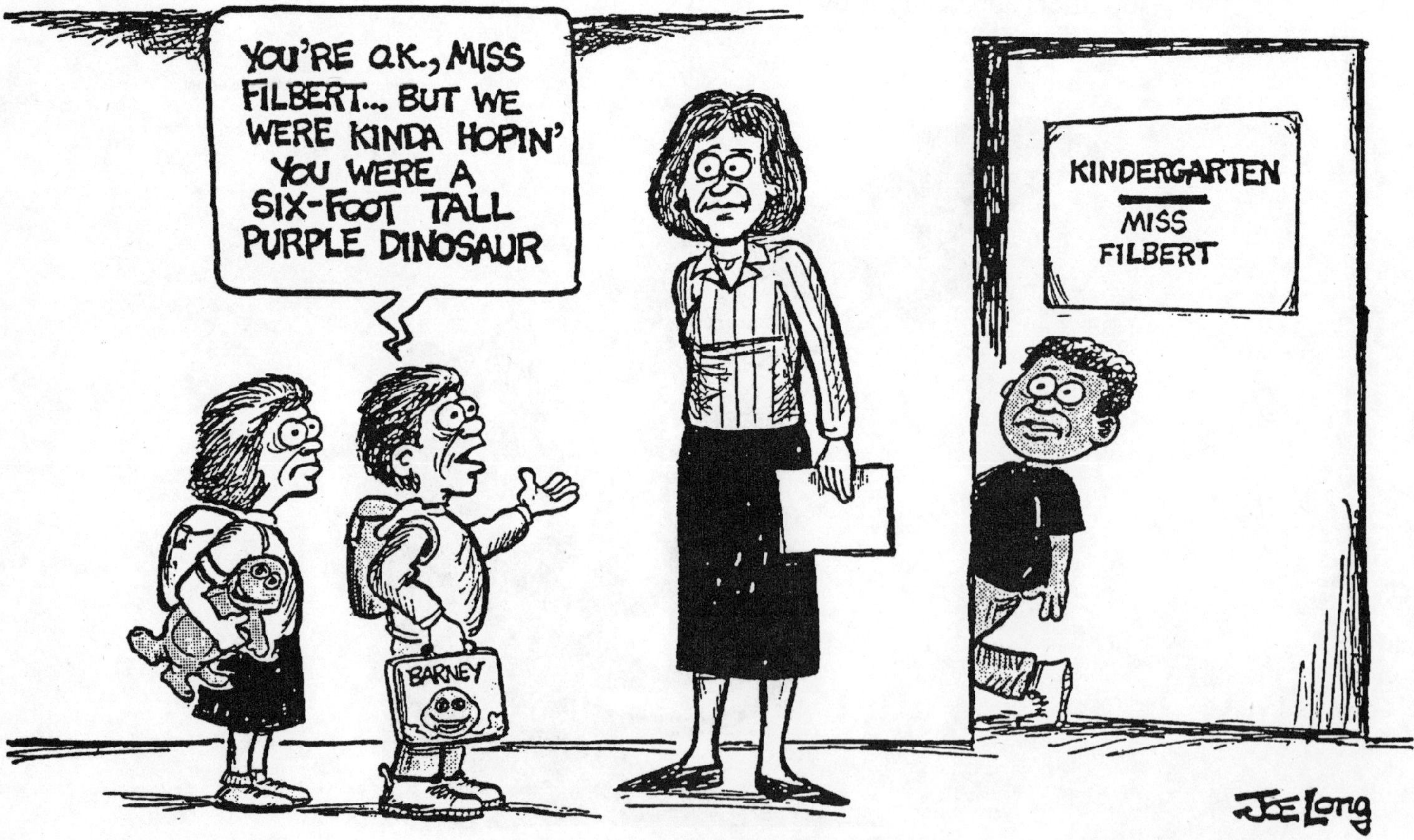
YOU'RE O.K., MISS FILBERT... BUT WE WERE KINDA HOPIN' YOU WERE A SIX-FOOT TALL PURPLE DINOSAUR
KINDERGARTEN
MISS FILBERT
BARNEY
JOE LONG

JOE LONG
Courtesy Little Falls Evening Times (N.Y.)

JIM JORDAN
Courtesy Courier News (Ill.)

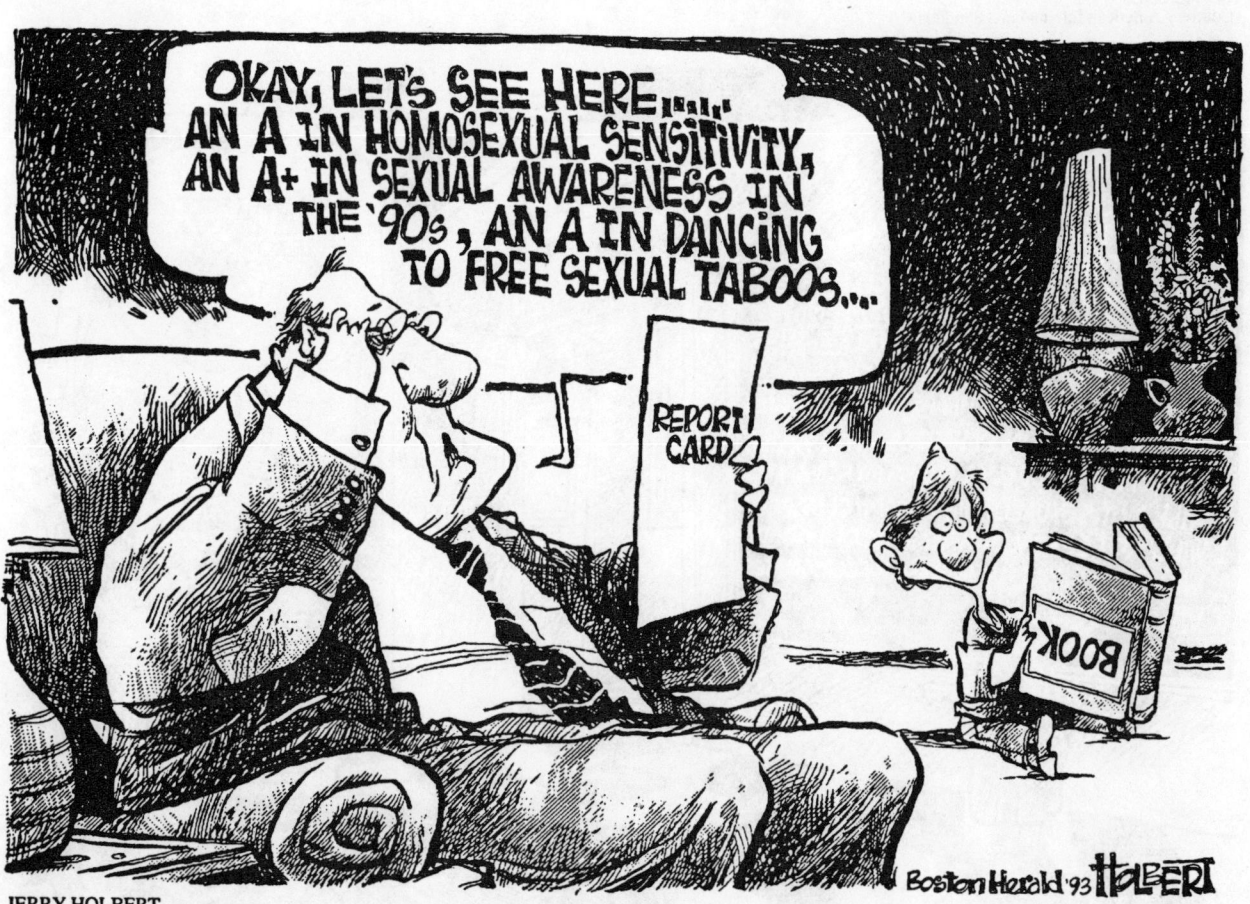

JERRY HOLBERT
Courtesy Boston Herald

STEVE NEASE
Courtesy Toronto Star

VIC CANTONE
Courtesy Rothco

CLAY JONES
Courtesy American International Syndicate

STEVE MCBRIDE
Courtesy Independence Daily Reporter (Kan.)

STEVE KELLEY
Courtesy San Diego Union

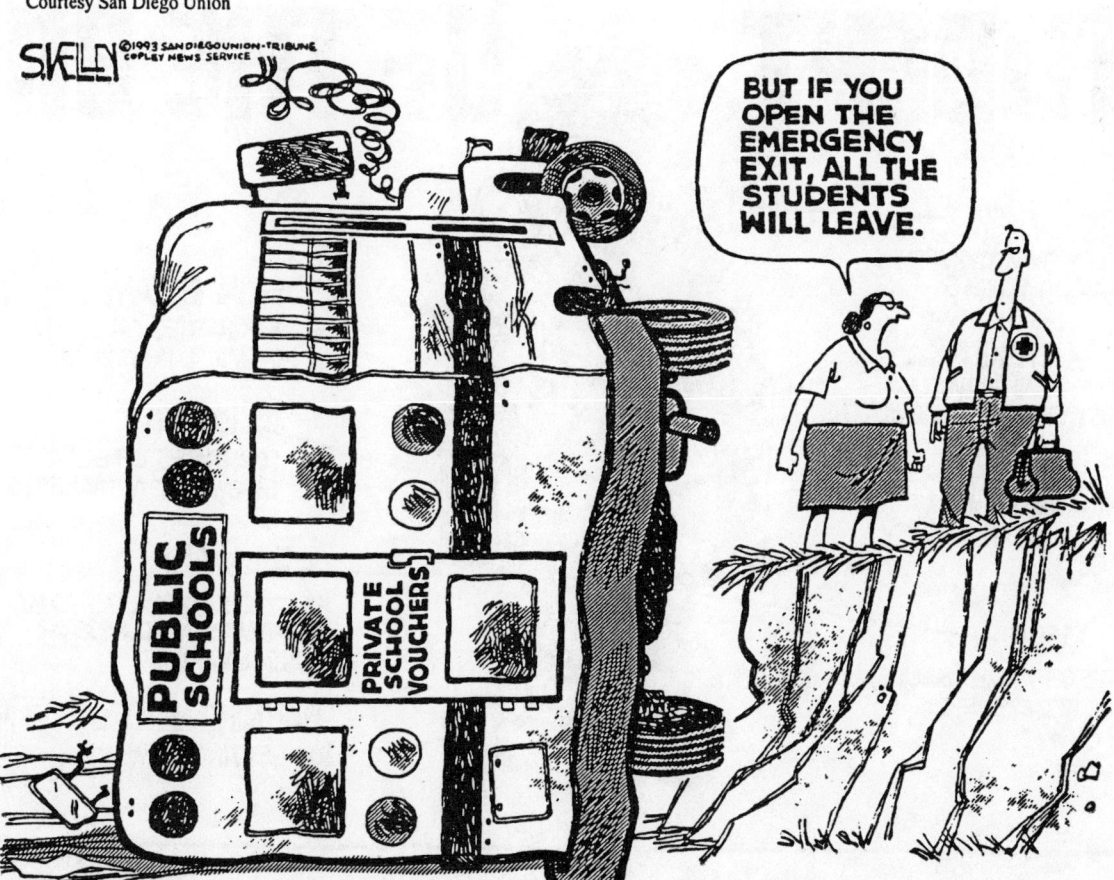

JIM MCCLOSKEY
Courtesy Staunton Daily News Leader

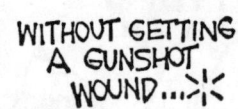

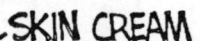

BRUCE MACKINNON
Courtesy Halifax Chronicle-Herald

DAVE COVERLY
Courtesy Bloomington-Herald-Times

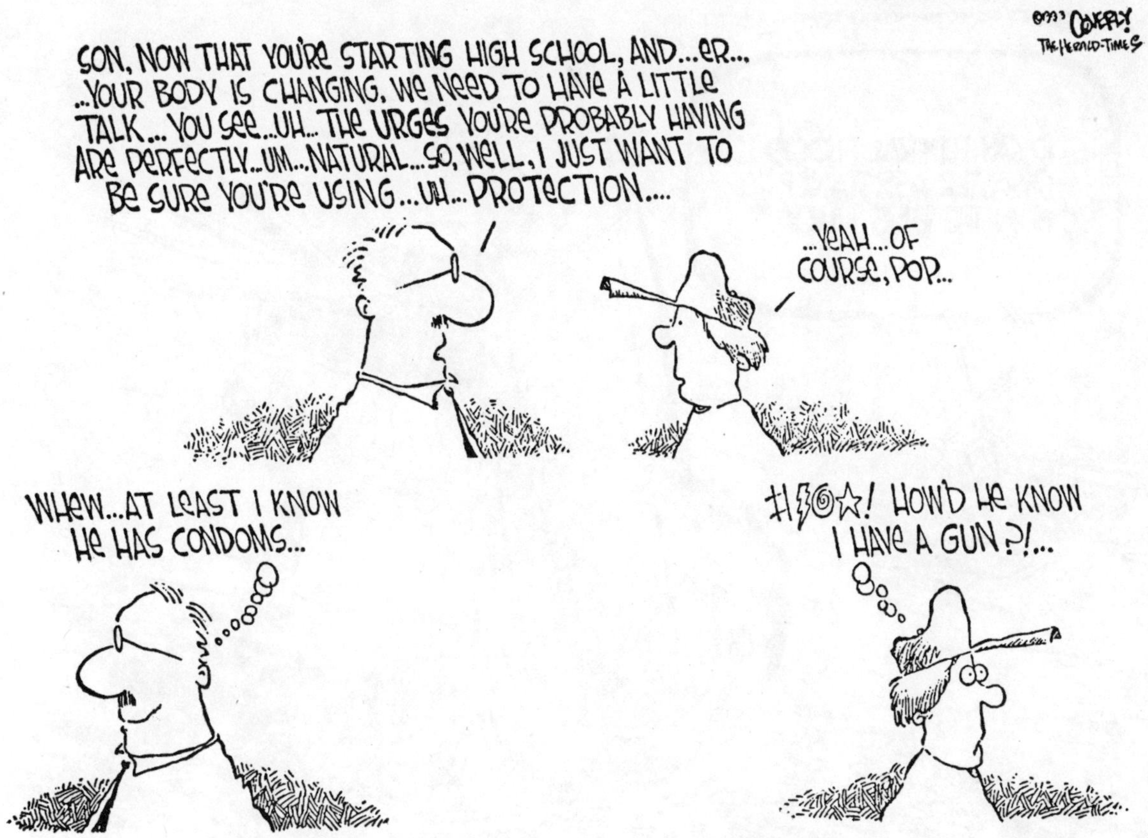

COVERLY THE HERALD-TIMES
SON, NOW THAT YOU'RE STARTING HIGH SCHOOL, AND...ER... ...YOUR BODY IS CHANGING, WE NEED TO HAVE A LITTLE TALK... YOU SEE...UH... THE URGES YOU'RE PROBABLY HAVING ARE PERFECTLY...UM...NATURAL...SO, WELL, I JUST WANT TO BE SURE YOU'RE USING...UH...PROTECTION....
...YEAH...OF COURSE, POP...
WHEW...AT LEAST I KNOW HE HAS CONDOMS...
#!@☆! HOW'D HE KNOW I HAVE A GUN?!...

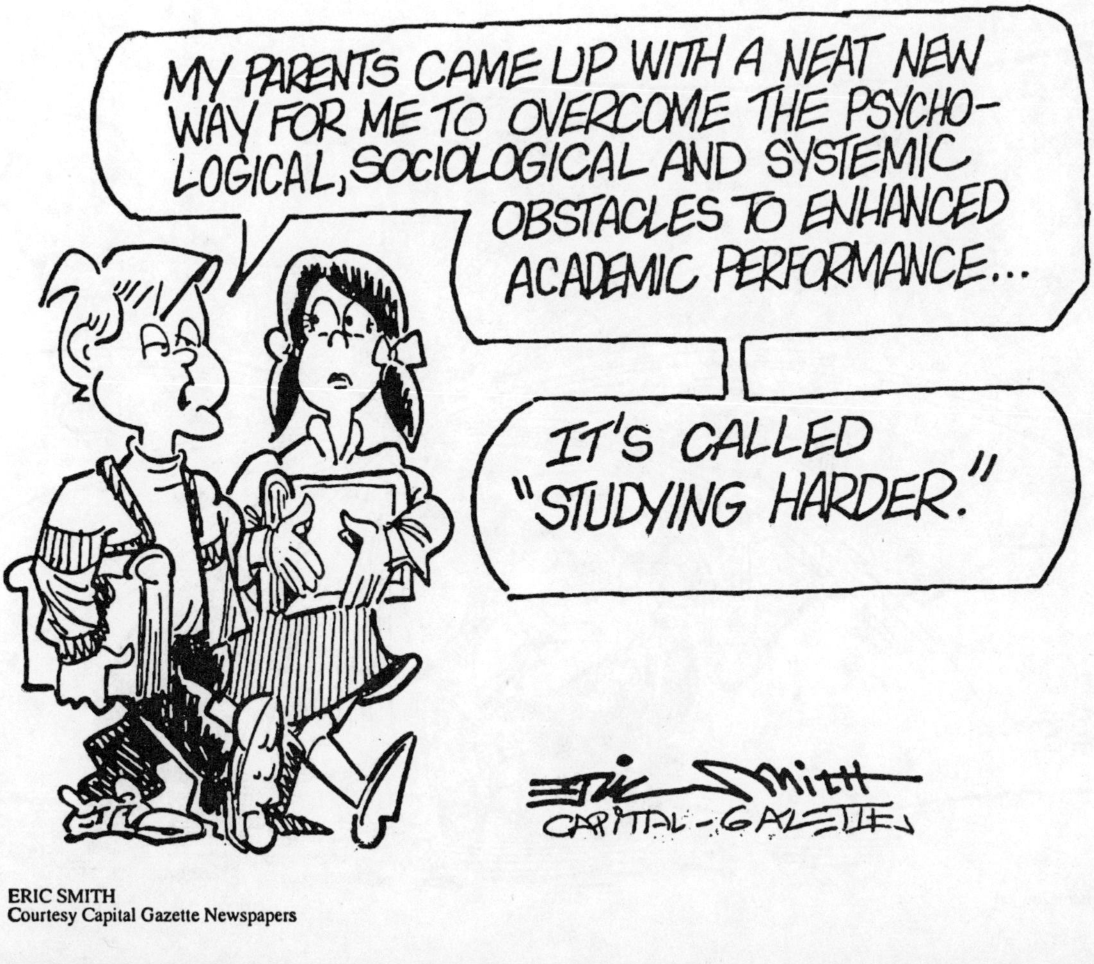

MY PARENTS CAME UP WITH A NEAT NEW WAY FOR ME TO OVERCOME THE PSYCHOLOGICAL, SOCIOLOGICAL AND SYSTEMIC OBSTACLES TO ENHANCED ACADEMIC PERFORMANCE...
IT'S CALLED "STUDYING HARDER."
ERIC SMITH CAPITAL-GAZETTE

ERIC SMITH
Courtesy Capital Gazette Newspapers

JACK OHMAN
Courtesy Portland Oregonian

MALCOLM MAYES
Courtesy Edmonton Journal

The Environment

The flood of the century hit Middle America in 1993. Heavy rains over a prolonged period left 48 dead, more than $10 billion in property damage, 70,000 people displaced, and 421 counties declared disaster areas. Farmlands twice the size of New Jersey were inundated, and the Mississippi River at St. Louis remained above flood stage for a record 80 days.

The year also spawned the snow blizzard of the century in the Southeast. In March, Birmingham, Alabama, was buried in 19 inches of snow. California again received its share of natural disasters. Fires in the southern part of the state burned 200,000 acres and 1,000 homes. That was followed by flooding and mudslides, which destroyed many other homes.

President Clinton's new plan to balance jobs and the environment in the Pacific Northwest apparently left both sides dissatisfied. The plan would establish reserves for the spotted owl and create no-logging buffer zones around streams to protect salmon. It also would allow the cutting of 1.2 billion board feet of timber from federal lands each year. Timber towns would receive $1.2 billion in aid over a five-year period. The specifics of the plan were to be worked out in 1994.

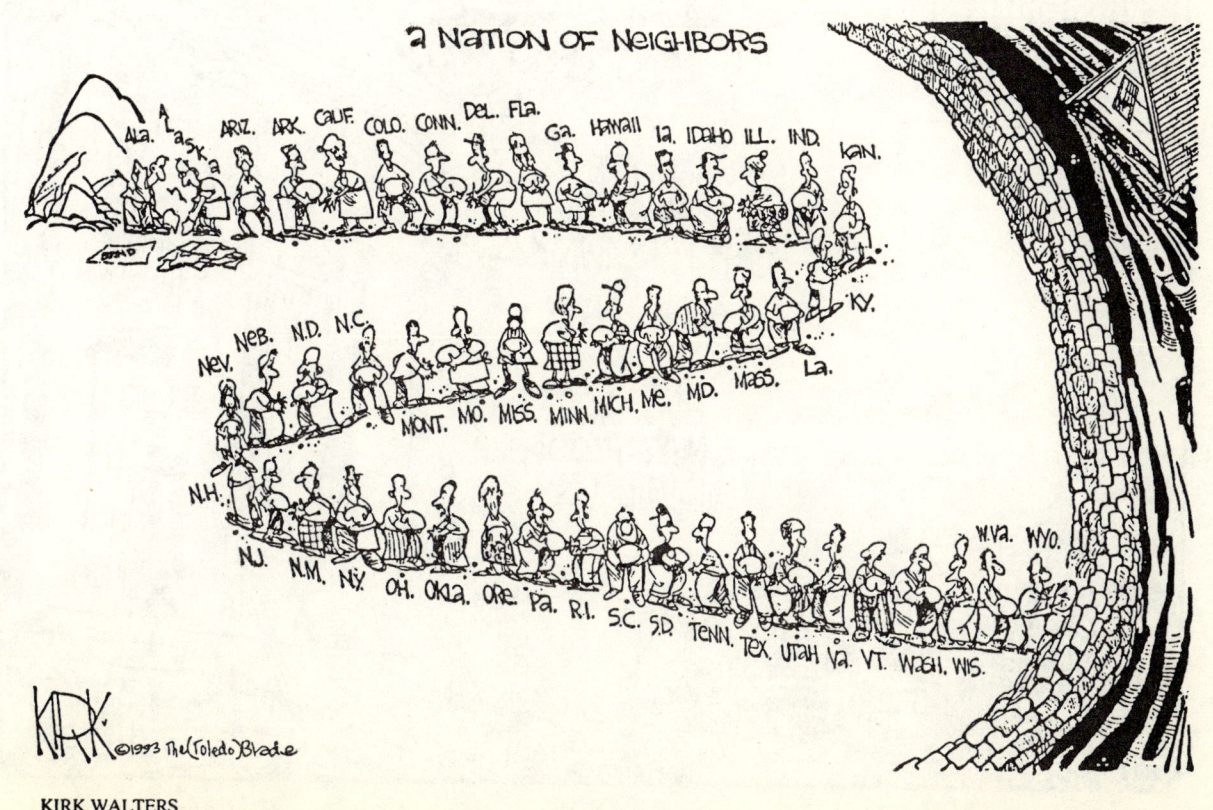

KIRK WALTERS
Courtesy Toledo Blade

NEIL GRAHAME
Courtesy Spencer Newspapers

THOMAS BOLDT
Courtesy Edmonton Journal

HUGH HAYNIE
Courtesy Louisville Courier Journal

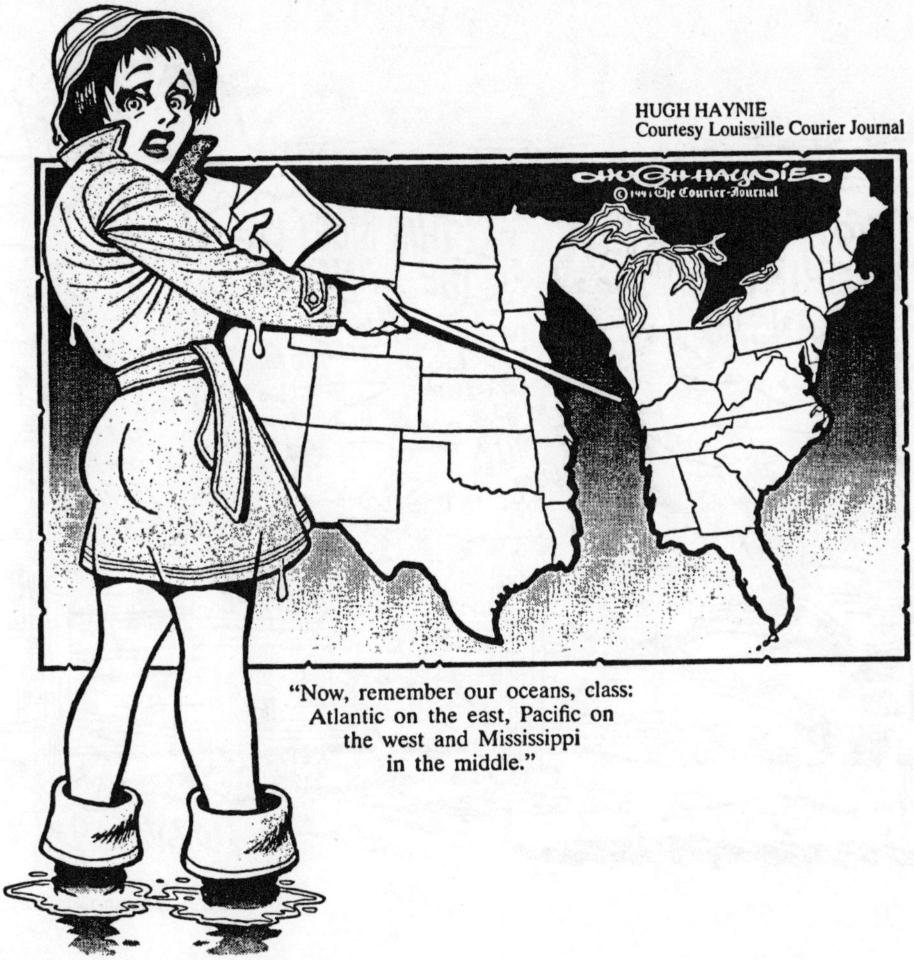
HUGH HAYNIE
© 1993 The Courier-Journal

"Now, remember our oceans, class:
Atlantic on the east, Pacific on
the west and Mississippi
in the middle."

JIM BORGMAN
Courtesy Cincinnati Enquirer

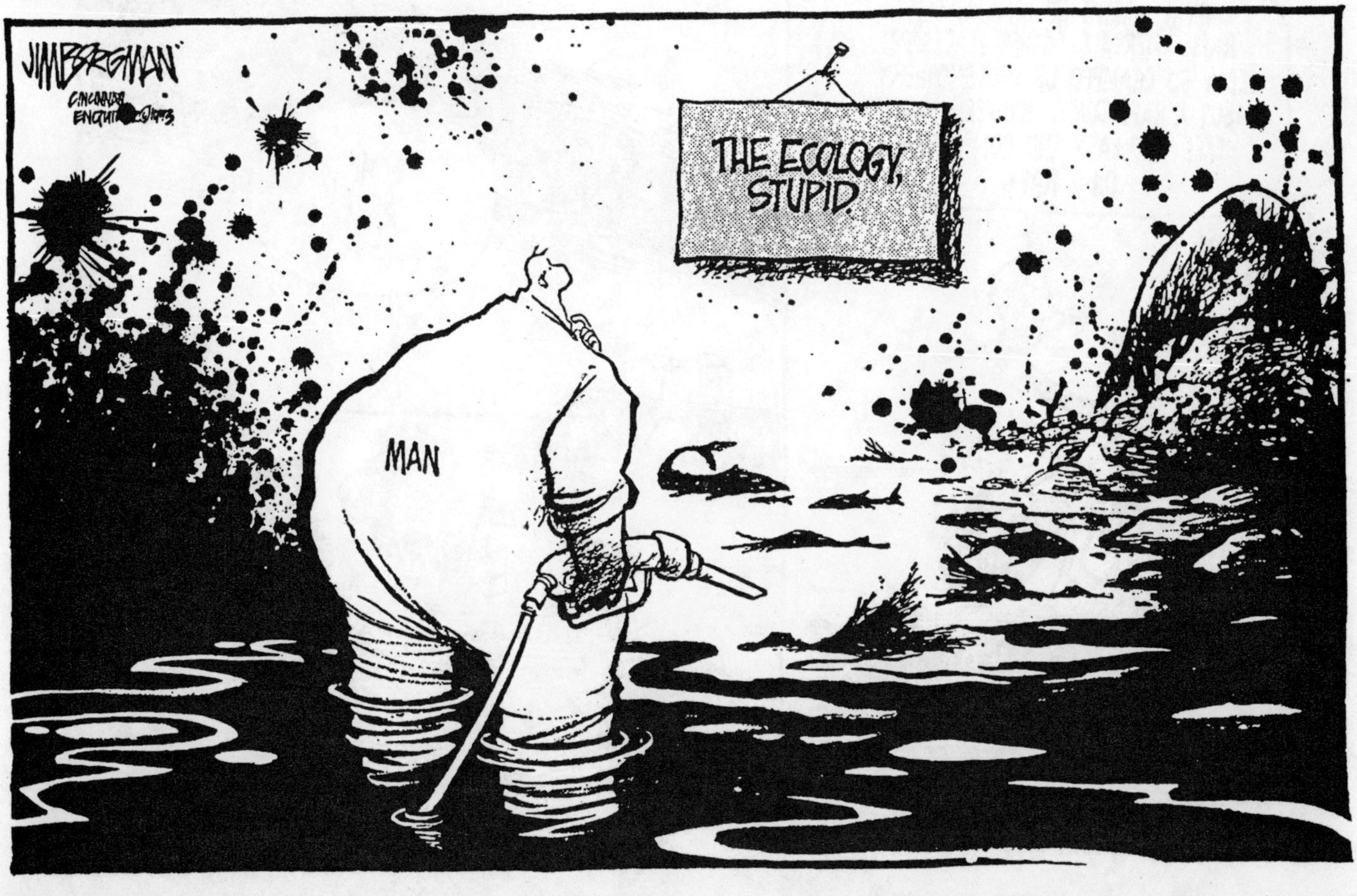
JIM BORGMAN
THE ECOLOGY, STUPID
MAN

GREG HORVAY
Courtesy Philadelphia Daily News

KEVIN SIERS
Courtesy Charlotte Observer

RANDY WICKS
Courtesy Valencia Signal (Calif.)

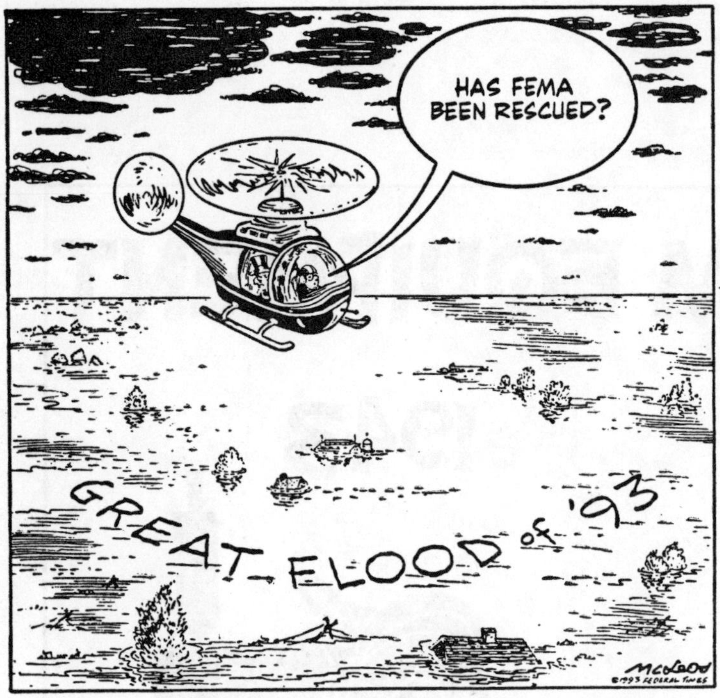
HAS FEMA BEEN RESCUED?
GREAT FLOOD of '93
McLEOD
©1993 FEDERAL TIMES

JACK MCLEOD
Courtesy Federal Times

TOM ENGELHARDT
Courtesy St. Louis Post-Dispatch

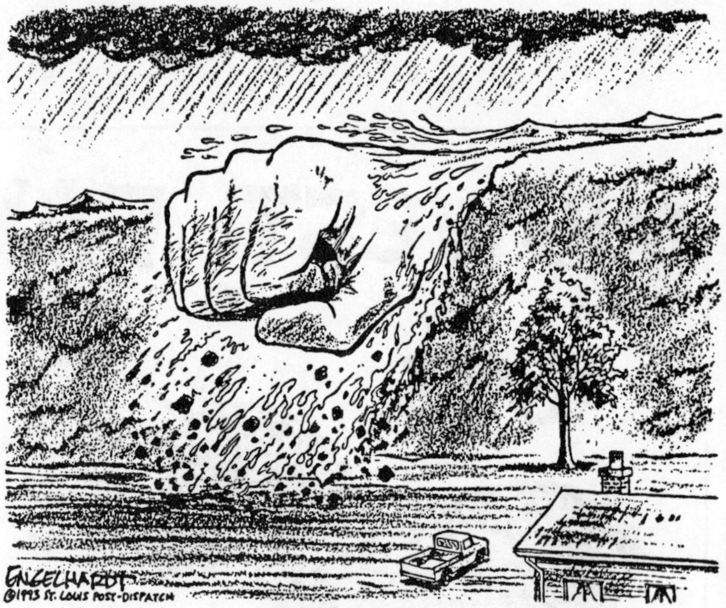
ENGELHARDT
©1993 ST. LOUIS POST-DISPATCH

Old Man River Takes Back His Flood Plain

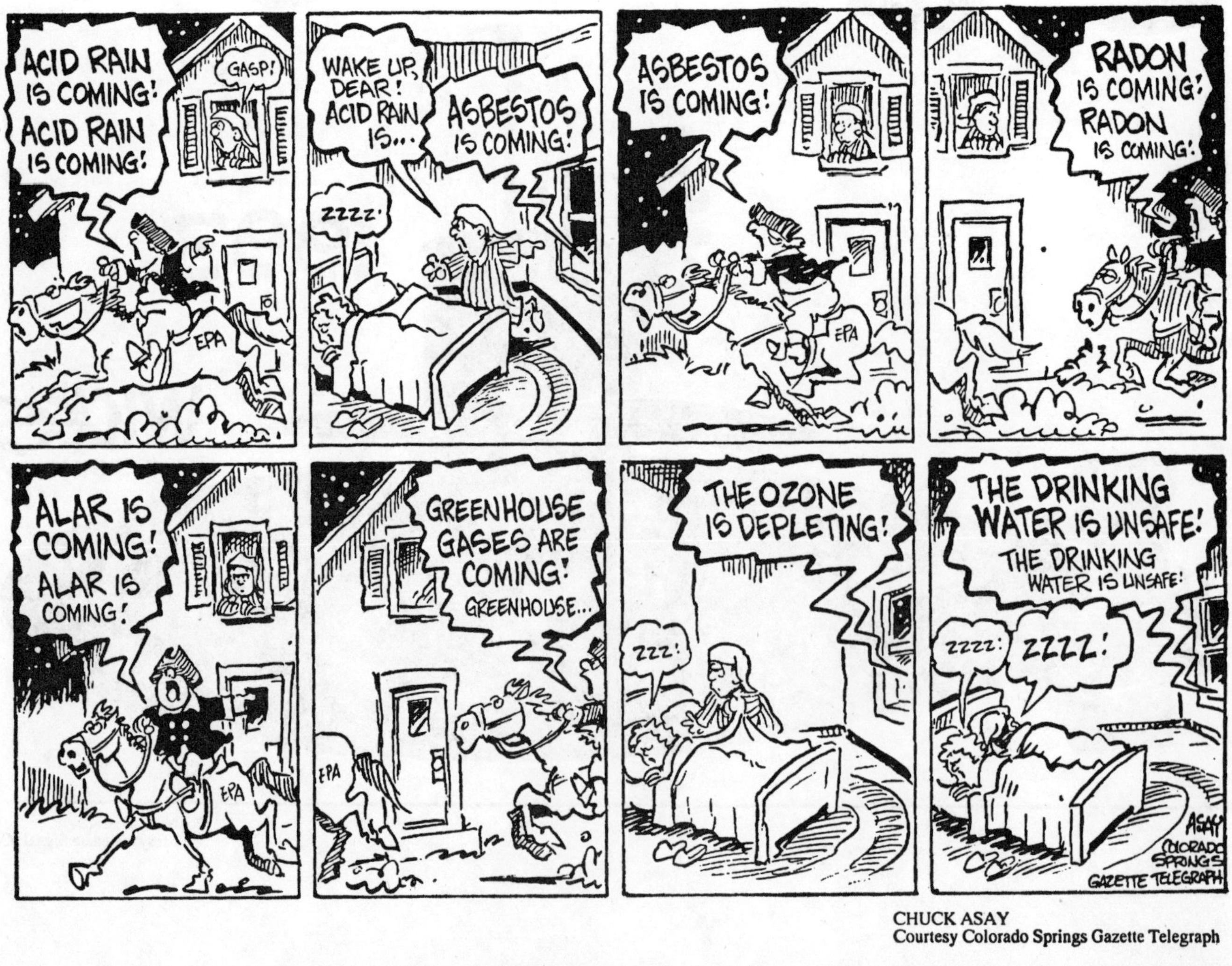
ACID RAIN IS COMING! ACID RAIN IS COMING!
GASP!
EPA
WAKE UP, DEAR! ACID RAIN IS...
ASBESTOS IS COMING!
ZZZZ!
ASBESTOS IS COMING!
EPA
RADON IS COMING! RADON IS COMING!
ALAR IS COMING! ALAR IS COMING!
EPA
GREENHOUSE GASES ARE COMING! GREENHOUSE...
EPA
THE OZONE IS DEPLETING!
ZZZ!
THE DRINKING WATER IS UNSAFE! THE DRINKING WATER IS UNSAFE!
ZZZZ!
ZZZZ!
ASAY
COLORADO SPRINGS GAZETTE TELEGRAPH

CHUCK ASAY
Courtesy Colorado Springs Gazette Telegraph

WAYNE STROOT
Courtesy Hastings Tribune

JERRY LEFLER
Courtesy Ventura County Star-Free Press

DENNY PRITCHARD
Courtesy Ottawa Citizen

MIKE SHELTON
Courtesy Orange County Register
and King Features Syndicate

Canada

In Canada's general election in late October, voters swept the Liberal party into power and installed a Quebecer, Jean Chrétien, as the new prime minister. Chrétien's immediate problem is the economy, which has gone through a severe recession, and increased trade competition brought on by the 1989 U.S.-Canada free-trade agreement. The new prime minister promised to renegotiate the free-trade pact and the North American Free Trade Agreement to satisfy Canadians who feel the U.S. enjoys an unfair advantage. After NAFTA was approved by the U.S. in November, Chrétien was anxious to meet with President Clinton to work things out.

Brian Mulroney, who had led his Conservative party to victories in 1984 and 1988, retired in June. His popularity finally hit bottom because of a combination of factors—an unpopular sales tax, the recession, and a defeat in the battle for a constitutional agreement between Quebec and the rest of Canada.

The Conservative party is now down to only two seats in Parliament. Quebec's Lucien Bouchard's party, the Bloc Quebecois, won the official opposition role in the election, and its platform pledges to separate Quebec from Canada.

ROY PETERSON
Courtesy Vancouver Sun

JAMES GRASDAL
Courtesy Edmonton Journal

JOSH BEUTEL
Courtesy St. John's Evening Telegram

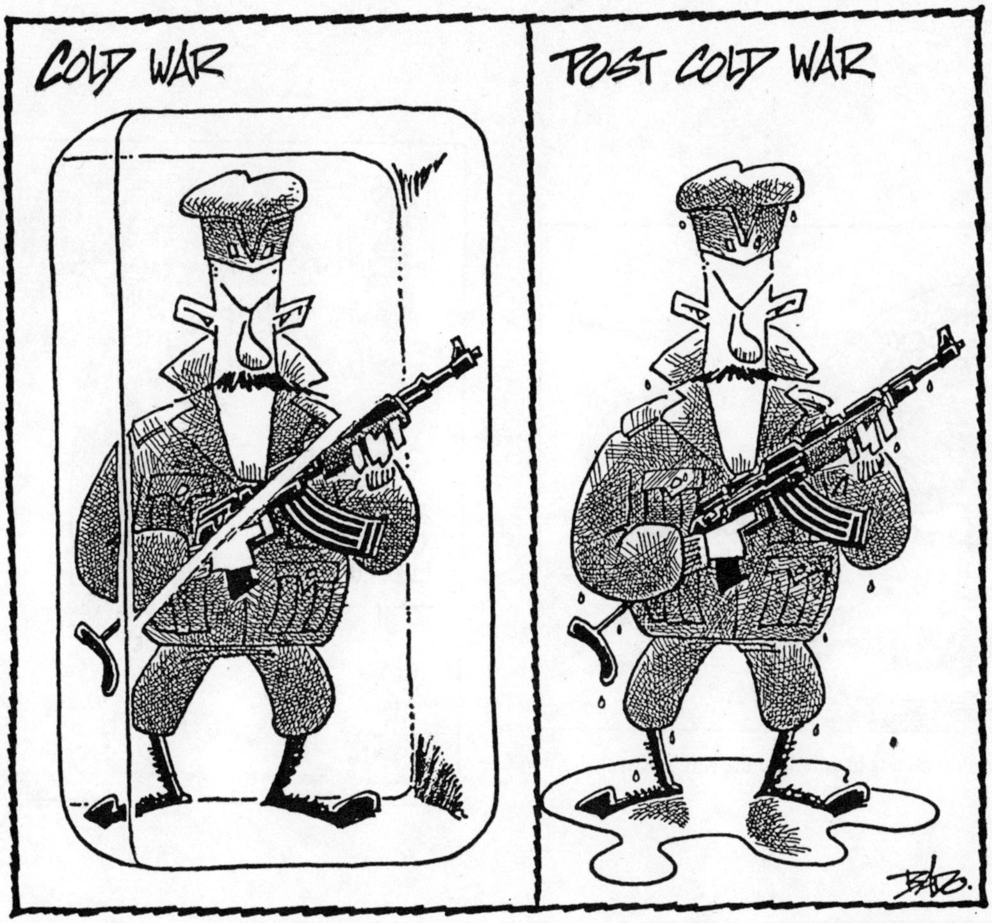
COLD WAR
POST COLD WAR

GUY BADEAUX
Courtesy Le Droit (Ottawa

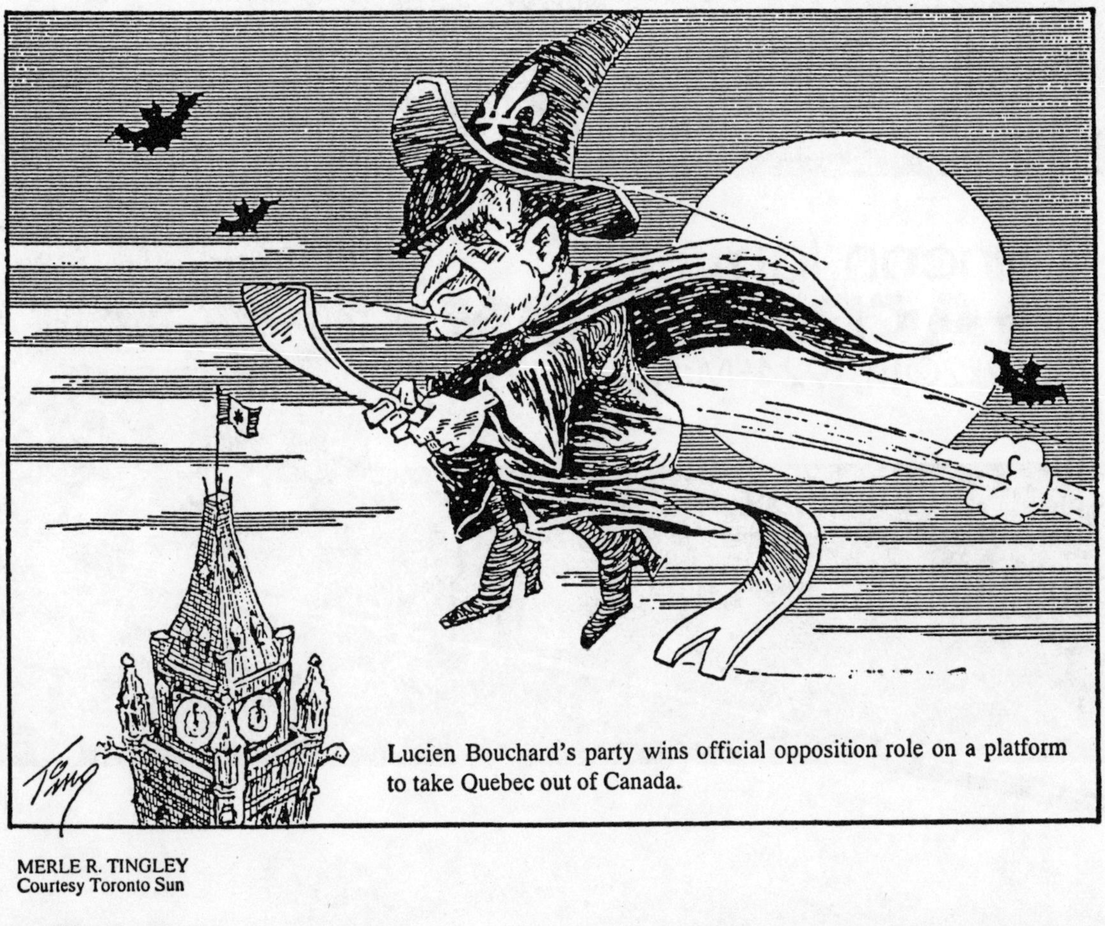

Lucien Bouchard's party wins official opposition role on a platform to take Quebec out of Canada.

MERLE R. TINGLEY
Courtesy Toronto Sun

MERLE R. TINGLEY
Courtesy Toronto Sun

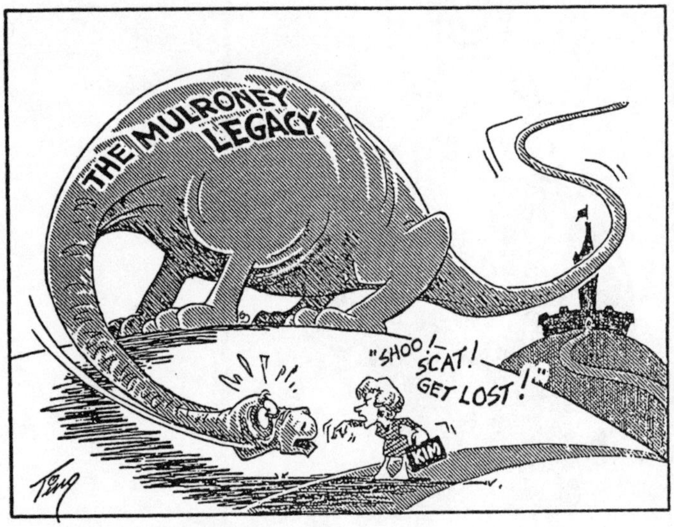
THE MULRONEY LEGACY
"SHOO! SCAT! GET LOST!"
KIM

Kim Campbell's leadership race is haunted by the retiring Mulroney.

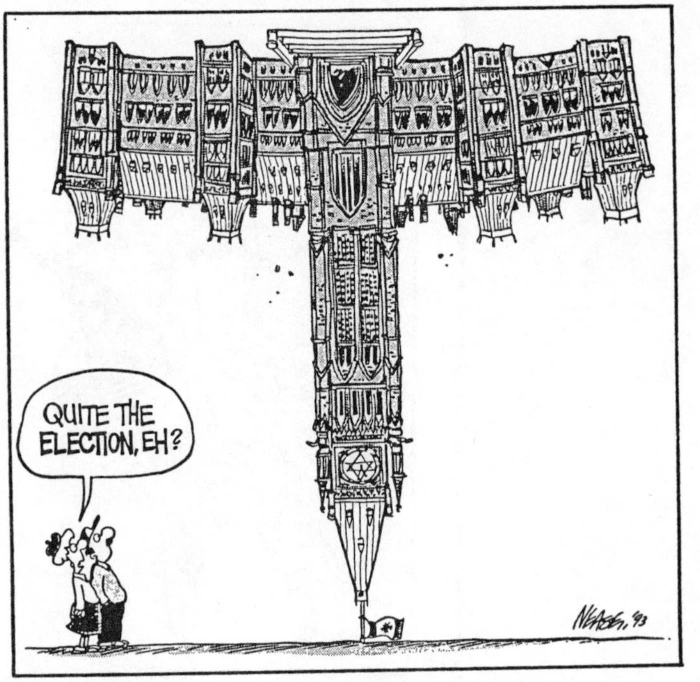
QUITE THE ELECTION, EH?

STEVE NEASE
Courtesy London Free Press

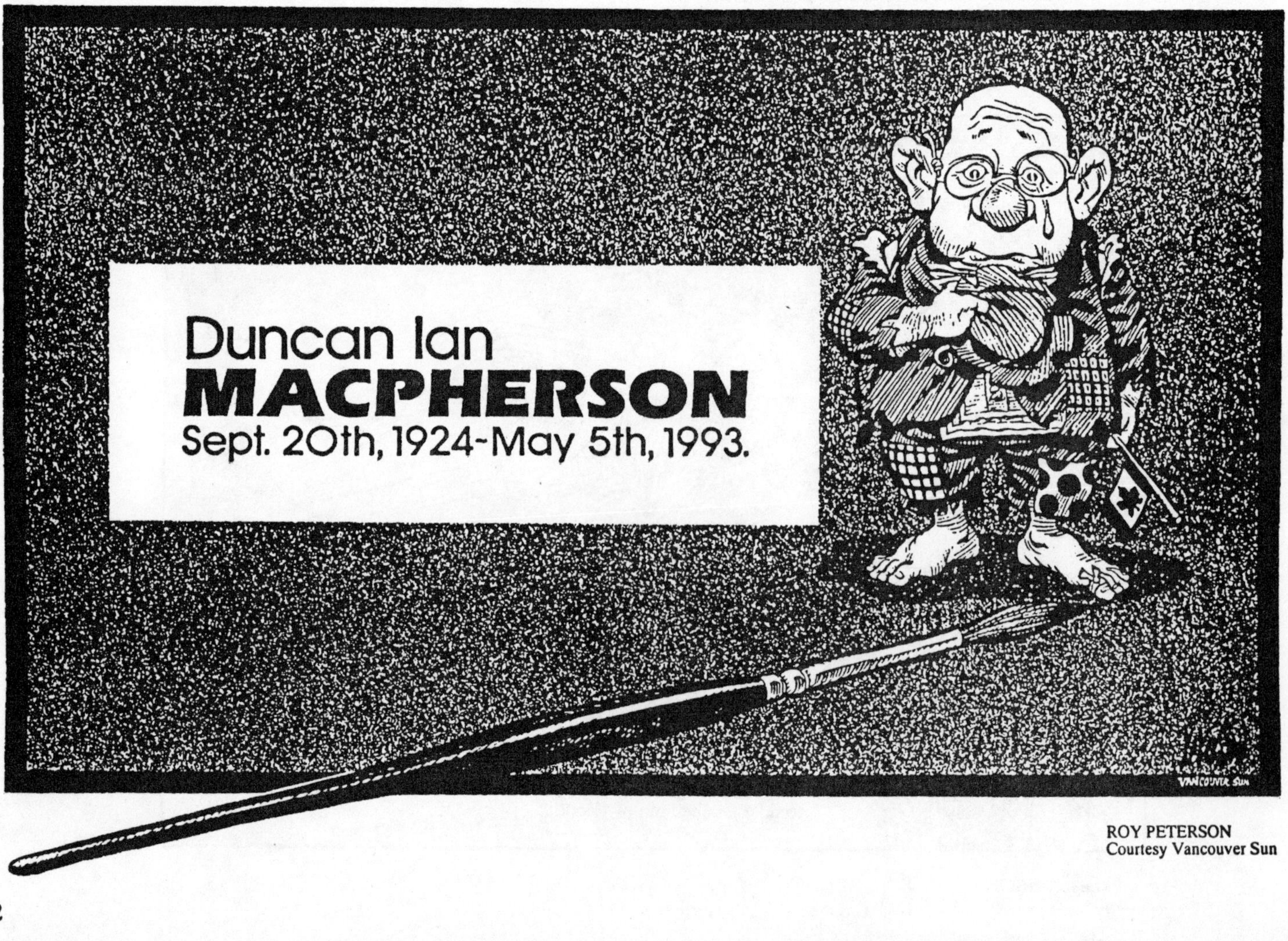
Duncan Ian
MACPHERSON
Sept. 20th, 1924-May 5th, 1993.

ROY PETERSON
Courtesy Vancouver Sun

MERLE TINGLEY
Courtesy St. Thomas Times-Journal

BRUCE MACKINNON
Courtesy Halifax Chronicle-Herald

BRIAN GABLE
Courtesy Toronto Globe and Mail

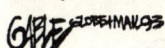

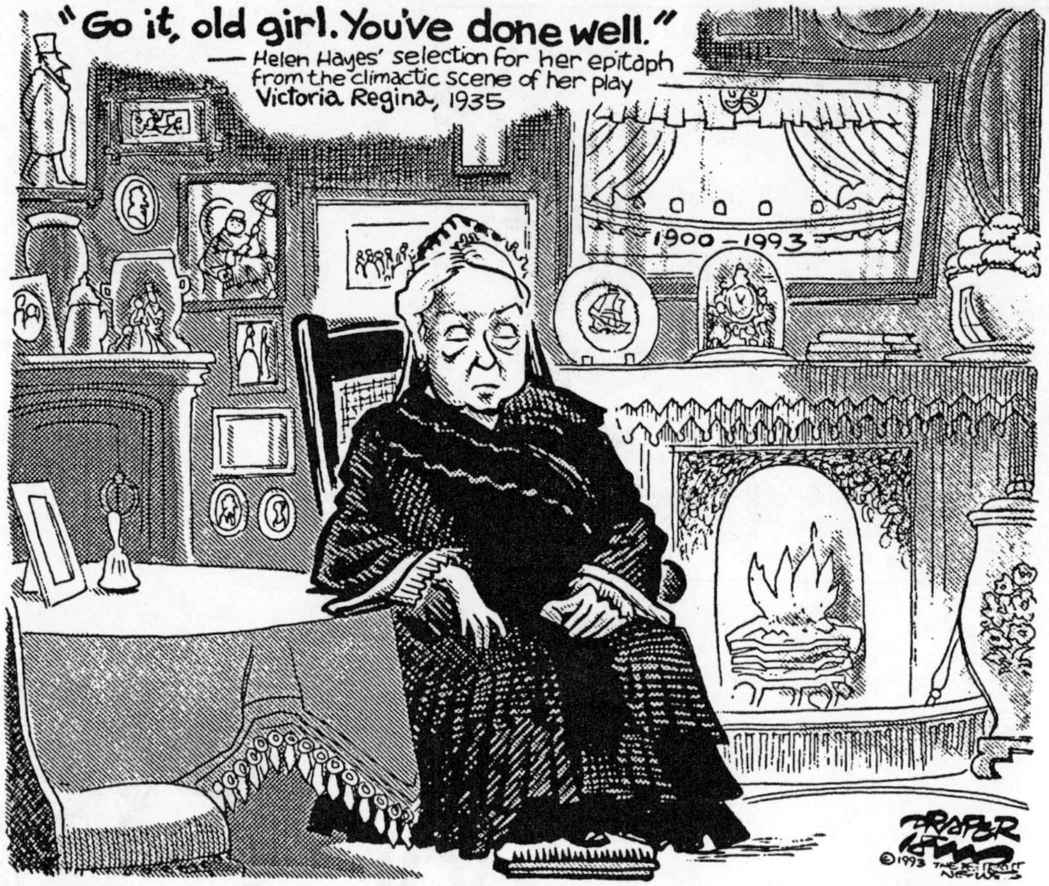
"Go it, old girl. You've done well."
— Helen Hayes' selection for her epitaph from the climactic scene of her play Victoria Regina, 1935
1900–1993
DRAPER HILL
©1993 THE DETROIT NEWS

DRAPER HILL
Courtesy Detroit News

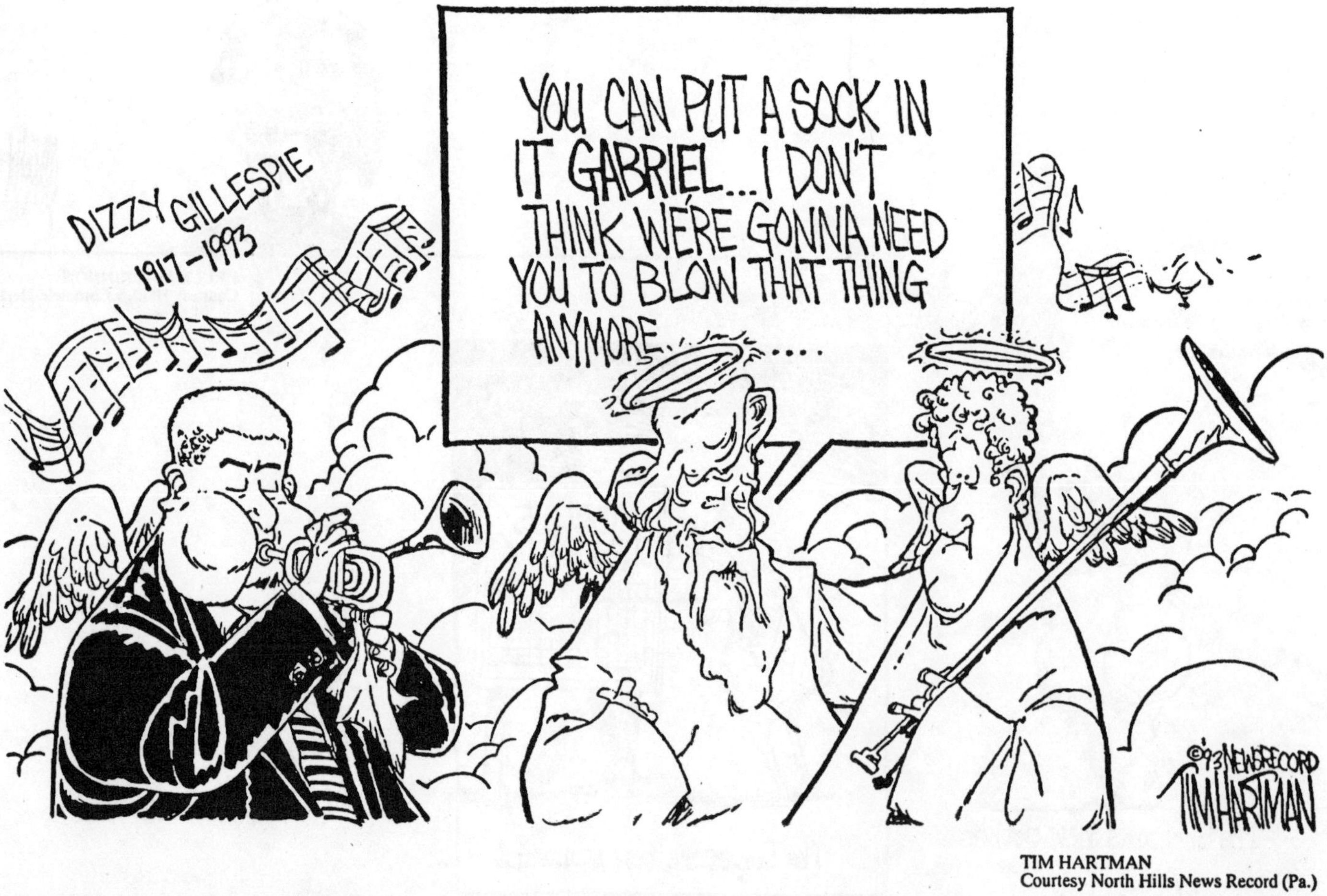
YOU CAN PUT A SOCK IN IT GABRIEL...I DON'T THINK WE'RE GONNA NEED YOU TO BLOW THAT THING ANYMORE.......
DIZZY GILLESPIE
1917–1993
©'93 NEWSRECORD
TIM HARTMAN

TIM HARTMAN
Courtesy North Hills News Record (Pa.)

...and Other Issues

Agents of the U.S. Bureau of Alcohol, Tobacco and Firearms on February 28 raided a compound outside Waco, Texas, where sect leader David Koresh and his followers were holed up. A fiery gun battle ensued, and four agents and at least two cult members were killed. After a standoff lasting nearly two months, agents attacked the compound walls with battering rams. A fire, allegedly set by Koresh's followers, broke out and quickly engulfed the compound, killing more than eighty people, including seventeen children.

NASA's reputation lost some of its luster when the Hubble Space Telescope was put into orbit with handicapped vision and the $1 billion Mars Observer quit working. Seven astronauts were able to restore Hubble to 20/20 vision. Eurodisney, an amusement park outside Paris, lost more than $700 million in 1993, and officials pondered the possibility of closing or downsizing operations. And a biography of the late Walt Disney claimed that he had served as a secret informer for the FBI.

The year marked the thirtieth anniversary of the assassination of John F. Kennedy and brought forth a new book, Case Closed, by Gerald Posner. But the controversy over his death rages on. More than half of all Americans still believe the case is not closed—that Lee Harvey Oswald did not act alone.

Notables who died during the year included: Thurgood Marshall, Gen. Matthew Ridgway, Raymond Burr, Audrey Hepburn, Helen Hayes, Dizzy Gillespie, Jim Valvano, Jimmie Doolittle, Arthur Ashe, Pat Nixon, and Marian Anderson.

JACK HIGGINS
Courtesy Chicago Sun-Times

TOM ENGELHARDT
Courtesy St. Louis Post-Dispatch

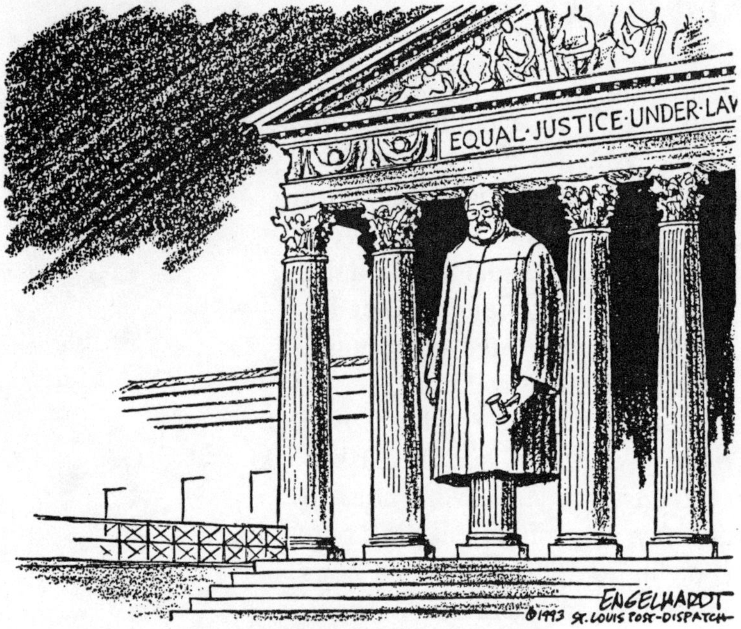

EQUAL·JUSTICE·UNDER·LAW
ENGELHARDT
©1993 ST. LOUIS POST-DISPATCH

Thurgood Marshall, 1908-1993

STEVE HILL
Courtesy Kansas City Star

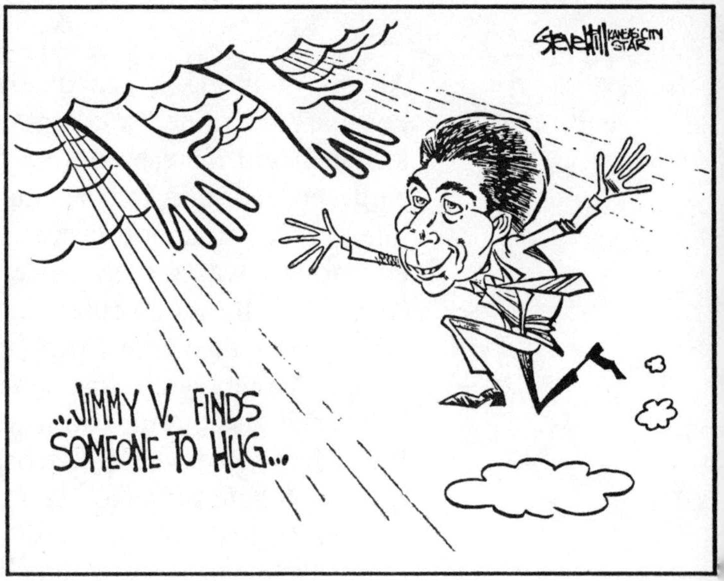

STEVE HILL KANSAS CITY STAR
...JIMMY V. FINDS SOMEONE TO HUG...

BILL HOGAN
Courtesy Times-Transcript
(N. Bruns.)

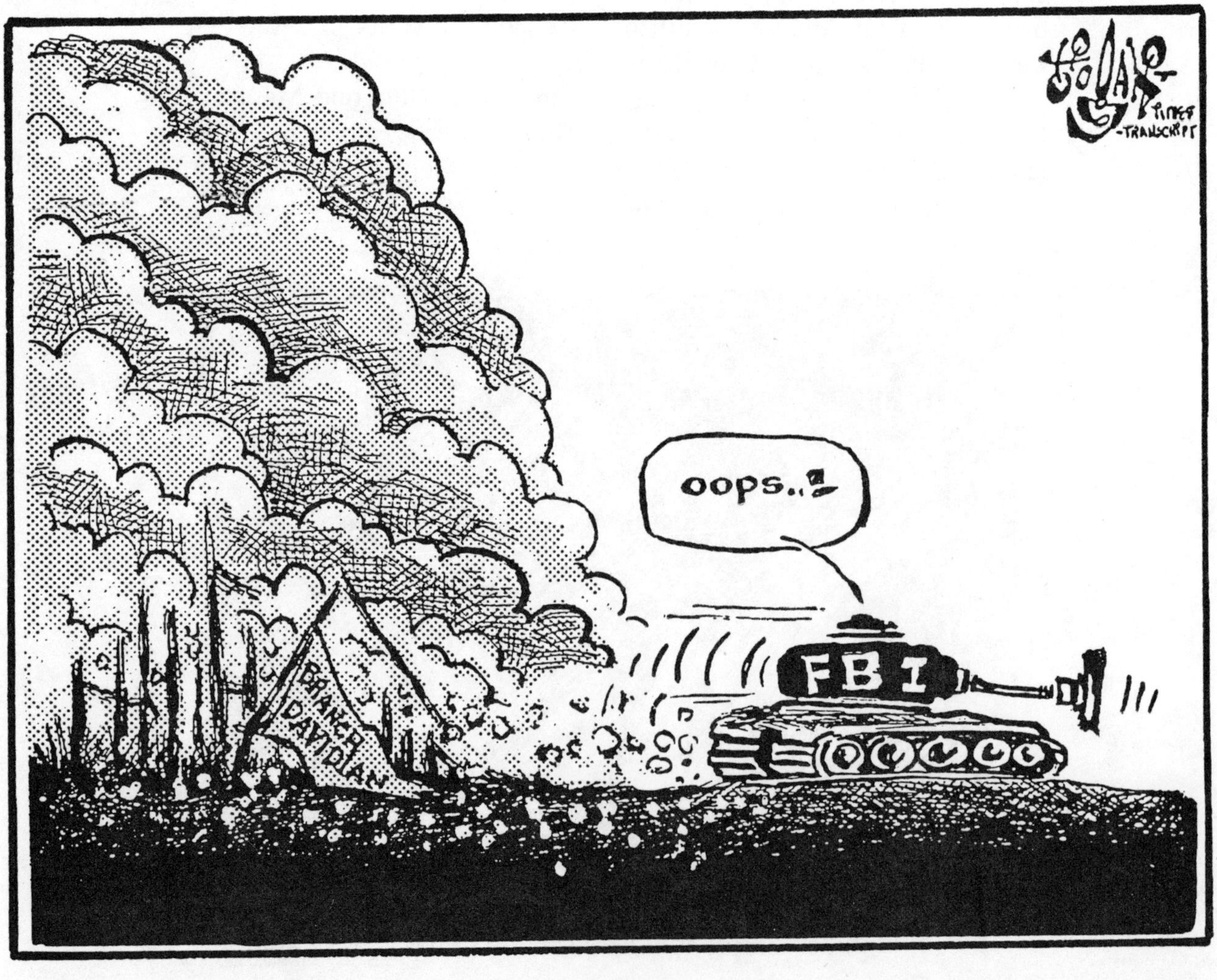

HOGAN TIMES-TRANSCRIPT
OOPS..!
FBI
BRANCH DAVIDIAN

DRAPER HILL
Courtesy Detroit News

STEVE HILL
Courtesy Oklahoma Gazette

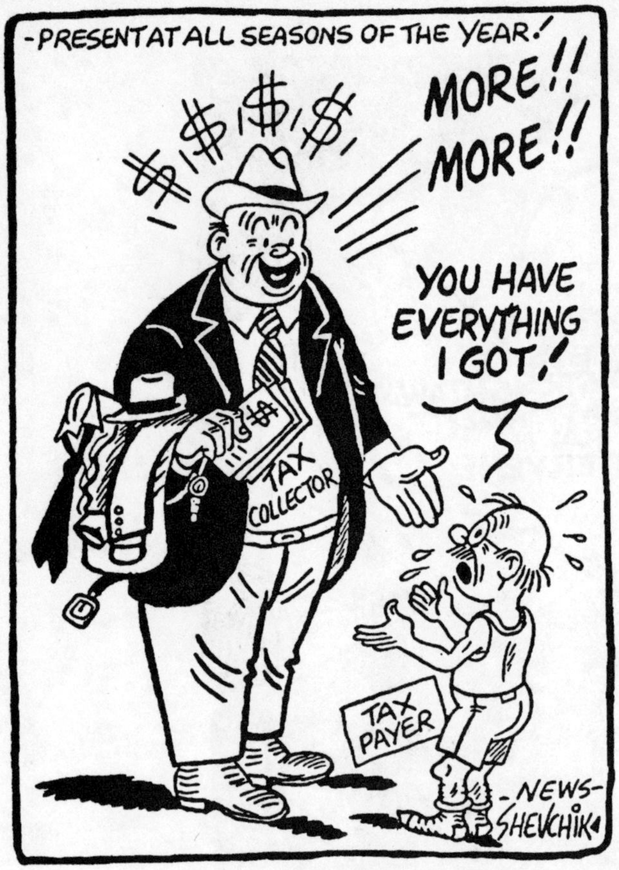
-PRESENT AT ALL SEASONS OF THE YEAR!
MORE!!
MORE!!
YOU HAVE EVERYTHING I GOT!
TAX COLLECTOR
TAX PAYER
-NEWS-
SHEVCHIK

JOHN SHEVCHIK
Courtesy Aliquippa News (Pa.)

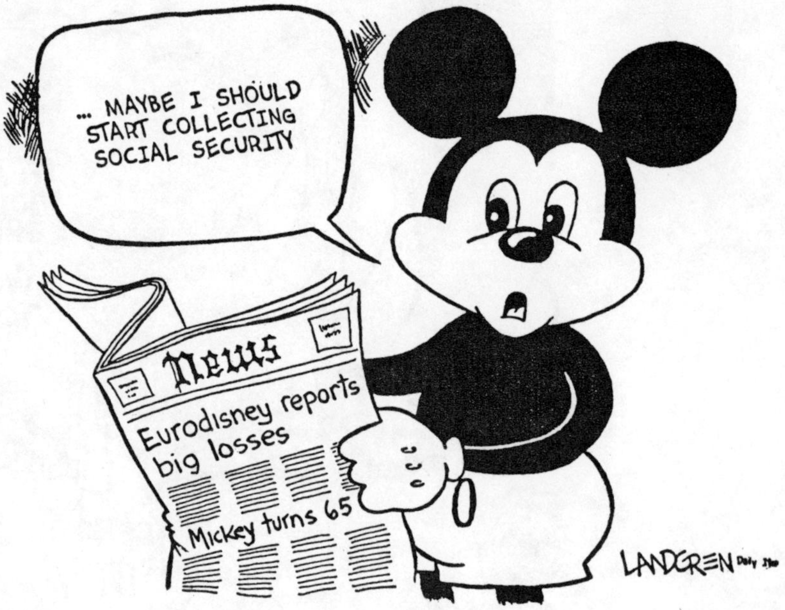
... MAYBE I SHOULD START COLLECTING SOCIAL SECURITY
News
Eurodisney reports big losses
Mickey turns 65
LANDGREN

DON LANDGREN, JR.
Courtesy Clinton Daily Item (Mass.)

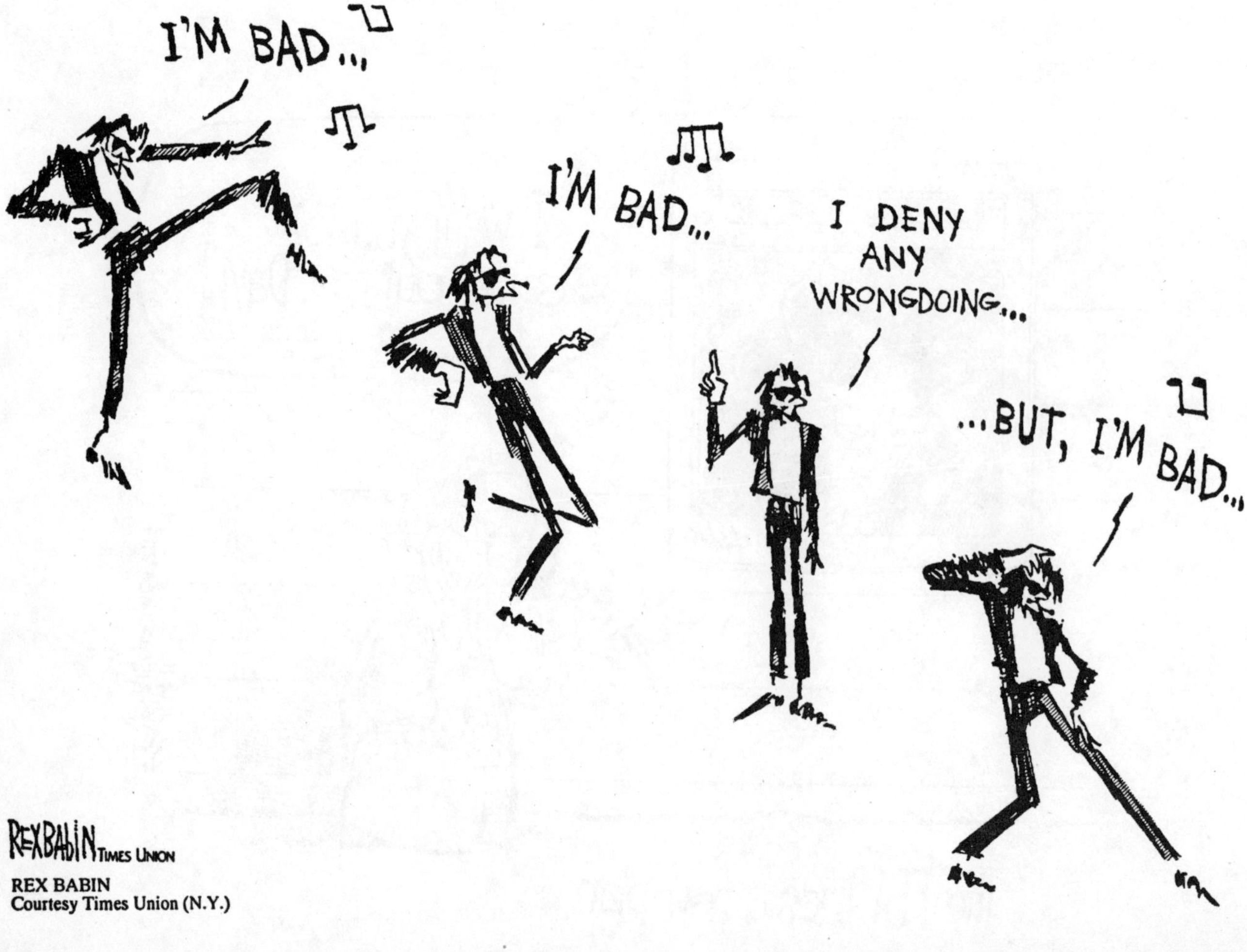
I'M BAD...
I'M BAD...
I DENY ANY WRONGDOING...
...BUT, I'M BAD...
REXBABIN TIMES UNION

REX BABIN
Courtesy Times Union (N.Y.)

MICHAEL RAMIREZ
Courtesy Memphis Commercial Appeal

NEA Self Portrait • with apologies to Mr. Rockwell.

LEN BOROZINSKI
Courtesy Phoenix Gazette

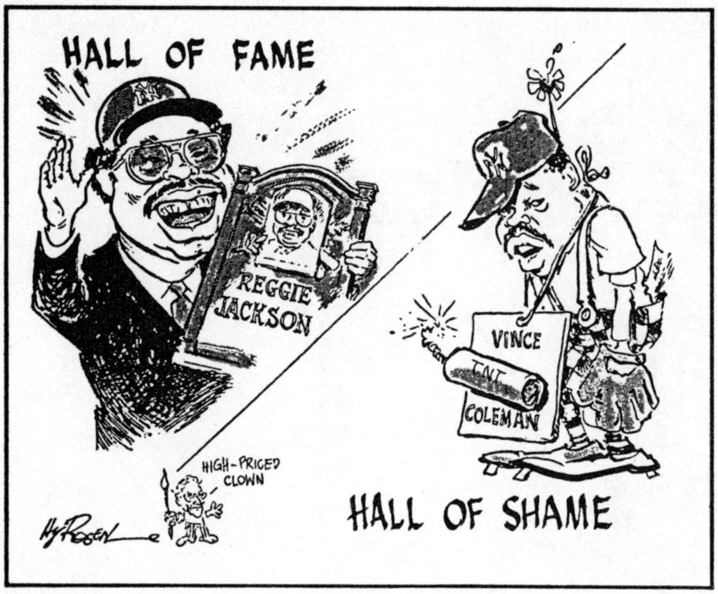
HALL OF FAME
REGGIE JACKSON
VINCE
TNT
COLEMAN
HIGH-PRICED CLOWN
HALL OF SHAME
Hy Rosen

HY ROSEN
Courtesy Albany Times-Union

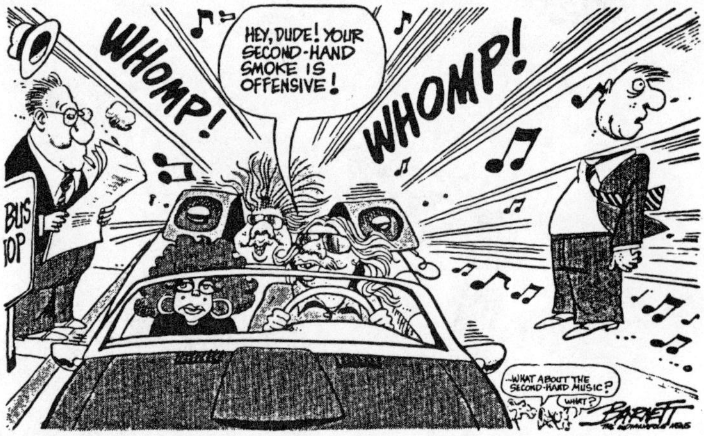
WHOMP!
HEY, DUDE! YOUR SECOND-HAND SMOKE IS OFFENSIVE!
WHOMP!
BUS STOP
—WHAT ABOUT THE SECOND-HAND MUSIC?
WHAT?
BARNETT

JERRY BARNETT
Courtesy Indianapolis News

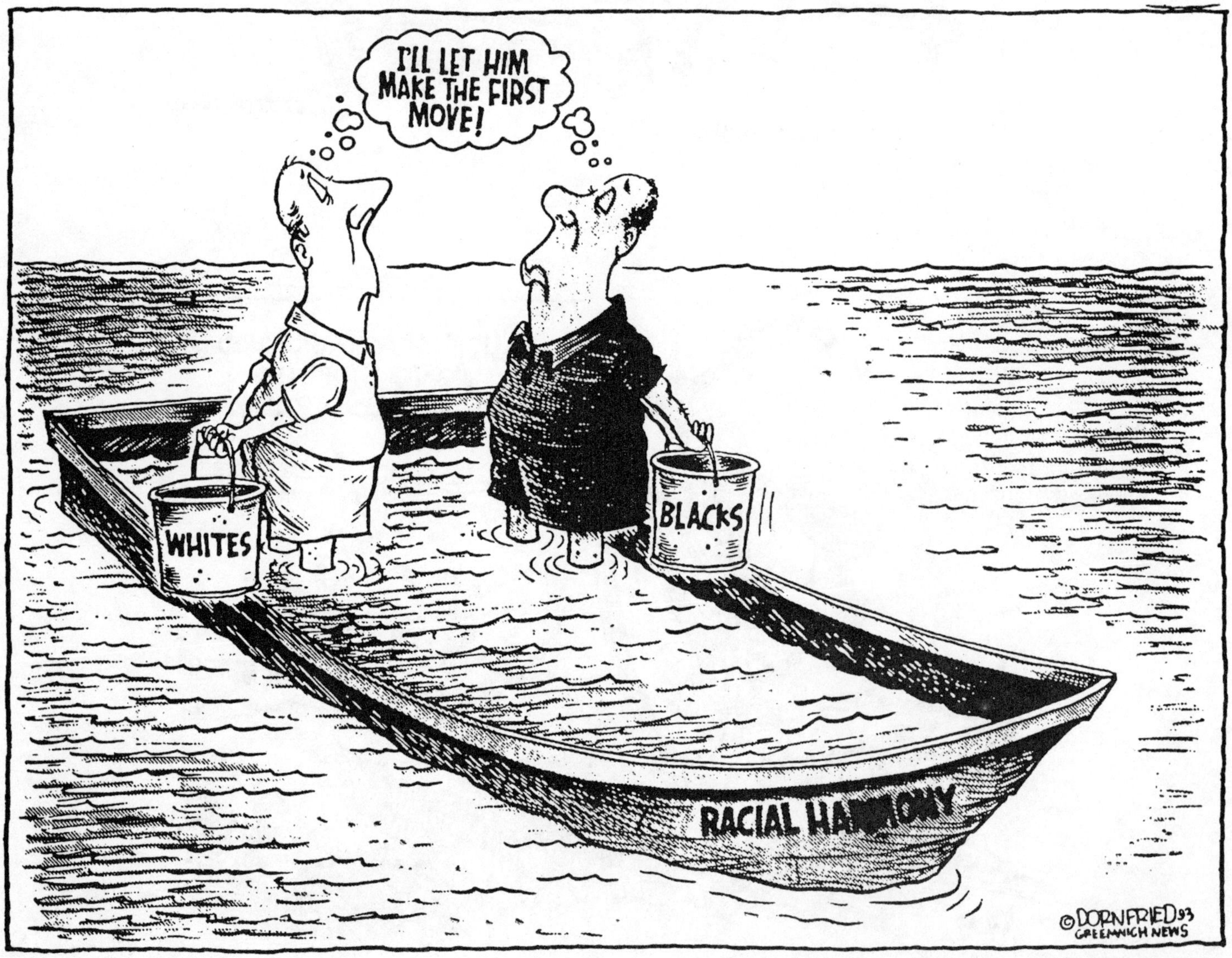
I'LL LET HIM MAKE THE FIRST MOVE!
WHITES
BLACKS
RACIAL HARMONY
©DORNFRIED'93 GREENWICH NEWS

BOB DORNFRIED
Courtesy Greenwich News

LEN BOROZINSKI
Courtesy Phoenix Gazette

J. R. ROSE
Courtesy Byrd Newspapers

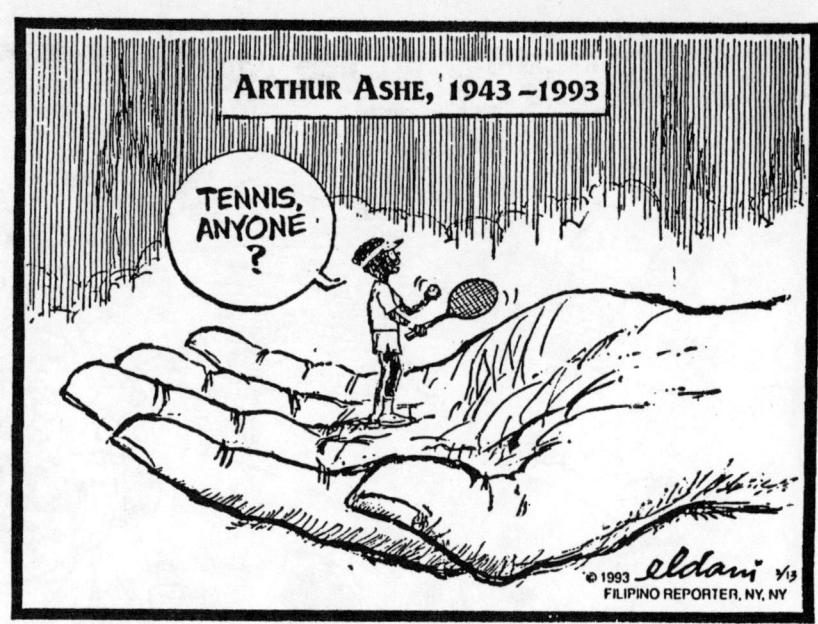

DANI AGUILA
Courtesy Filipino Reporter

MIKE SMITH
Courtesy Las Vegas Sun

GREG HORVAY
Courtesy Philadelphia Daily News

"HE WANTS TO KNOW, 'CAN YOU GET USED TO WRITING THE MAJORITY OPINION?'..."

Just did it.

MIKE LUCKOVICH
Courtesy Atlanta Constitution

ED STEIN
Courtesy Rocky Mountain News and NEA

GARY BROOKINS
Courtesy Richmond Times-Dispatch

ALAN VITELLO
Courtesy Colorado Editor

DAVID GRANLUND
Courtesy Middlesex News

TIM MENEES
Courtesy Pittsburgh Post-Gazette

JIM DOBBINS
Courtesy N.A.G.E. Reporter

Past Award Winners

NATIONAL SOCIETY OF PROFESSIONAL JOURNALISTS AWARD (SIGMA DELTA CHI AWARD)

1942–Jacob Burck, Chicago Times
1943–Charles Werner, Chicago Sun
1944–Henry Barrow, Associated Press
1945–Reuben L. Goldberg, New York Sun
1946–Dorman H. Smith, NEA
1947–Bruce Russell, Los Angeles Times
1948–Herbert Block, Washington Post
1949–Herbert Block, Washington Post
1950–Bruce Russell, Los Angeles Times
1951–Herbert Block, Washington Post, and
    Bruce Russell, Los Angeles Times
1952–Cecil Jensen, Chicago Daily News
1953–John Fischetti, NEA
1954–Calvin Alley, Memphis Commercial Appeal
1955–John Fischetti, NEA
1956–Herbert Block, Washington Post
1957–Scott Long, Minneapolis Tribune
1958–Clifford H. Baldowski, Atlanta Constitution
1959–Charles G. Brooks, Birmingham News
1960–Dan Dowling, New York Herald-Tribune
1961–Frank Interlandi, Des Moines Register
1962–Paul Conrad, Denver Post
1963–William Mauldin, Chicago Sun-Times
1964–Charles Bissell, Nashville Tennessean
1965–Roy Justus, Minneapolis Star
1966–Patrick Oliphant, Denver Post
1967–Eugene Payne, Charlotte Observer
1968–Paul Conrad, Los Angeles Times
1969–William Mauldin, Chicago Sun-Times
1970–Paul Conrad, Los Angeles Times
1971–Hugh Haynie, Louisville Courier-Journal
1972–William Mauldin, Chicago Sun-Times
1973–Paul Szep, Boston Globe
1974–Mike Peters, Dayton Daily News
1975–Tony Auth, Philadelphia Enquirer
1976–Paul Szep, Boston Globe
1977–Don Wright, Miami News
1978–Jim Borgman, Cincinnati Enquirer
1979–John P. Trever, Albuquerque Journal
1980–Paul Conrad, Los Angeles Times
1981–Paul Conrad, Los Angeles Times
1982–Dick Locher, Chicago Tribune
1983–Rob Lawlor, Philadelphia Daily News
1984–Mike Lane, Baltimore Evening Sun
1985–Doug Marlette, Charlotte Observer
1986–Mike Keefe, Denver Post
1987–Paul Conrad, Los Angeles Times
1988–Jack Higgins, Chicago Sun-Times
1989–Don Wright, Palm Beach Post
1990–Jeff MacNelly, Chicago Tribune
1991–Walt Handelsman, Times-Picayune
1992–Robert Ariail, Columbia State

NATIONAL HEADLINERS CLUB AWARD

1938–C. D. Batchelor, New York Daily News
1939–John Knott, Dallas News
1940–Herbert Block, NEA
1941–Charles H. Sykes, Philadelphia Evening Ledger
1942–Jerry Doyle, Philadelphia Record
1943–Vaughn Shoemaker, Chicago Daily News
1944–Roy Justus, Sioux City Journal
1945–F. O. Alexander, Philadelphia Bulletin
1946–Hank Barrow, Associated Press
1947–Cy Hungerford, Pittsburgh Post-Gazette
1948–Tom Little, Nashville Tennessean
1949–Bruce Russell, Los Angeles Times
1950–Dorman Smith, NEA
1951–C. G. Werner, Indianapolis Star
1952–John Fischetti, NEA
1953–James T. Berryman and
    Gib Crocket, Washington Star
1954–Scott Long, Minneapolis Tribune
1955–Leo Thiele, Los Angeles Mirror-News
1956–John Milt Morris, Associated Press
1957–Frank Miller, Des Moines Register
1958–Burris Jenkins, Jr., New York Journal-American
1959–Karl Hubenthal, Los Angeles Examiner
1960–Don Hesse, St. Louis Globe-Democrat
1961–L. D. Warren, Cincinnati Enquirer
1962–Franklin Morse, Los Angeles Mirror
1963–Charles Bissell, Nashville Tennessean
1964–Lou Grant, Oakland Tribune
1965–Merle R. Tingley, London (Ont.) Free Press
1966–Hugh Haynie, Louisville Courier-Journal
1967–Jim Berry, NEA
1968–Warren King, New York News
1969–Larry Barton, Toledo Blade
1970–Bill Crawford, NEA
1971–Ray Osrin, Cleveland Plain Dealer
1972–Jacob Burck, Chicago Sun-Times
1973–Ranan Lurie, New York Times
1974–Tom Darcy, Newsday
1975–Bill Sanders, Milwaukee Journal
1976–No award given
1977–Paul Szep, Boston Globe
1978–Dwane Powell, Raleigh News and Observer
1979–Pat Oliphant, Washington Star
1980–Don Wright, Miami News
1981–Bill Garner, Memphis Commercial Appeal
1982–Mike Peters, Dayton Daily News
1983–Doug Marlette, Charlotte Observer
1984–Steve Benson, Arizona Republic
1985–Bill Day, Detroit Free Press
1986–Mike Keefe, Denver Post
1987–Mike Peters, Dayton Daily News
1988–Doug Marlette, Charlotte Observer
1989–Walt Handelsman, Scranton Times
1990–Robert Ariail, The State
1991–Jim Borgman, Cincinnati Enquirer

PAST AWARD WINNERS

1992–Mike Luckovich, Atlanta Constitution
1993–Walt Handelsman, New Orleans Times-Picayune

PULITZER PRIZE

1922–Rollin Kirby, New York World
1923–No award given
1924–J. N. Darling, New York Herald Tribune
1925–Rollin Kirby, New York World
1926–D. R. Fitzpatrick, St. Louis Post-Dispatch
1927–Nelson Harding, Brooklyn Eagle
1928–Nelson Harding, Brooklyn Eagle
1929–Rollin Kirby, New York World
1930–Charles Macauley, Brooklyn Eagle
1931–Edmund Duffy, Baltimore Sun
1932–John T. McCutcheon, Chicago Tribune
1933–H. M. Talburt, Washington Daily News
1934–Edmund Duffy, Baltimore Sun
1935–Ross A. Lewis, Milwaukee Journal
1936–No award given
1937–C. D. Batchelor, New York Daily News
1938–Vaughn Shoemaker, Chicago Daily News
1939–Charles G. Werner, Daily Oklahoman
1940–Edmund Duffy, Baltimore Sun
1941–Jacob Burck, Chicago Times
1942–Herbert L. Block, NEA
1943–Jay N. Darling, New York Herald Tribune
1944–Clifford K. Berryman, Washington Star
1945–Bill Mauldin, United Features Syndicate
1946–Bruce Russell, Los Angeles Times
1947–Vaughn Shoemaker, Chicago Daily News
1948–Reuben L. ("Rube") Goldberg, New York Sun
1949–Lute Pease, Newark Evening News
1950–James T. Berryman, Washington Star
1951–Reginald W. Manning, Arizona Republic
1952–Fred L. Packer, New York Mirror
1953–Edward D. Kuekes, Cleveland Plain Dealer
1954–Herbert L. Block, Washington Post
1955–Daniel R. Fitzpatrick, St. Louis Post-Dispatch
1956–Robert York, Louisville Times
1957–Tom Little, Nashville Tennessean
1958–Bruce M. Shanks, Buffalo Evening News
1959–Bill Mauldin, St. Louis Post-Dispatch
1960–No award given
1961–Carey Orr, Chicago Tribune
1962–Edmund S. Valtman, Hartford Times
1963–Frank Miller, Des Moines Register
1964–Paul Conrad, Denver Post
1965–No award given
1966–Don Wright, Miami News
1967–Patrick B. Oliphant, Denver Post
1968–Eugene Gray Payne, Charlotte Observer
1969–John Fischetti, Chicago Daily News
1970–Thomas F. Darcy, Newsday
1971–Paul Conrad, Los Angeles Times
1972–Jeffrey K. MacNelly, Richmond News Leader
1973–No award given
1974–Paul Szep, Boston Globe
1975–Garry Trudeau, Universal Press Syndicate
1976–Tony Auth, Philadelphia Enquirer
1977–Paul Szep, Boston Globe
1978–Jeff MacNelly, Richmond News Leader
1979–Herbert Block, Washington Post
1980–Don Wright, Miami News
1981–Mike Peters, Dayton Daily News
1982–Ben Sargent, Austin American-Statesman
1983–Dick Locher, Chicago Tribune
1984–Paul Conrad, Los Angeles Times
1985–Jeff MacNelly, Chicago Tribune
1986–Jules Feiffer, Universal Press Syndicate
1987–Berke Breathed, Washington Post Writers Group
1988–Doug Marlette, Atlanta Constitution
1989–Jack Higgins, Chicago Sun-Times
1990–Tom Toles, Buffalo News
1991–Jim Borgman, Cincinnati Enquirer
1992–Signe Wilkinson, Philadelphia Daily News
1993–Steve Benson, Arizona Republic

NATIONAL NEWSPAPER AWARD / CANADA

1949–Jack Boothe, Toronto Globe and Mail
1950–James G. Reidford, Montreal Star
1951–Len Norris, Vancouver Sun
1952–Robert La Palme, Le Devoir, Montreal
1953–Robert W. Chambers, Halifax Chronicle-Herald
1954–John Collins, Montreal Gazette
1955–Merle R. Tingley, London Free Press
1956–James G. Reidford, Toronto Globe and Mail
1957–James G. Reidford, Toronto Globe and Mail
1958–Raoul Hunter, Le Soleil, Quebec
1959–Duncan Macpherson, Toronto Star
1960–Duncan Macpherson, Toronto Star
1961–Ed McNally, Montreal Star
1962–Duncan Macpherson, Toronto Star
1963–Jan Kamienski, Winnipeg Tribune
1964–Ed McNally, Montreal Star
1965–Duncan Macpherson, Toronto Star
1966–Robert W. Chambers, Halifax Chronicle-Herald
1967–Raoul Hunter, Le Soleil, Quebec
1968–Roy Peterson, Vancouver Sun
1969–Edward Uluschak, Edmonton Journal
1970–Duncan Macpherson, Toronto Daily Star
1971–Yardley Jones, Toronto Star
1972–Duncan Macpherson, Toronto Star
1973–John Collins, Montreal Gazette
1974–Blaine, Hamilton Spectator
1975–Roy Peterson, Vancouver Sun
1976–Andy Donato, Toronto Sun
1977–Terry Mosher, Montreal Gazette
1978–Terry Mosher, Montreal Gazette
1979–Edd Uluschak, Edmonton Journal
1980–Vic Roschkov, Toronto Star
1981–Tom Innes, Calgary Herald

PAST AWARD WINNERS

1982–Blaine, Hamilton Spectator
1983–Dale Cummings, Winnipeg Free Press
1984–Roy Peterson, Vancouver Sun
1985–Ed Franklin, Toronto Globe and Mail
1986–Brian Gable, Regina Leader Post
1987–Raffi Anderian, Ottawa Citizen
1988–Vance Rodewalt, Calgary Herald
1989–Cameron Cardow, Regina Leader-Post
1990–Roy Peterson, Vancouver Sun
1991–Guy Badeaux, Le Droit, Ottawa
1992–Bruce Mackinnon, Halifax Herald

FISCHETTI AWARD

1982–Lee Judge, Kansas City Times
1983–Bill DeOre, Dallas Morning News
1984–Tom Toles, Buffalo News
1985–Scott Willis, Dallas Times-Herald
1986–Doug Marlette, Charlotte Observer
1987–Dick Locher, Chicago Tribune
1988–Arthur Bok, Akron Beacon-Journal
1989–Lambert Der, Greenville News
1990–Jeff Stahler, Cincinnati Post
1991–Mike Keefe, Denver Post
1992–Doug Marlette, New York Newsday
1993–Bill Schorr, Kansas City Star

Index of Cartoonists

Aguila, Daniel, 129, 182
Anderson, Kirk, 72
Anderson, Nick, 41, 47, 88, 114
Ariail, Robert, 7, 53, 68-69, 93
Asay, Chuck, 16, 44, 52, 166
Ayers, Chuck, 50, 87

Babin, Rex, 102, 178
Badeaux, Guy, 63, 171
Bagley, Pat, 54, 74
Barnett, Jerry, 27, 136, 180
Bateman, Scott, 114
Beattie, Bruce, 49, 57
Beck, Chip, 24
Beck, Tom, 109
Bennett, Clay, 76, 113, 152
Benson, Steve, 6
Berry, Jim, 47, 89, 109, 122
Bertram, Jim, 27
Beutel, Josh, 61, 170
Bish, Randy, 70, 114
Bissell, Charles, 25, 86, 146
Bloom, Neal, 97
Boileau, Linda, 106, 150
Boldt, Thomas, 162
Borgman, Jim, 18, 163, 183
Borozinski, Len, 179, 181
Branch, John, 79, 134
Brewer, Mark, 108
Brookins, Gary, 35, 48, 184
Brown, Jonathan, 19
Buckley, Jerry, 90
Bush, Jim, 29, 41

Cammuso, Frank, 19
Cantone, Vic, 45, 156
Catalino, Kenneth, 118, 127, 148
Cavna, Michael, 183
Cleaves, Ann, 72
Commodore, Chester, 88, 132
Conrad, Paul, 12, 100, 149, 151
Costello, William, 23, 43
Coverly, David, 151, 159
Cox, David (Hardin), 84, 126
Crowson, Richard, 67, 82
Cullum, Mark, 99, 113
Curatolo, Fred, 55, 142

Danby, George, 32, 42, 56
Daniel, Charles, 29, 54
Darcy, Tom, 46, 83, 141
Deering, John, 15, 22
Der, Lambert, 17, 36, 138

Dobbins, Jim, 136, 186
Donar, David, 47
Dornfried, Bob, 37, 180
Draughon, Dennis, 57, 102
Duffy, Brian, 34, 94, 140
Duginski, Paul, 20, 115

Engelhardt, Tom, 56, 91, 166, 176

Fagan, Charles, 2, 54, 103
Fearing, Jerry, 126, 132, 141
Fischer, Ed, 14, 36, 85
Flint, Bubba, 26, 89
Foden, Glenn, 105
Fox, Gill, 30, 123
Fresquet, Lazaro, 94, 96

Gable, Brian, 147, 173
Gamble, Ed, 13, 17, 66, 122
Genn, Roman, 21
Germano, Eddie, 49
Gibb, Tom, 60, 130
Gillett, Michael, 110
Gorrell, Bob, 14, 76, 131
Grahame, Neil, 154, 162
Granlund, Dave, 58, 67, 103, 185
Grasdal, James, 53, 170
Greenberg, Steve, 81, 98

Handelsman, Walt, 10, 30, 33, 39, 133
Hartman, Tim, 174
Harville, Vic, 118
Haynie, Hugh, 16, 163, 101
Heller, Joe, 102, 121, 129
Henrikson, Arthur, 61, 71
Higgins, Jack, 45, 149, 175
Hill, Draper, 117, 174, 177
Hill, Steve, 176, 177
Hitch, David, 60, 89
Hoffecker, Joe, 31
Hogan, W. A., 176
Holbert, Jerry, 28, 155
Horsey, David, 92, 128
Horvay, Greg, 164, 182
Hughes, Jerry, 131
Hulme, Etta, 98, 134, 138

Jones, Clay, 156
Jordan, Jim, 155
Jurden, Jack, 24

Keefe, Mike, 95, 140, 146
Kelley, Steve, 32, 37, 130, 157
Knudsen, John, 48

INDEX OF CARTOONISTS

Koterba, Jeff, 19, 90

Lait, Steven, 29
Landgren, Don, Jr., 178
Lang, Bob, 22
Lange, Jim, 78, 138
Lee, Don, 39
Lefler, Jerry, 167
Lindstrom, Steve, 21
Locher, Dick, 42, 84, 107, back cover
Long, Joe, 154
Lowe, Chan, 20, 146
Luckovich, Mike, 28, 74, 125, 184
Lurie, Ranan, 63, 94, 105

MacGregor, Doug, 93
MacKinnon, Bruce, 9, 46, 158, 173
MacNelly, Jeff, 15, 18, 23, 75
Madan, Vikram, 86
Majeski, Joe, 108
Margulies, Jimmy, 40, 59, 137
Mayes, Malcolm, 147, 160
McBride, Steve, 112, 115, 157
McCloskey, James, 57, 110, 158
McClure, Hank, 87
McCoy, Gary, 120
McCoy, Glenn, 21, 128
McLeod, Jack, 117, 150, 166
Menees, Tim, 58, 186
Mercado, James, 100
Morin, Jim, 40, 82

Nease, Steve, 63, 156, 172
Nickel, Scott, 124

O'Brien, Dan, 62
OBrion, Chris, 79
Ohman, Jack, 127, 145, 160
O'Keefe, David, 76

Parker, Jeff, 132
Payne, Eugene, 96, 104
Peters, Mike, 38, 65, 120, 121
Peterson, Roy, 24, 169, 172
Plante, Bruce, 139
Pritchard, Denny, 85, 98, 168

Rall, Ted, 80, 86
Ramirez, Michael, 77, 179, front cover
Ramsay, Marshall, 70
Regalia, Douglas, 80
Rhoda, Michael, 140
Rice, Patrick, 135
Rich, Bob, 97

Richards, Jon, 104
Ritter, Mike, 95
Robinson, Jerry, 49, 55
Rogers, Rob, 81, 133
Rose, J. R., 181
Rosen, Hy, 62, 180

Sack, Steve, 73, 137
Sargent, Ben, 26, 38, 51
Scallion, Steve, 72
Schillerstrom, Roger, 66
Schorr, Bill, 8
Sebastian, Fred, 73, 96
Shelton, Mike, 168
Sherffius, John, 123
Shevchik, John, 178
Shingleton, J. Robert, 62
Siers, Kevin, 135, 164
Smith, Eric, 16, 99, 159
Smith, Mike, 64, 119, 182
Soller, Edgar, 136
Spencer, John, 71, 80
Stahler, Jeff, 25, 50, 145, 152
Stampone, John, 64, 100
Stayskal, Wayne, 43, 77, 78, 126
Stein, Ed, 32, 184
Stephanos, Dale, 78, 101, 116
Streeter, Mark, 92
Stroot, Wayne, 167
Summers, Dana, 43, 97, 105
Swann, David, 148
Szep, Paul, 27, 44, 104

Templeton, Stephen, 88
Terry, Craig, 139
Thomas, Gary, 108
Thompson, Michael, 31, 48
Tingley, M. R., 171, 172, 173
Trever, John, 52, 112, 143

Valtman, Edmund, 58
Varvel, Gary, 37, 70
Vitello, Alan, 185

Wallmeyer, Richard, 55, 153
Walters, Kirk, 116, 161
Warren, Rod, 124
Wells, Clyde, 111, 144
Werner, Chuck, 106, 117
Wicks, Randy, 33, 165
Wood, Art, 25
Wright, Dick, 46, 144
Wright, Larry, 31, 150

COMPLETE YOUR CARTOON COLLECTION

Previous editions of this timeless editorial cartoon series are available for those wishing to update their collection of the most provocative moments of the past twenty years. In the early days the topics were the oil crisis, Richard Nixon's presidency, Watergate, and the Vietnam War. Over time the cartoonists and their subjects have changed right along with presidential administrations. These days those subjects have been replaced by AIDS, Bill Clinton, Tailhook, and Desert Storm. But in the end, the wit and wisdom of the editorial cartoonists has prevailed. And on the pages of these op-ed galleries one can find memories and much more from the nation's best cartoonists.

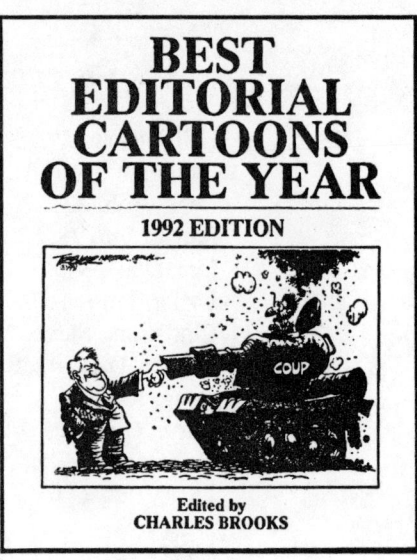

Select from the following supply of past editions

___ 1972 Edition out of print	___ 1981 Edition $12.95 pb	___ 1988 Edition $12.95 pb
___ 1974 Edition $16.95 hc	___ 1982 Edition $12.95 pb	___ 1989 Edition out of print
___ 1975 Edition $16.95 hc	___ 1983 Edition out of print	___ 1990 Edition $12.95 pb
___ 1976 Edition $16.95 hc	___ 1984 Edition $12.95 pb	___ 1991 Edition $12.95 pb
___ 1977 Edition $16.95 hc	___ 1985 Edition $12.95 pb	___ 1992 Edition $12.95 pb
___ 1978 Edition out of print	___ 1986 Edition $12.95 pb	___ 1993 Edition $12.95 pb
___ 1979 Edition out of print	___ 1987 Edition $12.95 pb	___ 1994 Edition $12.95 pb
___ 1980 Edition $16.95 hc	___ Please add me to the list of standing orders for future editions.	

Please include $1.75 for 4th Class Postage and handling or $3.25 for UPS Ground Shipment plus $.75 for each additional copy ordered.*

Total enclosed: _____

NAME _____

ADDRESS _____

CITY _____ STATE _____ ZIP _____

Make checks payable to:

 PELICAN PUBLISHING COMPANY
P.O. Box 3110, Dept. 2BCB
Gretna, Louisiana 70054

CREDIT CARD ORDERS CALL 1-800-843-1724

* Jefferson Parish residents add 8¾% tax. All other Louisiana residents add 4% tax.